AN AGENDA FOR A GROWING EUROPE

An Agenda for a Growing Europe

The Sapir Report

André Sapir, Philippe Aghion, Giuseppe Bertola, Martin Hellwig,
Jean Pisani-Ferry, Dariusz Rosati, José Viñals, and Helen
Wallace, with Marco Buti, Mario Nava, and Peter M. Smith

OXFORD
UNIVERSITY PRESS

OXFORD

UNIVERSITY PRESS

Great Clarendon Street, Oxford OX2 6DP

Oxford University Press is a department of the University of Oxford.
It furthers the University's objective of excellence in research, scholarship,
and education by publishing worldwide in

Oxford New York

Auckland Bangkok Buenos Aires Cape Town Chennai
Dar es Salaam Delhi Hong Kong Istanbul Karachi Kolkata
Kuala Lumpur Madrid Melbourne Mexico City Mumbai Nairobi
São Paulo Shanghai Taipei Tokyo Toronto

Oxford is a registered trade mark of Oxford University Press
in the UK and in certain other countries

Published in the United States
by Oxford University Press Inc., New York

First published 2004

British Library Cataloguing in Publication Data
Data available

Library of Congress Cataloging in Publication Data
Data available
ISBN 0-19-927148-8 (hbk.)
ISBN 0-19-927149-6 (pbk.)

1 3 5 7 9 10 8 6 4 2

Typeset by Newgen Imaging Systems (P) Ltd., Chennai, India
Printed in Great Britain
on acid-free paper by
Biddles Ltd., King's Lynn, Norfolk

Letter of Transmission to Romano Prodi, President of the European Commission

Dear President,

In July 2002 you invited a High-Level Group of independent experts to analyse the consequences of the two strategic economic goals set by the European Union (EU) for the decade ending in 2010: to become the most competitive and dynamic knowledge-based economy with sustainable economic growth and greater social cohesion (the so-called Lisbon Agenda); and to make a success of the pending enlargement by rapidly raising living standards in the new Member States. The Group was asked to review the entire system of EU economic policies and to propose a strategy for delivering faster growth together with stability and cohesion in the enlarged Union.

The Group was invited to seek inspiration from a report by Tommaso Padoa-Schioppa and others, whom the Commission had invited in 1986 to reflect on the economic consequences of the Single Market Programme and of the southern enlargement. The Padoa-Schioppa Report was extremely influential. It laid down the intellectual foundation for the construction of a coherent economic edifice resting on three pillars: the Single Market, to improve economic efficiency; an effective monetary arrangement, to ensure monetary stability; and an expanded Community budget, to foster cohesion.

All three pillars were gradually put in place: the Single Market became a reality in 1993, although problems of coverage and implementation still remain; the Community budget and the share allocated to cohesion were somewhat expanded; and, even more remarkably, a European Monetary Union was set up in 1999.

The present Report finds that, despite the considerable institutional achievements of the EU, its economic performance is mixed. While macroeconomic stability has considerably improved during the 1990s and a strong emphasis on cohesion has been preserved, the EU system has failed to deliver a satisfactory growth performance. This underperformance is striking because it contrasts not only with expectations but also with past EU performance and recent US accomplishment. In the EU, there has been a steady decline of the average growth rate decade after decade and per capita GDP has stagnated at about 70 per cent of the US level since the early 1980s.

Growth must become Europe's number one economic priority—not only in the declarations of its leaders, but first and foremost, in their actions. A more dynamic EU will help the integration of new Member States and strongly growing new members will contribute to more dynamism. A more dynamic EU will also be a better partner for other European and Mediterranean neighbouring countries, and in the global system.

Faster growth is paramount for the sustainability of the European model, which puts a high premium on cohesion. Sustainability is under threat from rapid developments in demography, technology, and globalisation, all of which increase the demand for social protection. Failure to deliver on the commitments of the Lisbon Agenda would endanger the present European contract and could lead to its fundamental revision, thereby threatening the very process of European integration. Fortunately, however, technology and globalisation, like enlargement, also hold the potential for faster growth throughout Europe.

The Group views Europe's unsatisfactory growth performance during the last decades as a symptom of its failure to transform into an innovation-based economy. It has now become clear that the context in which economic policies have been developed changed fundamentally over the past thirty years. A system built around the assimilation of existing technologies, mass production generating economies of scale, and an industrial structure dominated by large firms with stable markets and long-term employment patterns no longer delivers in the world of today, characterised by economic globalisation and strong external competition. What is needed now is more opportunity for new entrants, greater mobility of employees within and across firms, more retraining, greater reliance on market financing, and higher investment in both R&D and higher education. This requires a massive and urgent change in economic policies in Europe.

The Group considers that the three pillars upon which the European economic edifice is now built are fundamentally sound. At the same time, it feels that the design of each of the pillars, which together constitute the EU system of economic policies, must be improved. In particular, greater coherence— across instruments, across decision-makers and jurisdictions, and over time— is absolutely essential to ensure that the system delivers on the objectives.

Expanding growth potential requires first reforms of microeconomic policies at both the EU and national levels. However, there is also a need to revise features of the current macroeconomic policy setting and to redesign cohesion policies at both the EU and national levels. Growth, stability, and cohesion must go together. Well-designed macroeconomic and cohesion policies help to achieve sustainable growth. At the same time, significant growth is necessary to maintain stability and cohesion.

To trigger those changes, we should reconsider the relationship between the EU as such and the Member States. While the role of EU institutions in enforcing commonly-agreed disciplines remains essential, they must increasingly take on the role of a facilitator. Sticks must be used when needed, but a policy system that essentially relies on the threat of sanctions is neither efficient nor sustainable. Nor is a system viable that leaves so much to depend on loose and uncertain agreements from the Member States to deliver on commonly-agreed objectives. The Report therefore suggests moving towards a more incentive-based approach that treats Member States as partners. It also recommends refocusing the EU budget to make it consistent with this approach, while respecting the current budget ceiling of 1.27 per cent of GNP. And it proposes a number of changes in methods of governance in order to make this partnership much more effective.

The Report puts forward a six-point agenda focusing on where EU policies and their economic management can make the greatest contribution to achieving the declared objectives of sustainable growth with more and better jobs, continuing price stability, and greater economic and social cohesion in the enlarged EU. This agenda calls on the EU and its members:

(1) to make the Single Market more dynamic;
(2) to boost investment in knowledge;
(3) to improve the macroeconomic policy framework for EMU;
(4) to redesign policies for convergence and restructuring;
(5) to achieve effectiveness in decision-taking and regulation; and
(6) to refocus the EU budget.

For each of these six items, precise recommendations are spelled out in the Report. These recommendations address solely EU policies, even though the Group strongly believes that reforming national policies, especially in the area of social affairs, public investment, and taxation, is absolutely crucial to ensure that the EU economic system achieves higher sustained growth. Equally, our recommendations address only the economic and social dimensions of sustainability, although the Group recognises the importance of the environmental dimension. Taking up the details of other national and environmental policies would have been outside the Group's area of competence.

Between the beginning and the end of our work, two important developments have taken place in the EU. The first is the draft Treaty establishing a Constitution for Europe submitted by the President of the Convention to the European Council meeting in Thessaloniki in June 2003. Most of our work had already been completed when the Convention released its final proposal. Our recommendations and the Convention proposals converge on some aspects of economic governance, but on several other our recommendations require treaty changes, on which the draft constitutional treaty is silent.

The second is the current macroeconomic situation. In the span of one year, the economic situation has deteriorated to a considerable extent. It was not within the mandate of the Group to offer responses to this problem. Nor was it to provide a solution to the difficulty of several countries, which, having failed to create the necessary room for manoeuvre during good years, now find their fiscal policy increasingly constrained by the 3 per cent of GDP deficit ceiling. The Group, however, suggests a possible way to combine, in the present juncture, the necessary commitment to growth and to fiscal discipline. In particular, the Group proposes some measures to try and reconcile the need to reduce budgetary deficits and to undertake growth-enhancing public expenditures.

The members of the Group have reached a common diagnosis on the seriousness of the economic situation in the EU and the risks involved in a continuation of current trends. Based upon this diagnosis, they have formulated common proposals. While all members of the Group share the thrust of the full set of proposals, individual members may retain their own particular perspective on some specific aspects of individual proposals.

In closing, I want to emphasise that this Report is the joint product of an extraordinary team, which comprises not only the members of the Group and the rapporteurs, but also Ricardo Franco Levi, the Director of the Commission's Group of Policy Advisors. All of us are grateful to you, Mr President, for the opportunity and the privilege to work—with your support and in full independence—on the very complex and challenging matters that lie at the heart of the European economic integration process.

André Sapir
Chairman of the Group
Brussels, July 2003

Contents

List of Figures

List of Tables

List of Boxes

Composition of the Group

Chairman

André Sapir, Université Libre de Bruxelles and Group of Policy Advisers, European Commission

Members

Philippe Aghion, Harvard University

Giuseppe Bertola, Università di Torino and European University Institute

Martin Hellwig, Universität Mannheim

Jean Pisani-Ferry, Université Paris-Dauphine

Dariusz Rosati, Szkolą Glówną Handlową w Warszawie and Narodowy Bank Polski

José Viñals, Banco de España

Helen Wallace, Robert Schuman Centre for Advanced Studies, European University Institute, and Sussex European Institute

Rapporteurs

Marco Buti, Mario Nava and **Peter Smith**, Group of Policy Advisers, European Commission.

The Group met eight times between July 2002 and June 2003, in Brussels, Florence, Paris, and Warsaw. It benefited greatly from the constant support of the staff of the Group of Policy Advisers at the European Commission. In particular, it wishes to acknowledge research assistance provided by Kirsten Lemming-Christensen and Peer Ritter as well as administrative support from Pamela Cranston and Guy Wilmes. It also thanks Bob Taylor for editorial assistance.

All members of the Group participated in a personal capacity. Views expressed in the Report should not be attributed to any of the institutions with which they are affiliated.

The Report was submitted to the President of the European Commission in July 2003.

1

Overview

Over the past decade, the process of European economic integration has witnessed considerable institutional success, with the establishment of the Single Market in 1993, the launch of the euro in 1999 and the decision to welcome ten new Member States into the European Union (EU) in 2004. The economic performance of the EU, however, is more varied. While macroeconomic *stability* has considerably improved and a strong emphasis on *cohesion* has been preserved, the EU economic system has failed to deliver a satisfactory *growth* performance.

Europe needs to grow, not only in area but also in dynamism. A more dynamic EU will help the integration of new Member States and strongly growing new members will contribute to more dynamism. A more dynamic EU will also be a better partner for other European and Mediterranean neighbouring countries, and for the global system. Faster growth is also paramount for the sustainability of the European model, which puts a high premium on cohesion. Sustainability is under threat from rapid developments in demography, technology, and globalisation, all of which increase the demand for social protection. Fortunately, however, technology and globalisation, like enlargement, also hold the potential for faster growth.

It is against this background that the Group was asked to review all three facets of the EU economic system—the Single Market and complementary microeconomic policies, macroeconomic policies inside the monetary union, and the EU budget—and to assess their suitability in the context of enlargement. It was also asked to propose a blueprint for a EU economic system capable of delivering faster growth together with stability and cohesion in the enlarged Union.

The EU system of economic policies is very complex. It encompasses not only a large number of instruments, but also a wide array of decision-makers, ranging from local to national and supranational actors, which often share responsibilities for the many instruments. Moreover, these instruments and actors often operate with different time horizons. Coherence—across instruments and objectives, across decision-makers and jurisdictions, and over time— is therefore difficult to achieve inside the EU system. At the same time, however, coherence is absolutely necessary in order to ensure that the system delivers.

The Report is in three parts. The first contains an assessment of economic performance in terms of growth, stability, and cohesion. The second part

looks at the challenges facing the Union in the years to come. The final part of
the Report builds on the previous two to distil a series of recommendations for
the future.

1.1. Assessment

European Union policies (Chapter 3)
Judged by the progress made in the integration process, there is no doubt that
the period of the last fifteen years has been a tremendous success. A number
of flagship policies have been successfully implemented. The Single Market
Programme was a major step forward, even if a number of problems of coverage and implementation remain. The remit of competition policy was widened
to include merger control and the Uruguay Round of trade negotiations has led
to significant trade liberalisation. Even more remarkable were the smooth
creation of the Economic and Monetary Union (EMU) and the pooling of
monetary sovereignty in the European Central Bank (ECB).

Growth (Chapter 4)
By removing barriers to the mobility of goods, services, labour, and capital,
the Single Market Programme was intended to foster competition, to boost
productivity and to accelerate growth. Yet, growth has been mediocre, with
Europe's performance deteriorating—both absolutely and in comparison with
the United States. It is as if Europe has become stuck in a rut. That is all the
more surprising since the size of the home market, the high level of human
resources, capital, and infrastructure, the potential for catching up with the
United States and the efforts made to promote more competition should
together have provided a solid basis for sustaining above average growth over
a number of years.

It has now become clear that the context in which economic policies have
been developed changed fundamentally over the past thirty years. A system
built around the assimilation of existing technologies, mass production generating economies of scale, and an industrial structure dominated by large firms
with stable markets, and long-term employment patterns no longer delivers in
the world of today, characterised by economic globalisation and strong
external competition. What is needed now is less vertically integrated firms,
greater mobility within and across firms, more retraining, greater flexibility of
labour markets, greater availability of external finance—in particular equity
finance, and higher investment in both R&D and higher education. In other
words, what is required is a massive change in economic institutions and
organisations, which has not yet occurred on a large scale in Europe.

Stability (Chapter 4)
In the field of macroeconomic policy, the period of the 1990s could best be
qualified as one of 'cleaning up the balance sheet'. Overall, stability has been

greatly enhanced by the achievement of low inflation and lower budget deficits. However, while the United States has been able to achieve greater economic stability without any apparent reduction in growth, the EU progress towards stability has been accompanied by lower growth, thus prolonging the unsatisfactory growth trend of the previous decade. Furthermore, not all Member States have recently pursued stability-oriented policies with the same enthusiasm as in the run up to monetary union. As a result, those countries that failed to create the necessary room for manoeuvre under the 3 per cent deficit ceiling when growth conditions were favourable are now in trouble. They find themselves required to undertake major structural reforms with little room for manoeuvre on the macroeconomic side.

Cohesion (Chapter 4)

Convergence has occurred both at the level of Member States and at that of the macro regions. At a more disaggregated regional level, however, the evidence is less clear-cut. Efforts by the EU through the structural funds and the cohesion fund to promote convergence can only be a complement to other factors. They must be accompanied by national policies to put in place a favourable environment for investment and for human capital formation. The varied administrative capacities of Member States have proved decisive in facilitating growth not least by their use of funds from the EU budget. This experience has obvious implications for enlargement where new members will need to achieve very high rates of growth over a sustained period in order to converge with the more developed Member States.

Economic trade-offs (Chapter 5)

Policies to promote growth, stability, and cohesion may be mutually supportive or they may undermine each other. The extent to which they are supportive or not depends to a great extent on the existence of trade-offs. Concerning the relationship between macroeconomic stability and growth, a major effort to bring inflation and public deficits under control preceded monetary union. This effort may have had a short-term negative impact on economic activity in some cases but in the medium term it provided a much-improved framework for growth. Growth may have a negative effect on cohesion if market forces lead to a widening of the income gaps between regions or between individuals. In the case of economic convergence between regions there is little evidence of such effects and, on the contrary, lagging regions have provided a boost to overall EU growth. As regards interpersonal distribution, market forces have tended to increase the inequality of incomes. Member States have generally reacted with higher levels of tax and transfers to maintain the previous post-tax and transfer distribution of income. Such policies have been good for cohesion, but at the expense of lower incentives for growth.

Economic governance (Chapter 6)
How economic policies are managed in the EU has become a key issue in recent years. Currently, a patchwork of different arrangements for managing economic policies in the EU is in place. Four basic approaches have been adopted: delegation, commitment, coordination, and autonomy of national policies. Not only are there different approaches, but also many different instruments are used to execute policy, ranging from hard collective rules to milder instruments of persuasion and soft procedures for cooperation and dialogue. The picture that emerges is one of confusion and tension—confusion created by the complexity of the system and diversity of the roles performed, and tension in the gap between goals and means.

1.2. Challenges

Sustainability (Chapter 7)
The dilemma facing European policy-makers is likely to increase in the years ahead. The current combination of low growth and high public expenditure is not sustainable, and will become less so in future. Europe's population has aged considerably but is set to age even more, leading to higher public expenditure for pensions and for health care. Innovation and change will open the prospect of higher productivity, higher wages, and improved living standards. But they will continue to be disruptive and costs will be concentrated in the short run, while the benefits will take longer to materialise. Skill-biased technological change reduces the demand for unskilled workers leading to higher income inequality in the United States and higher long-term unemployment among unskilled workers in Europe. With less employment, the burden of ageing is made worse. Globalisation produces the same effects as technological change, reinforcing its impact.

Enlargement (Chapter 8)
The eastward enlargement of the EU presents both similarities and differences when compared with the southern enlargement to Mediterranean countries in the 1980s. In terms of size (population, GDP) relative to the EU total of the time, both rounds are quite similar. However, the income gap between the new Member States and the current EU is much larger than the one between the Mediterranean countries and the then EU. The accession of ten more countries also adds a dimension of complexity and heterogeneity that was not present in the previous round. At that time, enlargement increased the number of members by one-third, whereas now the EU faces a cumulative doubling of its membership.

Because of the gap in income, convergence between the new Member States and the current EU members is more than ever the key to successful enlargement. Neither theory nor the experience of earlier enlargement convincingly supports a hypothesis of automatic convergence. Convergence occurs only in the presence of certain key growth factors and supporting policies. Identification of these factors and assessing the extent to which they are present in the new Member States are necessary to answer the question whether they are well equipped for rapid and sustained growth. On the one hand, the new Member States have relatively high levels of human capital. On the other hand, they have a legacy of old industrial investment, environmental damage, and poor public administration to remedy.

The new Member States are not only poorer; they are also structurally different. Against this background, it may be assumed that their economic priorities can differ, not only from those in the EU-15, but also among themselves. This poses a double challenge with respect to EU-wide macroeconomic policy: first, how to ensure the necessary degree of fiscal discipline and coordination in a grouping of twenty-five countries with quite diverse macroeconomic and structural characteristics; and, second, how eventually to conduct a single monetary policy in a euro area with increased economic heterogeneity.

Enlargement will further increase the heterogeneity of the EU. The model of governance of the EU was initially conceived for a Community, which was small and homogenous as regards levels of economic development. Successive rounds of enlargement, increasing yet uneven market integration and the growing number of policy domains and instruments have made the task of governance more and more complex. Challenges are already apparent in a wide range of policy domains, ranging from regulatory policies to the macroeconomic field. They could trigger a hollowing out of the intermediate layers of governance based on commitment and coordination to the benefit of the two 'corner solutions' of delegation and Member States autonomy, unless the EU is able to achieve significant efficiency gains in making coordination and cooperation work.

1.3. Recommendations

Principles (Chapter 10)
Transforming the EU system of economic policy-making, so as to deliver higher growth, will require redesigning policies and revising their modes of delivery, as embodied in governance methods and the EU budget.

We follow four principles in recommending new policy designs:

1. To expand growth potential requires first and foremost reforms of microeconomic policies. However, there is also a need to revise some features of the current macroeconomic policy setting and to redesign cohesion policies at both the EU and national levels.
2. Well-functioning and competitive markets for labour, capital, goods, and services foster growth. Appropriate market regulation also plays a crucial role. Improving the functioning of product and factor markets requires action at both the EU and national levels.

3. Quite often in the EU economic system, policy instruments are assigned two objectives at the same time: for example, fostering growth and improving cohesion. It would be better to assign one objective to each policy instrument.
4. New policy designs should improve the functioning of the enlarged Union and be geared towards increasing growth both in general and in the new Member States.

We also follow four principles in recommending new modes of delivery:

1. Methods need to be better matched to tasks. Some tasks need methods of delegation that are crystal clear, consistent, and capable of well-specified implementation. Others depend on building up cooperation over time and on leaving space for decentralised experimentation and more local dynamics.
2. Effective implementation of EU policy frequently depends on the willingness of national and sub-national government bodies to set their own priorities and develop their own agenda in accordance with EU priorities. Promoting the EU's role as a facilitator requires not only sticks but also carrots, including through the EU budget.
3. Whatever the incentives from the top, EU priorities can translate into policy actions by the Member States or by economic and social actors only if they develop a sense of shared ownership.
4. In an enlarged Union, variable geometry is likely to become a natural response to differences of situation or preference. In order to make it functional, clarity about basic organising principles will be of utmost importance.

But before presenting its detailed recommendations, the Report sets out an agenda for a growing Europe to achieve its two strategic economic goals for the years to 2010 in terms of, on the one hand, creating the most competitive and dynamic knowledge-based economy, and, on the other hand, rapidly raising standards of living in the new Member States.

The agenda contains six points which focus on where EU policies and their economic management can make the greatest contribution to achieving the declared aims of sustainable growth with more and better jobs, continuing price stability and greater economic and social cohesion. The six-point agenda calls on the EU and its members to:

(1) make the Single Market more dynamic;
(2) boost investment in knowledge;
(3) improve the macroeconomic policy framework for EMU;
(4) redesign policies for convergence and restructuring;
(5) achieve more effectiveness in decision-taking and regulation; and
(6) refocus the EU budget.

The Report contains a series of recommendations for each agenda item. The recommendations are divided into policies (items 1–4) and modes of delivery (items 5 and 6).

Policies for promoting growth (Chapter 11)

1. *Make the Single Market more dynamic.* Here the main recommendations are for better coordination between regulatory and competition policies to encourage market access for new entrants and to introduce a more proactive policy to support labour mobility within the Union. A third recommendation is to develop infrastructure to connect up the broader European economy.

2. *Boost investment in knowledge.* The specific recommendations in this context are to increase government and EU spending in research and post-graduate education, to allocate research grants according to the highest scientific standards, to create an independent European Agency for Science and Research, and to encourage private-sector R&D through tax credits.

3. *Improve the macroeconomic policy framework for EMU.* The recommendations here go in the direction of improving the incentives for countries to secure surpluses in good times, while increasing the room for manoeuvre for fiscal policies in bad times within a framework of strengthened budgetary surveillance and more effective and flexible implementation of the Stability and Growth Pact (SGP), while sticking to the 3 per cent ceiling. The Commission should reinforce its surveillance and be given more responsibility to interpret the rules of the SGP. Also, budgetary responsibility would be enhanced by establishing independent Fiscal Auditing Boards in the Member States. At the same time, a higher degree of country differentiation based on the level of public indebtedness should be introduced and the conditions under which the 3 per cent deficit threshold can be breached should be modified. Another set of recommendations concerns policy coordination: there should be greater coordination among national budgeting processes and more dialogue between the president of a newly-established euro-area Council, the relevant EU commissioner and the ECB president.

4. *Redesign policies for convergence and restructuring.* In this context, the Report recommends that EU convergence policy should concentrate on low-income countries rather than low-income regions, and that eligibility for access to EU assistance should be reviewed at the end of each programming period. In addition, convergence funds allocated to low-income countries should focus on two areas: (*a*) institution building, and (*b*) investment in human and physical capital, leaving beneficiaries free to decide how to allocate resources across different national projects. The Report also recommends EU restructuring support for workers who lose their job and need support to retrain, relocate, or start a new business, as a complement to national welfare policies. Part of the restructuring efforts should also be devoted to the agricultural sector.

Modes of delivery: Governance and the budget (Chapter 12)

1. *Achieve effectiveness in decision-taking and regulation.* Here the Report makes a series of recommendations: the assignment of competences between the EU and national levels of governance should be more flexibly and coherently defined; the devolution of some funding, economic law enforcement, and regulatory functions from the Commission to independent European bodies; further movement towards decentralised implementation of market regulation by developing both steered networks of national and EU bodies operating within the same legal framework and partnerships of autonomous national bodies cooperating with each other and with EU bodies; improvement in the management of the Single Market; strengthening EU methods for implementing the common growth and social cohesion agenda; institutional reform aimed at strengthening the strategic capabilities of EU institutions, including a leaner Commission (fifteen members) and more qualified majority voting (QMV) on economic issues in the Council; and extension of the possibilities for developing more intensive cooperation among subsets of Member States, without defining an a priori threshold for the number of participants.

2. *Refocus the EU budget.* The idea is to reorganise radically that part of the budget for economic actions within the EU. There should be three funds: a growth fund, a convergence fund, and a restructuring fund. Eligibility for each kind of spending will be based on separate, but fair and transparent criteria. This restructuring would enable the budget to play a more clearly defined role in achieving the Union's 2010 objectives. If the total budget amount remains unchanged, this will imply a major cut in agricultural spending and the devolution of spending for rural policy to the Member States. Financing the budget should move away from national contributions to sources with a clear EU dimension. Along with changes in expenditures and revenues, the Report recommends changes in budgetary procedures, including the devolution of some responsibility for budget execution to actors other than the Commission.

2

A conceptual framework

This Report aims first at assessing whether and how economic policy as implemented in the European Union (EU) has been able to achieve its objective. It does so by analysing historical evidence in the context of a rapidly changing political and economic environment. In the recent past, change has been driven by new technologies, globalisation, German reunification, and the process of European integration itself. The Report then assesses how the EU's policy-making framework can best adapt to further challenging developments in the form of continued globalisation and enlargement, set against a background of an ageing population.

The Report seeks to make recommendations for adapting the EU policy-making framework based on clear principles for policy evaluation. This opening chapter outlines a conceptual framework for policy assessment, on the basis of clearly outlined trade-offs and interactions between objectives, between instruments, and over time in a changing environment.

The process through which supranational institutions and policies emerged in Europe was motivated by a variety of politico-economic objectives. In the aftermath of the Second World War, the original six members chiefly wished to organise their mutual relationships in a way that would prevent future wars. Accession by Spain, Portugal, and Greece had important implications for those countries' commitment to democracy, while EU membership also has obvious political implications for the formerly communist countries of central and eastern Europe. Thus, a variety of different, if similarly strong, political reasons for European accession led the member countries towards 'ever closer union.'

The scope and depth of integration have been increasing along with the number of Member States in areas like defence and external representation. But the process of European integration so far has been driven essentially by economics. Economic policy instruments and economic policy goals have played the central role in the framework of the European Community: by stimulating trade, competition, and factor mobility, resources will be allocated more efficiently and aggregate incomes will rise. An efficient allocation of economic activity, however, need not necessarily be equitable and politically acceptable. Market pressure can be perceived to be unfair when markets are imperfect. The European continent has in the last century witnessed wars, revolutions, hyperinflation, and excessive fluctuations, resulting in episodic social and political crises. Hence, it is far from surprising that national and supranational policy-makers should be concerned not only with economic growth but also with cohesion (to the extent that divergent economic circumstances could foster social conflict) and with stability (to prevent excessive fluctuations of economic, monetary, and fiscal circumstances from provoking political crises).

In the history and practice of European economic policies, accordingly, the efficiency (or 'growth') implications of economic integration and other institutional developments are intimately intertwined with 'cohesion' and 'stability' objectives. Throughout this Report, the final goal of EU economic policies is taken to be that of achieving higher incomes and faster growth, in a macro-economically stable and cohesive Union of as many states as historical circumstances allow, in the light of political as well as economic objectives.

2.1. On policy coherence

Throughout the world, and in all history, economic and social outcomes are shaped by the interaction of market forces and collectively-decided policies. Market interactions are imperfect in various respects, and a variety of policy instruments can effectively alter market-driven outcomes, positively as well as negatively.

It is possible, however, to identify reasons why policies and the relevant governance processes may fail to yield socially desirable outcomes. The resulting conceptual framework will be brought to bear on assessing the performance of the complex historical web of political and economic features that characterise the EU policy-making system, and will be useful in outlining how policy may best be configured so as to deal with the special challenges facing Europe now and in the near future.

To this end, it will be useful to focus on the relationship between the *scope* of *policies* and the *governance process* that implements policy instruments. Policy decisions and implementation can be defective when the scope of policies and of decision-making processes is imperfectly coherent across policy effects and policy decisions, either at a point in time, or over time. Coherence can be looked at on three levels:

- coherence at the level of instruments and objectives;
- coherence at the level of decision-makers and jurisdictions; and
- coherence over time for a given decision-maker and/or jurisdiction.

The following three subsections offer general definitions and practical examples of the desirability and possible lack of coherence for each of these dimensions.

2.1.1. *Coherence at the level of policy instruments and objectives*

Policies lack coherence between instruments and objectives when they effectively address a specific objective in a positive direction, but have adverse effects on other objectives.

There may not be a general trade-off between growth, stability, and cohesion, in the sense that the three objectives can be met simultaneously by an appropriate set of policies in favourable economic circumstances. However, trade-offs can easily emerge when specific instruments are designed and implemented to reach these objectives. For instance, stability can foster growth if it is conducive to long-horizon investment and innovation decisions by economic agents. But it may be that a particular policy instrument, such as the strict limits to government deficits envisaged by the Stability and Growth Pact (SGP), does foster stability at the expense of growth in specific circumstances (e.g. if it prevents desirable reforms in the face of demographic changes). Similarly, growth and cohesion may be achieved together in principle, but may conflict in practice if, for example, regional policies reduce the intensity of reallocation and restructuring (hence overall growth and efficiency) for the sake of cohesion.

Even when policy instruments have conflicting implications for the basic growth, stability, and cohesion objectives, policies may still coherently pursue the EU's broad objectives if the three objectives are traded off against each other according to a well-defined set of priorities. In terms of the two examples given above, it may be perfectly sensible for instruments such as the SGP or regional policies to sacrifice some growth if the stability and cohesion they afford is valuable.

A set of policy instruments lacks coherence in a deeper and disturbing sense, however, when it fails to achieve its objectives efficiently. For example, cohesion may be pursued by instruments that reduce efficiency more than would be necessary to achieve a given level of cohesion. This is arguably the case when regional policies work against (rather than in favour of) the structural adjustments based on comparative advantage called for by economic integration processes. It should also be kept in mind that policies can reinforce or offset each other's desirable effects. Market liberalisation may, for instance, foster faster growth, but other policies (such as the enforcement of property rights) are needed to ensure that liberalisation results in desirable outcomes.

2.1.2. *Coherence at the level of decision-makers and jurisdictions*

Policies lack coherence when the decision-making process fails to address the full scope of their effects across interconnected geographic and political entities.

Lack of coherence in this sense can result from *different policy objectives* across levels of government and across constituencies. The nature of the resulting policy failure is intimately related to the mechanism underlying undesirable outcomes of laissez-faire interactions among individual economic agents. Just as imperfect factor and goods markets can fail to balance appropriately the sometimes conflicting objectives of economic agents, so imperfect political interactions between collective decision-makers with differing objectives can result in undesirable policy configurations. Conflicts of interests between policy-making entities may lead to attempts to undo the effects of policies implemented at higher or lower levels.

But lack of coherence can also be brought about by more subtle failures of policy coordination. Even policy-makers who share an ultimately common view of what would constitute desirable outcomes may fail to take appropriate action. When implementing policies that have effects beyond their immediate constituency, each may rely on others to implement costly actions in pursuit of a *common good*, and inaction may result even when all share similar views on appropriate actions. Again, the nature of the relevant policy failure is similar to what may be observed when interactions at the individual level fail to address public-good aspects appropriately: just as individuals cannot be expected to pay taxes spontaneously in the absence of collective enforcement, so policy-makers cannot be expected to implement the tax, subsidy, and regulatory policies that would be optimal from the viewpoint of a large integrated area when their constituency is smaller than the scope of those policies.

In both cases, the failure to see policy trade-offs in their entirety can imply that policy implementation fails to address them appropriately. When this happens, poor coordination results in outcomes that are unsatisfactory from the constituents' and policy-makers' own point of view. Just as market interactions can fail to support efficient outcomes when some markets fail to exist or function properly, so imperfect coordination of policy implementation can fail to yield efficient allocations in a given market environment.

2.1.3. *Coherence over time*

Policies lack coherence over time (or *sustainability*) if political choice and implementation processes lack foresight, and fail to take into account consistently their own ultimate consequences. Coordination of individual innovation efforts and orderly exchanges in the factor and product markets can be fostered by an appropriately sustainable policy-making environment, able to deliver appropriate incentives to entrepreneurship, as well as by low and predictable interest rates, and by public institutions conducive to the enforcement of property rights and the rule of law.

Imperfect coherence of policy decisions over time can undermine growth and efficiency, however. For both individual and collective decision-makers, excessive commitment to the status quo can result in stagnation, just as easily as opportunistic behaviour can yield instability. Political decision-making processes need not in general be better able than individual actions to achieve the degree of foresight needed to take proper account of forward-looking considerations. Financial and fiscal instability, for example, can certainly reduce investment and innovation incentives through heightened uncertainty and higher real interest rates.

2.2. A perspective on economic policies in the European Union

The European Union's *system of economic policies* includes a wide variety of decision-making powers and policy instruments, ranging from local to national and supranational constituencies; across executive, legislative, and jurisdictional aspects; and from microeconomic market regulation to macro-economic fiscal and monetary stance.

In the following chapters, the Report will assess in some detail the extent to which the EU has been able to achieve its main growth, stability, and cohesion objectives. Before proceeding with this assessment, it will be useful to discuss briefly how the general conceptual framework may offer a constructive perspective on the role of policies and reforms in shaping the well-known features of broad economic outcomes. If cooperation among European nations was originally meant to avoid war, this fundamental objective has undeniably been achieved. But the EU policy-making record is mixed as regards the economic and social objectives pursued by the economic instruments adopted by national and supranational institutions. As we will see, economic integration has proved to be able to foster convergence across countries in the EU in the long run (but less across regions within countries, while equity among individuals appears increasingly difficult to achieve). But the growth and employment performance of EU economies has been broadly disappointing.

By means of a detailed assessment of different performances of different countries, regions, and sectors in different respects, the Report focuses on how lack of growth and efficiency may be remedied by more appropriate use of available policy instruments, in ways consistent with cohesion and stability objectives. The broad coherence-based perspective proposed above can be very helpful in ascertaining why imperfect policy-making processes can result in outcomes that appear not only to sacrifice growth for the sake of other objectives, but also to achieve less growth and efficiency than European policy-makers and citizens appear to find desirable.

2.2.1. *Policy incoherence and low-growth malaise*

It is easy to blame policies and institutions for the disappointing growth and employment performance of European countries. High levels of taxation and redistribution, stringent regulation, and anti-competitive market structures are widespread in European industry and services, and all are theoretically and empirically associated with low levels of economic activity.

To the extent that tax, spending, and regulatory policy instruments aim at objectives other than economic growth and formal employment, of course, it is not surprising or disturbing to find that they fail to foster growth. The policy instruments blamed for low employment and growth outcomes may not only contribute to achieving cohesion (through redistribution) and stability (by restraining turbulent competition), but might also reflect a preference for leisure over material production.

However, as will be apparent in the assessment exercise of Chapter 4, in many instances government policies and other forms of collective action lack coherence in both the static and dynamic dimensions discussed above. Policies implemented by different instruments or by different decision-makers some-times tend to counteract, rather than strengthen, each other's desirable effects. And many policies and regulations stifle change and reduce economic effi-ciency, by discouraging entrepreneurship and encouraging self-production rather than efficient market exchange.

Coherence at the level of objectives and instruments is doubtful when policies that restrain market efficiency have similarly adverse effects on cohesion and stability. Of course, incoherent policies are endogenously determined in politico-economic equilibrium. Conflicting economic interests easily lead to poorly coordinated policy implementation, and entrenched agents all too readily stand in the way of market competition and economic efficiency. However, to the extent that these outcomes are not uniformly satisfactory, the conceptual framework outlined above indicates that the roots of disappointing performance have to be sought in inappropriate allocation of decisions and/or in a political process that does not correctly address the relevant dynamic trade-offs. The difficulty of addressing policy issues at the appropriate level of scope need not lead European citizens and policy-makers to accept the status quo situation passively. A clear understanding of the relevant static and dynamic trade-offs can lead policy-making processes to target their objectives more effectively, and offer a credible alternative to pleasant, but static, economic conditions.

Coherence at the level of jurisdictions and decision-makers may also be particularly difficult to achieve in the EU system of economic policies. The EU is a multi-tier government system, where each of the three policy instrument sets mentioned in the first section of this chapter have both Community and national dimensions. The Single Market—encompassing goods, services, and capital—is a Community programme, but labour market regulation as well as many flanking initiatives rest with the national authorities and are subject to different degrees of coordination. The income redistribution function is spread across the EU level and the national level; the former dealing mainly with interregional and intercountry cohesion, the latter with interpersonal cohesion. The tools of macroeconomic stabilisation are also spread across the two levels: monetary policy is centralised for countries belonging to the euro area, but fiscal discipline is decentralised to the national level, subject to Community rules. In summary, the largest part of fiscal policy (be it for allocative, redistributive, or stabilisation purposes) is a national responsibility subject to an EU constraint (the SGP). However, a small part of fiscal policy (the EU budget) has been allocated to the EU subject to national constraint (resources transferred from Member States). At present, no coordination exists between the two levels.

Coherence over time is a very desirable and very elusive feature of economic policies everywhere. It may be particularly difficult to achieve in the EU context, however, because a young and evolving institutional framework naturally finds it difficult to adopt an appropriately long horizon in its policy implementation and institutional reform processes. An obvious example of incoherence over time in the EU policy framework is of course that emphasised by the landmark 1987 Padoa-Schioppa Report between monetary, exchange rate, and capital control policies. Fixing exchange rates in the absence of appropriate supporting policies or institutions, that is under independent monetary policies and free capital mobility, led to frequent realignments in the Exchange Rate Mechanism (ERM), and ultimately to unsustainable instability. Now that Economic and Monetary Union (EMU) has successfully addressed this type of incoherence, many Europeans may appear happy not to grow, but stagnation can hardly be a sustainable outcome. While resistance to change is often understandable from the point of view of individual economic agents, the resulting stagnation can easily lead the same agents to regret not taking action. Increasing unhappiness at the lack of growth and jobs is an indication that the status quo may precipitate a crisis rather than maintain stability, while a policy framework that fosters low growth lacks coherence over time.

It is not surprising to see signs of policy incoherence in the resulting system of economic and political interaction. Offsetting market failures by appropriate tax-and-subsidy or regulation policies (in the social and labour market area as well as in financial and other markets) can be difficult when decision-making is decentralised, and policy-making authorities are accountable to constituencies that are small relative to the scope of economic interaction across a large integrated area. As discussed above, the resulting framework can easily lack coherence as each policy-maker focuses on a small portion of aggregate trade-offs, or relies on others to provide common goods. For example, if factor and product market integration makes tax bases react very elastically to taxation and lets social benefits be paid to members of other jurisdictions (directly, through immigration, or indirectly, through product market interaction), it is difficult for uncoordinated local jurisdictions to achieve the redistribution they deem desirable in the light of financial market imperfections and political cohesion objectives. Local decision-making, unfettered integration of factor and product markets, and a desire to protect one's own citizens from poverty are the three elements of an inconsistent trinity. One of the three aspects (or part of each) must be sacrificed: decision-making must be centralised or coordinated to preserve both redistribution and economic integration; alternatively, redistribution can be abandoned—a 'race to the bottom' outcome with little political acceptability in Europe — or economic integration may remain imperfect. A policy-making framework maintaining all three elements as basic principles is internally incoherent and doomed to failure, while uncertainty regarding which of the three will be the odd-member-out of the trinity adds dynamic incoherence to it. As mentioned in Section 2.1, redistribution can be excessive, and can go in the wrong direction, and is certainly not liked by all. From the collective point of view, however, there can be no presumption that policies are in general beneficial or in general harmful. Only a clear understanding of the relevant trade-offs can lead to adequate policies. If markets imperfectly address the relevant issues, relying on automatic competition among equally imperfect policy-making systems, they are unlikely to foster better outcomes than a well-informed, coherent policy-making framework.

The EU system of economic policies addresses coordination and coherence problems on the basis of the subsidiarity principle. Policy decisions and implementation should respect the principle of 'economic subsidiarity', and be delegated to the lowest level of government able to balance benefits and costs of the relevant policy. In practice, of course, the effects of all policies spill across the borders of local constituencies, and when the interests and objectives of different jurisdictions are heterogeneous the application of the principle of subsidiarity is subject to a political check. Political constraints might translate into an implementation level higher or lower than the optimal one. If changing tier proves politically unfeasible or too costly, coordination may be second best for centralisation and differentiation second best for decentralisation. From the perspective proposed above, markets often fail to deliver desirable outcomes, but government intervention does not necessarily deliver unambiguously better outcomes. Hence, the extent to which policy governance processes can best interpret economic and social preferences needs to be taken into account along with standard diversity and accountability criteria when allocating policies to various levels of government. Not only heterogeneous policy preferences, but also rent-seeking temptations can get in the way of appropriately coherent harmonisation, and governance institutions should be carefully designed so as to guarantee that policy trade-offs are addressed appropriately rather than myopically.

PART I

ASSESSMENT

3

Policy implementation

Since the mid-1980s, the Community has been implementing policies to respond to low growth, high inflation, and low levels of employment. A legislative programme, often called the Single Market Programme, was launched in the hope that removing barriers would reallocate resources and foster competition, thus boosting productivity and raising real incomes. The full liberalisation of capital flows, a cornerstone of this programme, was among the primary reasons that eventually led to the creation of the Economic and Monetary Union (EMU) in 1999, flanked by provisions introducing new disciplines on national budgetary policies. In order to benefit from the growth effects of the Single Market, a number of conditions needed to be met. To ensure that all Member States would be able to meet those conditions, spending on cohesion policy was expanded.

This chapter sketches the developments between the mid-1980s and 2003 under four main headings: growth, stability, cohesion, and the budget (Molle 2001; Pelkmans 2001; Tsoukalis 1997).

3.1. Growth

Single market
The White Paper *Completing the Internal Market* (European Commission 1985) started the Single Market process with the explicit aim of completing it by the end of 1992.

On 1 January 1993, border controls for goods were indeed eliminated as foreseen in the 1985 White Paper. The Single Market for goods has been largely achieved. Frictions still arise as a result of the diversity of national technical regulations, despite the principle of mutual recognition. A cornerstone of the Single Market Programme, this posits that Member States are requested to recognise regulations drawn by other EU countries as being equivalent to their own, allowing economic activities that are lawful in one Member State to be freely pursued throughout the Community. Member States are often reluctant to recognise this equivalence. Harmonisation represents an alternative approach to mutual recognition either where mutual recognition does not work or for areas for which it is not appropriate. Under the new approach, the EU sets out essential requirements which can be met in different ways, for the most part by the development of EU product standards.

Since 1987 the 'home bias' in public procurement of goods (but also of services) has been addressed progressively through EU-wide rules on the issuing of tenders. The total value of public procurement represents about 16 per cent of the EU GDP. The value of public contracts actually awarded to bidders from another Member State, which was 6 per cent of total tenders in 1987 had risen to 10 per cent in 1998 (European Commission 2003e).

Services are regulated in much more diverse ways than goods. Legal barriers include restrictions on the number of providers of particular services and their qualifications, licensing rules, legal form, etc., while the identity of the regulator varies from local administrations to professional associations. Furthermore, many services are provided by bodies under public ownership, whether as social and local services or as public utilities. The Single Market Programme strategy for service liberalisation was based around home country control, which can be considered a counterpart to mutual recognition. The Commission also took a sectoral and gradualist approach to liberalising services, often relying on case law from the European Court of Justice, competition policy, and following technological developments in some markets. Using competition policy, the Commission gradually reduced the scope of legal monopolies. Liberalisation of certain services requires ongoing regulation in addition to a given set of rules established by statute, for instance network industries and financial services. In these cases the Commission did not set up European regulators, but is providing national regulators with some mandatory rules, ranging from requirements of regulatory independence to licensing and pricing principles. In spite of active EU policies for the liberalisation of network industries, some EU countries have a different degree of commitment to utility liberalisation and progress has been uneven.

The recognition of diplomas and professional qualifications is a very substantial barrier to the freedom to provide certain types of service. Whereas directives regulate the recognition of university degrees, ensuring equivalence of professional qualifications has proved a much harder exercise. Directives shaped a general system of mutual recognition of professional qualifications, but rules taking account of the specifics of individual professions have also been necessary, because Member States often refuse to acknowledge equivalence of each other's qualifications.

The free movement of capital involves the cross-border transfer of ownership of assets (both financial capital and foreign direct investment). A directive implemented the principle in 1988, which specified the types of capital movements to be freed by 1 June 1990. The Treaty of Maastricht makes the freedom of capital movement directly applicable among Member States and between Member States and third countries; discrimination between different forms of movements was ended. With capital liberalisation, some Member States complained of an erosion of tax revenues concerning the direct taxation of personal savings and company taxation. While proposals to harmonise company tax bases or rates have been on the table for decades, their adoption has been blocked by the requirement of unanimity in the Council. Limited measures have been adopted. In 1997, the Council agreed on a code of conduct for business taxation, followed by a list of harmful tax practices in 1999, which are addressed under the Community state-aid rules. The taxation of personal savings is by country of residence, so that interest income from accounts in other Member States often went undeclared, benefiting in many cases from local provisions on banking secrecy. Member States have provisionally agreed that from 2004, they will either implement a system of automatic information exchange on the savings income and interest on non-resident accounts or a system of automatic withholding tax.

Flanking policies
The EU competition policy since the mid-1980s can be characterised by three developments.

1. An active *ex ante* control of mergers was introduced by a regulation in 1990, as it had not been provided for in the Treaty (Seabright 2001).
2. Since the late 1980s the Commission has been using competition policy as a tool for liberalising markets. Member States often granted legal monopolies to companies for public policy goals, as in telecommunications, transport, postal services, gas, and electricity. In order to maintain wide public access to these services, the Treaty exempts service providers from EU competition rules under certain conditions. The Commission increasingly questioned whether a legal monopoly was indeed necessary to ensure public access, gradually forcing open monopoly markets.
3. Furthermore, the Treaty foresees that the Commission exercises control over state aid to avoid distortions of competition through subsidies to national companies. The Commission has been active in promoting a reorientation from aid to individual companies or sectors to less distortive horizontal regimes addressing specific market failures.

EU trade policy has pursued a two-pronged approach. Multilateral trade policy is conducted through the World Trade Organisation (WTO), created as a result of the Uruguay Round, which took place from 1986 to 1994. As to regional trade policy, the European Economic Area (EEA) was created in 1994 to integrate those western European countries that wished to benefit from the Single Market while remaining outside the EU, although implementation was largely overtaken by the 1995 enlargement and the EEA has not proved attractive to third countries. So-called Europe Agreements have been concluded with the accession countries. Starting in 1991, the EU has progressively liberalised trade with these countries on a reciprocal basis. Furthermore, the EU has been consistently expanding free trade agreements with third countries.

The EU promotes R&D by maintaining its own research facilities and by financial support for third-party research. Since 1984, the latter is organised in

multi-annual research framework programmes, where many individual projects involving multiple European partners are co-financed by the Commission. Since 2000, the Commission has shifted the focus of the R&D
framework programmes towards supporting networks of excellence, whereby
larger grants will be given to a few established research institutions colla-
borating on a European scale. After thirty years of discussion, the Council
reached agreement in March 2003 on the Community Patent. It will be
granted by the European Patent Office and litigation will take place before a
judicial panel, subject to review by the European Court of Justice. Growth-
oriented policies to develop physical infrastructure are targeted on the one side
at particular countries and regions as part of cohesion policy. But a second
infrastructure policy focuses on the elimination of bottlenecks in advanced
regions and the creation of access in peripheral regions. These Trans-European
Networks for transport, energy, and telecommunications were introduced by
the Maastricht Treaty.

3.2. Macroeconomic stability

In the days before the Single Market, Member States had developed only
limited forms of monetary coordination. However, the growing trade between
them, the need for capital mobility, and the coexistence of asymmetric
monetary policies revived the debate on monetary union in the late 1980s,
which eventually led to the creation of the Economic and Monetary Union
(EMU). (De Grauwe 2003a; Eijffinger and de Haan 2000; Corsetti and Pesenti
1999).

Monetary policy
In the mid-1980s, when the Single Market Programme was launched, most
European currencies were part of the Exchange Rate Mechanism (ERM) of the
European Monetary System (EMS). With capital mobility, the preservation of
a high degree of exchange rate stability became incompatible with the pursuit
of autonomous national monetary policies. This led to the Treaty of Maastricht
in 1992, which fixed the convergence criteria for joining EMU and set a
calendar for its creation. EMU started on 1 January 1999, with all Member
States participating except for Denmark, Sweden, and the United Kingdom.
Greece was not initially a member, but joined EMU in 2001. The Treaty gave
the European Central Bank (ECB) independence and enshrined price stability
as the primary objective of the single monetary policy.

Fiscal policy
With the Treaty of Maastricht, Member States set up provisions limiting the
scope of their budgetary policies. First, convergence criteria had to be fulfilled
to qualify for the final stage of EMU. The fiscal requirements are that
Member States should have budget deficits at or below 3 per cent of GDP and
government debt at or below 60 per cent of GDP (or a tendency towards it) to

join the euro area. These criteria are used by the Commission and the Council to determine whether a Member State runs an 'excessive deficit'. The Stability and Growth Pact (SGP), adopted in 1997, reinforces the excessive deficit procedure by defining more precisely the criteria and circumstances which permit exceptions, sets a timetable for adjustments to be made by Member States, and finally provides for sanctions in case of non-compliance.

3.3. Cohesion

Cohesion policies can be grouped into three categories. The first is convergence policy which aims at promoting regional convergence mainly by allocating development funding to countries and regions on a non-competitive basis. Second comes social policy which targets both the individual employment situation (basically driven by non-discrimination and health concerns) and seeks to develop an active labour market policy. The third policy, agricultural policy, although not conceived as an instrument for interpersonal redistribution, has been turning into one over time. These three policies were substantially reshaped in response to the southern enlargement of the 1980s, which widened income differentials across the Community, to the Single Market and monetary union, whose gains were perceived as flowing unevenly across the Community as well as to the forthcoming eastern enlargement.

Convergence policy
With the 1986 Single European Act, the goal of 'economic and social cohesion' was inserted into the Treaty, driven by concerns that some areas in the Community would not be able to participate in the economic dynamics expected from the completion of the internal market. The convergence of regions has been addressed through the European Regional Development Fund (ERDF), one of the Structural Funds.[1] Its financial endowment grew in 1988, and it concentrated on two instruments. The first covers structural support for regions lagging behind in development, which are selected according to an income per capita criterion relative to the EU average (the so-called objective 1 regions). The other instruments target specific problems throughout the Community, such as regions with a declining industrial base, the need for cross-border cooperation between administrations, and urban and rural development.

The convergence of countries has been addressed through the Cohesion Fund. It was introduced in 1993 to make financial contributions to projects in the field of the environment and transport. Subject to the eligibility condition of a GDP per head of less than 90 per cent of the Community average, four countries (Greece, Ireland, Spain, and Portugal) have benefited from it.

---

[1] See also Box 4.3 in Chapter 4. The other Structural Funds are the European Social Fund (ESF), the European Agricultural Guidance and Guarantee Fund (EAGGF, Guidance Section) and the Financial Instrument for Fisheries Guidance (FIFG).

Social policy
The Single European Act bolstered social policy by facilitating the adoption of labour legislation. Labour law harmonisation in regard to health and safety could be adopted in the Council by qualified majority. While this was seen as a move complementary to the Single Market Programme, some Member States have remained hesitant towards further integration of social policy. The Treaty of Maastricht contained a protocol to draft binding legislation on social policy, which was extended to include all Member States by the Treaty of Amsterdam. However, most social legislation still requires unanimous approval by the Council.

Spending by the European Social Fund (ESF) has been used by the Community to conduct active labour market policies, not least in response to the Single Market, EMU and persistent high unemployment, and to focus on the objectives of combating long-term unemployment, integrating the young into the labour market, and improving the adaptability of the workforce to technological change.

Agricultural policy
The Uruguay Round negotiations exerted pressure for opening European markets to world agricultural products at the same time as overproduction was leading to higher budgetary outlays. In 1992, the Commission initiated a move away from the price support for farmers linked to volume produced to a system of direct aids. In addition a small part of available funds could be used for premiums for those using less intensive production methods for environmental reasons. These reforms were further developed in 1999 in the Agenda 2000 package. In June 2003, the EU Council adopted a fundamental reform of the Common Agricultural Policy (CAP), which partially decouples income support from production and links it, instead, to statutory environmental, food safety, and plant and animal welfare standards.

3.4. The budget

At regular intervals, every five or seven years, the EU heads of state and government set the multi-annual framework for Community finances, when they agree the so-called Financial Perspectives which define the budget guidelines for the ensuing period. The Financial Perspectives, adopted by unanimity, set the Community's spending ceiling for each year of the financing period for each category of spending. Within this multi-annual framework, the Commission proposes a draft annual budget. The Council decides on the so-called compulsory expenditure, which covers obligations arising from the Treaty (mainly the expenditure on agriculture), while the European Parliament and the Council decide on the non-compulsory expenditure, which covers the rest of the budget. The European Parliament finally adopts the annual budget. The Commission is responsible for the execution of the budget, meaning that it takes responsibility for its sound financial management. Every year, the Court of Auditors delivers a technical opinion on the execution of the previous year's budget, upon which (and other considerations) the European Parliament formally discharges the Commission for its stewardship. The growing responsibilities of the Community and a shift in priorities have been reflected in the budget, whose size and composition have changed over the years (Buti and Nava 2003).

The so-called Delors-I financial package (1988–1992) reduced the weight of agriculture in the budget by expanding structural expenditure and created room for further spending. In 1988, farm support took up 60 per cent of the budget, while the Structural Funds accounted for only 17 per cent. By 1992, these shares had shifted to 52 per cent and 27 per cent, respectively. The budget for research was doubled in this time period, although it was still only about 4 per cent of the total budget in 1992. The package added a fourth source of budgetary income, a share of the Member States' GNP, to the three existing own resources of the Community. These were agricultural levies, customs duties, and a share of harmonised Value Added Tax (VAT) revenue of the Member States. The financial perspectives of the Delors-I package laid down a ceiling for the Community's own resources revenue of 1.15 per cent of the Community GDP in 1988, rising to 1.20 per cent in 1992.

The Delors-II financial package (1993–1999) took account of the policies adopted in the Maastricht Treaty. The need to offset the effects of fiscal discipline required for EMU across Member States, in particular the southern countries, led to the creation of the Cohesion Fund. In addition, spending policies to enhance growth were introduced, giving priority to Trans-European Networks. By 1999, the structural policies represented 35 per cent of the total budget, with agriculture down to 45 per cent. The ceiling on total own resources was gradually raised to reach 1.27 per cent of the EU's GDP, where it stands today.

The next budgetary package, Agenda 2000 (2000–2006), reflected the coming eastern enlargement. Its financial impact was expected to be substantial since all candidate countries have incomes per head below the EU average, while their agricultural sector is much larger. For the EU-15, agricultural expenditure was kept roughly at the level of 1999 (thus decreasing its share in the total budget over time), while cohesion spending was lower than the 1999 level. For the accession and candidate countries, the pre-accession aid was set at about 3.5 per cent of the total budget, containing agricultural and structural aid as well as technical assistance. To allow the entry of ten new members in 2004, adjustments to the Agenda 2000 framework were made in 2002. Direct income support for farmers in the new Member States will be phased in until 2013. Structural Fund spending will start for the new Member States from 2004. For 2004–2006, they are allocated an amount corresponding to roughly 25 per cent of the structural expenditure going to the current Member States. In spite of enlargement, the ceiling for the EU's own

Table 3.1. *The budgets of the Community and the Member States, 2000*

	Member States		EU		Total	
	Euro bn	% EU GDP	Euro bn	% EU GDP	Euro bn	% EU GDP
General public services	500	5.8	9.4	0.1	436[b]	5.1
of which transferred to EU[a]	73	0.8	—	—	—	—
Defence	153	1.8	0.0	0.0	153	1.8
Public order and safety	137	1.6	0.1	0.0	137	1.6
Economic affairs	331	3.9	53.3	0.6	384	4.5
Environment protection	62	0.7	5.4	0.1	67	0.8
Housing and community amenities	85	1.0	0.1	0.0	85	1.0
Health	477	5.6	0.1	0.0	477	5.6
Recreation, culture, and religion	70	0.8	0.1	0.0	70	0.8
Education	430	5.0	1.9	0.0	432	5.0
Social protection	1,648	19.2	24.4	0.3	1,672	19.5
Total net of transfers to EU	3,820	44.7	94.8	1.1	3,915	45.7
Total	3,893	45.5	—	—	—	—

[a] The national transfers to the EU budget are the VAT and the GNP resources.
[b] National general public services minus the transfers to the EU plus EU expenditure on general public services.

Source: Eurostat New Cronos database (Classification of the Functions of Government (COFOG)), European Commission (2001*b*, 1*d*) and own calculations. The EU budget figures are payment appropriations authorised.

resources was not raised, owing to the unfavourable macroeconomic situation at the time, fiscal tightening for EMU and because of the dissatisfaction of some current members at their position as net contributors to the EU budget. The composition of the revenue raised from the different sources saw a lowering of the share raised by members' VAT contributions and a rise in the GNP-related payments. The new Member States will make full contributions to the EU budget after joining, but will receive compensation so that they are no worse off in terms of budget receipts than during the pre-accession period.

Table 3.1 shows the budgets of the Member States and the EU for the year 2000 allocated according to ten functions of government. The Community expenditure mainly focuses on economic activities (which consist of the Structural Funds, half of the Cohesion Fund, agricultural market subsidies and several internal policies) and on social protection (the interpersonal redistributive component of CAP). Expenditure on external policies and administration are classified within general public services.

4

Economic performance: Growth, stability, and cohesion

4.1. Growth

4.1.1. *European Union economic performance in a long-term perspective*

The desire to improve poor European economic performance has driven European Union (EU) policy over a long period. The need to combat perceived 'Euro-sclerosis' in the mid-1980s (Giersch 1985; Lawrence and Schultze 1987) gave rise to the Single Market Programme and the Padoa-Schioppa Report (Padoa-Schioppa et al. 1987). A similar perception led to the Lisbon process at the beginning of the current decade and, of course, to the present Report. What are the durable features behind this performance record and what has changed? More specifically, what explains Europe's poor growth performance over the last decade, especially when compared to the United States?

Levels
The United States achieves higher per capita GDP than the EU through both higher labour productivity and higher employment input. This should imply that there is room for the EU to grow faster than the United States through the assimilation of existing technology and organisational practices and that there should be no trade-off between employment and productivity. Instead, after a phase of very rapid catching-up with the United States in the early post-war period, convergence in the levels of per capita GDP at current prices and in purchasing power standards (PPS) came to an end at the beginning of the 1980s and has remained unchanged since at around 70 per cent of US level (Fig. 4.1).

Behind this story lies the strong divergence between EU and US performance on employment and labour productivity both absolutely and relatively over the last thirty years (Fig. 4.2). While the US jobs machine was generating employment as well as maintaining working hours, Europe's employment performance was weak and working hours fell consistently. On labour productivity the reverse occurred. As a result, the steep fall in the numbers of hours worked per head of population in Europe compared to the United States exactly compensated for the rise in relative labour productivity per hour.

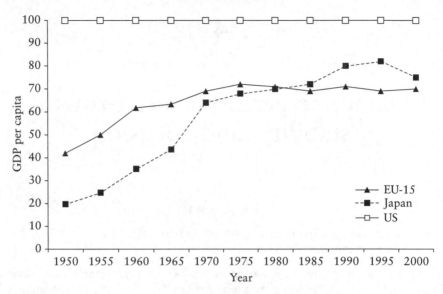

Figure 4.1. *GDP per capita at current market prices and PPS during 1950–2000: EU-15, Japan, and US (US = 100)*

Source: European Commission, AMECO database; Maddison (1995); and own calculations.

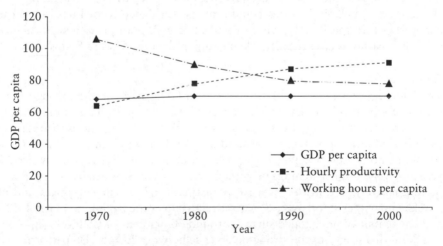

Figure 4.2. *EU per capita GDP, US = 100*

Source: European Commission, AMECO database.

By 2000, about one-third of the difference in per capita GDP can be attributed to lower European labour productivity, one-third to lower working hours, and one-third to lower employment rates. In 1970, all of the difference could be attributed to lower labour productivity (Table 4.1). The overall

Table 4.1. *GDP per capita, in PPS US = 100*

	GDP/head population		GDP/working hour		Working hours per person employed		Employment/working-age population		Working-age population/population	
	1970	2000	1970	2000	1970	2000	1970	2000	1970	2000
Austria	65.2	79.3	53.7	95.7	101.6	80.8	120.3	97.4	99.4	105.2
Belgium	68.3	75.3	66.2	113.7	107.5	82.7	94.2	78.7	101.8	101.8
Denmark	84.6	83.9	77.2	95.5	87.3	82.0	120.6	103.4	104.1	103.6
Finland	61.6	73.2	52.9	91.9	93.8	87.1	115.9	87.9	107.0	104.0
France	73.2	70.7	73.2	105.2	99.4	82.0	102.2	83.5	98.4	98.2
Germany[a]	78.7	74.2	70.8	93.4	100.9	81.6	107.2	92.2	102.8	105.5
Greece	42.8	47.6	42.9	60.3	112.4	103.5	85.9	72.9	103.5	104.7
Ireland	41.9	81.7	39.2	97.7	116.2	90.5	98.9	88.8	93.1	104.1
Italy	65.0	73.5	74.7	104.0	97.9	87.0	85.2	77.5	104.2	104.8
Netherlands	76.3	79.4	74.8	104.9	93.5	71.7	108.0	100.1	101.1	105.3
Portugal	34.7	51.6	24.8	54.1	107.7	93.5	130.3	94.9	99.8	107.4
Spain	49.8	57.5	47.1	73.2	105.8	97.1	98.9	76.2	101.1	106.2
Sweden	83.8	71.0	76.4	83.1	89.5	86.4	115.9	99.2	105.7	99.8
United Kingdom	70.8	70.2	58.7	80.3	103.5	88.0	114.8	97.9	101.5	101.5
EU-15[b]	69.0	70.3	64.8	90.7	101.0	85.6	103.6	87.6	101.7	103.4
USA	100	100	100	100	100	100	100	100	100	100

[a] 1970 West Germany
[b] 1970 including West Germany.

Source: European Commission, AMECO database.

picture is confirmed on a Member State basis at least with regard to employment. In 2000, all countries were below 90 per cent of the US labour input of hours per capita, while four countries achieve higher productivity per hour (Belgium, France, Italy, Netherlands). Even countries with higher or similar employment rates to the United States (Denmark, Netherlands, Sweden, United Kingdom) are well below when hours worked are taken into consideration. This raises the issue of the extent to which the difference in levels of per capita GDP reflect different preferences for leisure on each side of the Atlantic.

Although the lower average number of hours worked per year may indicate a higher European preference for leisure, it is difficult to argue that the lower employment rate (the share of the working population with a job) represents such an indicator (Table 4.2). The rates for prime age males vary comparatively little across European countries and between Europe and the United States. Employment rates for prime age females increased substantially on both sides of the Atlantic and by around the same amount, but the US rate continues to exceed that of the EU by 8 percentage points because of the higher initial rate in the United States. Major differences in employment rates can be found in both the younger (age 15–24) and older (55–64) age groups. In the United States, employment rates for young males fell only slightly over the last twenty years while those for young females increased over the same period. In the EU, employment rates for both young males and young females fell

Table 4.2. *Employment rates by age group,*
1980–2000 (% of population in the age group)

	Age group			
	15–24	25–54	55–64	15–64
EU-8[a]				
1980				
Male	51	92	64	78
Female	40	48	28	43
Total	45	70	44	60
1990				
Male	45	88	49	73
Female	37	55	23	46
Total	41	71	36	59
2000				
Male	42	87	47	72
Female	33	64	27	52
Total	37	76	37	62
EU-15				
2000				
Male	45	88	49	73
Female	37	66	28	54
Total	41	77	39	64
USA				
1980				
Male	64	89	70	80
Female	54	60	40	55
Total	59	74	54	67
1990				
Male	63	89	65	81
Female	56	71	44	64
Total	60	80	54	72
2000				
Male	62	89	66	81
Female	58	74	50	68
Total	60	81	58	74

[a] Germany, Finland, France, Italy, Netherlands,
Portugal, Spain, and Sweden.

Source: OECD 'Labour Force Statistics' database and
own calculations.

consistently so that by 2000 there was a 17 percentage point gap for males and a 21 percentage point gap for females. Similar developments can be observed for older workers so that by 2000 there was a 17 percentage point gap for older males between the EU and the United States and a 22 percentage point gap for females.

Since the lower employment rate and lower labour productivity accounted for just under two-thirds of the difference in per capita GDP, preferences for shorter working time could account for at most one-third of the difference. The major differences in working time can be attributed to a greater tendency towards part-time working in Europe along with longer paid and unpaid leave. In the United States, the share of part-time working in total employment was a fifth lower than in Europe in 2000 (12.8 per cent compared with 16.3 per cent) while a decade earlier the share had been about the same around 13.5 per cent. The drop in the US share of part-time workers occurred for both men and women while in Europe it rose for both sexes. According to the Organisation for Economic Cooperation and Development (OECD), in most EU countries, the greatest contribution to the overall change in hours came from the increase in the number of part-timers. Changes in the hours worked by part-timers contributed relatively little while in several countries changes in the hours of full-timers made a significant contribution. In Denmark and Greece that contribution was positive so that only in France, The Netherlands, and Portugal did a fall in the hours of full-timers make a major contribution to overall changes in hours worked.

It appears that Europeans work part-time to a greater extent than Americans because of lack of employment opportunities rather than because of preference. Just under 8 per cent of Americans in 1997 said they worked part-time because they could not find full-time work compared with nearly 20 per cent in Europe. That employment opportunities affect working time is illustrated by the fall in involuntary part-time work in Europe between 1997 and 2000 as overall employment performance improved. Even then, involuntary part-time work still stood at double the rate of the United States in 1997. In conclusion, the major difference in working hours would not appear to stem from preferences but rather from the opportunities on offer for full-time employment.

Growth

Macroeconomic performance of the EU during the 1990s has been disappointing both in absolute terms and with regard to the United States (Table 4.3). Overall growth slowed from the 1980s, which itself had slowed from the 1970s, in spite of the implementation of far-reaching reforms in both the macro-environment (consolidation of public finances and lower inflation, Economic and Monetary Union (EMU)) and micro-environment (Single Market Programme, Uruguay Round and to a certain extent labour market reform). During the first half of the 1990s, restructuring led to heavy labour-shedding and a strong increase in productivity in spite of low overall growth.

Table 4.3. *Growth of GDP, labour input (annual number of hours worked), and labour productivity (GDP per hour) (% per annum)*

	GDP		Labour input		Labour productivity	
	EU	US	EU	US	EU	US
1970–1980	3.0	3.2	−0.5	1.8	3.5	1.4
1980–1990	2.4	3.2	0.0	1.7	2.4	1.4
1991–2000	2.1	3.6	0.3	1.9	1.8	1.7
1991–1995	1.5	3.1	−0.9	1.8	2.4	1.3
1995–2000	2.6	4.1	1.2	2.0	1.4	2.0

Source: European Commission, AMECO database and OECD employment outlook (various years). 1970–1990 includes former West Germany; 1991–2000 includes Germany.

During the rebound in the second half of the decade, the strong increase in employment (measured by the total number of hours worked) came at the expense of increases in labour productivity.

Spurred by a successful transition to the knowledge-based economy, the United States posted a higher growth rate than during the previous two decades. Labour supply in the United States increased substantially both because of demography (natural increase and immigration) and higher participation rates. While the EU population grew by a mere 0.4 per cent per annum between 1991 and 2000, that of the United States increased by 1.2 per cent. At the same time, the EU employment rate (the share of the population of working age actually employed) increased by only 1 percentage point while that of the United States increased by over 5 percentage points. With average working hours also increasing, US labour input continued to rise strongly throughout the decade, but in the latter part growth was stimulated in addition by a strong increase in labour productivity. For the first time in three decades, growth in US labour productivity outstripped that of the EU, an extraordinary performance for a country at the leading edge of the production possibility frontier.

While demographic trends have certainly been more favourable in the United States than in the EU, it would be too simplistic to view them as the main explanation for the GDP growth differential between the two sides of the Atlantic. As shown in Table 4.3, this GDP growth differential has widened considerably from the 1970s to the 1990s, while the population growth differential has barely increased. Moreover, demographic trends clearly cannot be considered as fully exogenous to growth.

Within the EU, performance during the 1990s was by no means homogeneous (Fig. 4.3). Four countries were classified as cohesion countries at the beginning of the decade because of their noticeably lower-than-average level of development. These countries were expected to exhibit higher rates of growth and thereby to converge on the EU average. They did indeed contribute more

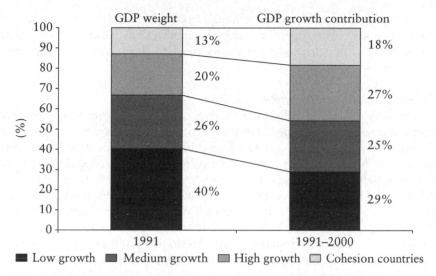

Figure 4.3. *Growth performance by groups of countries in the EU*
Source: European Commission, AMECO database.

to total growth (18 per cent) than their share in GDP at the beginning of the period (13 per cent). However, the other EU members also turned in quite different growth performances. A slow-growth group, made up of Germany and Italy, had a significant impact on the overall outcome because of their high weighting in the EU economy (around 40 per cent). A high-growth group, composed of Finland, The Netherlands, and the United Kingdom, represented a much smaller weight in the EU economy (20 per cent) but contributed a significant part of total growth (27 per cent).

Another way of looking at the growth performance of the EU is to see what the outcome would have been on removing the lower growth performers. Without Italy and Germany, EU average growth would have been 2.5 per cent per annum instead of 2.1 per cent during the 1990s. Taking just the two above-average groups of performers would bring the EU to 2.9 per cent, still below the Lisbon target of 3 per cent per annum. Even the cohesion countries with strong potential did not manage quite to attain the 3 per cent during the 1990s, well below what was needed for them to converge on the EU average. Ireland was the exception with its average annual growth of around 7 per cent during the 1990s.

Even though performance differed quite markedly between EU Member States, certain common structural characteristics remain. Up to the mid-1990s, growth remained driven by labour productivity rather than employment—a continuation of the secular tendency. However, the employment content of growth in Europe has been rising steadily and the second half of the decade marks something of a break with previous periods, producing a much improved employment performance. A few countries (Denmark, Italy, Netherlands and Spain) even saw employment-led growth (employment increased faster than productivity) although productivity continued to drive growth in the other Member States.

The productivity–employment paradox

Another way of looking at EU performance concerns the relationship between productivity and labour input between European countries with similar levels of overall development. It should be possible for countries with higher productivity to increase employment and converge on the United States. It should also be possible for countries with higher employment rates to increase productivity and similarly converge. As a typical manifestation of less developed status, cohesion countries exhibit both low labour productivity and low employment and should be able to raise both simultaneously.

For EU countries with similar levels of development (all except the cohesion countries), we observe a negative correlation between labour productivity and labour input measured as number of hours per capita (Fig. 4.4). This implies a trade-off, with low productivity countries compensating by working longer hours and/or higher employment rates.

The trade-off is not only structural but also temporal. It seems that countries in Europe have been incapable of improving employment performance without reducing productivity and vice-versa. Such a situation points to an overall limit on the EU's potential growth rate at a time when it is still trying to catch up with the United States and when very fast technological change should provide a fillip to growth potential (see also Gros et al. 2001).

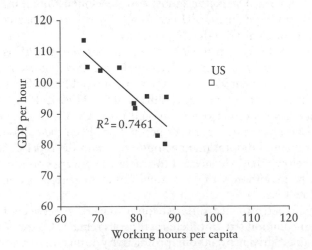

Figure 4.4. *Labour productivity and labour input in EU countries, excluding cohesion countries 2000, US = 100*

Source: European Commission, AMECO database.

Since EU countries with output per hour at or above US levels leave a substantial part of their potential labour force unoccupied, an exclusion of low productivity workers from the labour force rather than the existence of particularly productive workers in similar occupations would appear to be a better explanation. European workers employ substantially more capital than those in the United States, so that labour productivity is also distorted by capital/labour substitution. The existence of a trade-off would appear to indicate European economies operating inside or at best along the production possibility frontier rather than an ability to grow by pushing out the frontier.

4.1.2. *Why has Europe been growing so slowly?*

Innovation, the driver of economic growth
In the first three decades after the Second World War, Europe established an enviable reputation for both high growth and a high level of social protection. As indicated, growth subsequently deteriorated in each successive decade. In order to mitigate the adverse social effects of poor employment performance, ever higher levels of social transfers were required to achieve acceptable outcomes in terms of income inequality. Since such expenditure cannot continue to rise indefinitely, the sustainability of the European model(s) of development is increasingly challenged without a viable alternative in view.

The interrelated set of institutions and policies in the economic and social spheres developed after the war were appropriate to the conditions of the time and in turn met with the success mentioned. Their declining ability to deliver in terms of both efficiency and equity can be attributed essentially to a fundamental change in the conduct of economic activities. To understand properly why the institutions and policies that worked so well in the post-war period are no longer appropriate requires deeper analysis of how the economy has changed over time and how certain fundamental characteristics of the contemporary economy differ from those of the immediate post-war period.

The long post-war expansion had been built on the basis of the generalisation of an already mature technological trajectory with well-known organisational implications and rapid diffusion of best practice. In short, Europe was catching up with the United States both through investment and factor accumulation, and through imitation of leading-edge technologies. Standardised, mass market products that could be made with long production runs brought significant economies of scale, resulting in an industrial structure dominated by large firms. Assembly-line production proved well able to absorb large quantities of unskilled labour coming off the land in those years and some substantial intra-European migration from the Mediterranean. With rather stable and predictable cash flows, retained earnings, and bank finance largely sufficed to fund investment.

The innovation process was heavily incremental in nature. Codified knowledge and organisational routines developed by large firms were important in maintaining quality and managing the process. Technology-based industries relied on large central R&D laboratories exploiting the advances made in fundamental science since the end of the nineteenth century. They were typified by the chemical and pharmaceutical industries building new and better molecules on the basis of inorganic chemistry. New entry and the competitive drive that entry gave were not crucial in this period.

The settlement associated with the post-war welfare state favoured the establishment of long-term labour relations and human capital investments through mutual commitment between firms and their employees. Particularly in continental Europe, but to some extent also elsewhere, the dominant form of social protection was built on the Bismarckian insurance principle with provision financed by social security contributions rather than the Beveridge universalist principle financed out of general taxation. The incentive for the firm to invest not only in firm-specific but also transferable skills increased with the strength of this mutual commitment of labour and capital.

Macroeconomic management could direct itself to aggregate demand in a stable and non-inflationary environment. Microeconomic management dealt with the unwanted side effects of greater concentration and the concomitant power wielded by large firms. The instruments used to restrain such power included the public ownership of enterprises operating in industries characterised as natural monopolies, direct regulation, and anti-trust action. For its part, public education systems concentrated on primary and secondary education, sometimes combined with extensive apprenticeship systems. Tertiary education, often separated from research activities, played an elite-forming role for top managers, civil servants, and the liberal professions. R&D policy tended to target strategic sectors and/or firms with direct subsidies often built around major prestige projects.

The breakdown of the post-war system did not come suddenly and it remains in place in significant areas. To begin with, the easy gains from assimilating existing technologies became exhausted and demand became saturated for the output of leading industries. Because the technology was now widely available and the knowledge required largely codified, such industries were peculiarly susceptible to offshore production in middle-income newly-industrialising countries (NICs) with educated workforces and lower labour costs, first in south-east Asia and Mexico, then in China and in central Europe after the fall of the Berlin wall.

Firms in Europe reacted to the erosion of their competitive advantage through a variety of strategies including retreating into higher quality, higher margin segments, substituting capital for labour, and greater outsourcing. This enabled them to maintain profits but generally at the expense of employment.

More fundamentally, the post-war system came under attack because the patterns of both consumption and production had shifted in favour of different types of product requiring a different form of industrial organisation. Higher educational standards and changing consumer preferences led to greater demand for less standardised, more customised products. No longer was growth driven by volume but by composition. The macro-effects of this shift in consumption are reflected in the growth of the service sector as well as the changing composition of demand for both types of good and services. Between 1980 and 2000, the share of services in the EU economy increased by 13 percentage points to 70 per cent.

Contrary to the post-war period where growth and catching-up with the United States could largely be achieved through factor accumulation and imitation, once European countries had moved closer to the technology frontier and also with the occurrence of new technological revolutions in communication and information, innovation at the frontier has become the main engine of growth (see Box 4.1). This in turn called for new organisational forms, less vertically-integrated firms, greater mobility both intra- and inter-firm, greater flexibility of labour markets, a greater reliance on market finance

Box 4.1. *Innovation versus imitation*

In this box we briefly explain why the importance of innovation as opposed to imitation should depend on a country's distance to the technological frontier.

Let A_t denote a country's productivity at date t. Let $A_t^{\max}$ denote frontier productivity at date t. Then the convergence process of the country towards the frontier can be described by an equation of the form:

$$A_t = \eta A_{t-1}^{\max} + \gamma A_{t-1}$$

where $\eta A_{t-1}^{\max}$ is imitation of frontier technology, γA_{t-1} is innovation upon previous local technology, and $\eta < 1$, $\gamma > 1$.

Suppose the frontier grows at rate g, that is, $A_t^{\max} = A_{t-1}^{\max}(1+g)$. Combining the above, one obtains:

$$\frac{A_t}{A_t^{\max}} = a_t = \frac{1}{1+g}(\eta + \gamma a_{t-1}),$$

where a_t measures the country's distance to the technological frontier. In particular, when the country is far from the frontier, that is, when a_t is close to zero, then imitation (i.e. the term η) is the main source of productivity growth as measured by a_t/a_{t-1}. But as the country moves closer to the frontier, that is, as a_t becomes closer to 1, innovation (i.e. the term γa_{t-1}) becomes important for growth. The occurrence of a new technological wave (like the Information and Communication Technology (ICT) revolution) will further increase the importance of innovation by increasing γ. In other words: the closer the country is to the world frontier, that is the closer a_{t-1} is to 1, the more innovation matters for growth relative to imitation, and therefore the more important it is to establish innovation enhancing institutions and policies.

Source: Acemoglu et al. (2003).

and a higher demand for both R&D and higher education (Geroski and Jacquemin 1985). However, these necessary changes in economic institutions and organisations have not yet occurred on a large scale in Europe and it is this delay in adjusting our institutions, which accounts to a large extent for our growth deficit.

Key requirements for innovation
The balance between imitation and innovation has thus shifted decisively in favour of the second. In addition, a greater proportion of that innovation is radical rather than incremental. Growth becomes driven by innovation at the frontier and fast adaptation to technical progress.

Now, as new growth theories suggest, most innovations result from entrepreneurial activities or investments—typically, investments in R&D—which involve risky experimentation and learning. The incentive to engage in innovative investments is itself affected by the economic environment. In particular research investment is encouraged by:

- a good system to protect intellectual property rights on innovations;
- a high productivity of R&D, which itself requires a good education and research subsidy system
- low interest rates as R&D investments are forward-looking; this in turn calls for a stable macroeconomy;
- product market competition, low entry costs, and market openness to stimulate innovation by incumbents;
- good access to risk capital by new start-up firms; and
- more flexible labour market institutions, so that new innovators can quickly find workers that match their new technologies.

In the remaining part of the chapter we consider these elements in turn.

4.1.3. *Knowledge*

As an economy gets closer to the educational frontier, the greater the importance of higher education becomes (Box 4.2). While the basic requirement for the post-war economy was secondary education, that of an innovation-driven economy is higher education (Table 4.4). Overall, the United States has a larger share of population aged 25–64 years who have completed higher education than any EU Member State—over one-and-a-half times the current EU average. The future share of graduates is driven by current enrolment and expenditure on higher education. Here the present situation is clearly inadequate to generate the future numbers of graduates that will be required in an innovation-driven economy (Table 4.5). The United States already spends a higher share of GDP on higher education from public sources than the EU average, but the addition of very substantial private sources means that the United States spends more than double the EU average on higher education and more than any Member State.

Box 4.2. *Education and growth*

The growing importance of human capital for innovation at the frontier is illustrated by the results of the following regression:

- Nineteen OECD countries, 1960–2000, with observations every 5 years
- Output, investment data: Penn World Tables 6.1 (2002)
- Human capital data: Barro-Lee (2000)

$$g_t = \alpha_0 + \alpha_1 d_{t-1} + \alpha_2 s_{t-1} + \alpha_3 s_{t-1}{}^* d_{t-1} + \varepsilon_t$$

where

g = total factor productivity (TFP) growth over five years,
d = distance to productivity frontier,
s = share of population with higher education.

	TFP
d_{t-1}	−0.28 (.08)*
s_{t-1}	−0.43 (.24)
$s_{t-1}{}^* d_{t-1}$	1.11 (.30)*

Note: Standard errors in parentheses; *indicates that the coefficient is significant at 1%

Thus, the coefficient of the interaction term between distance to the technological frontier and skilled labour is positive and significant. This demonstrates the importance of higher education for growth, the closer a country is to the world technology frontier.

Source: Aghion et al. (2003).

The growing premium for college graduates over all other educational levels in the United States is an illustration of this requirement. Where labour market conditions permit, unskilled workers can still find jobs in the market for 'industrialised', low skilled service jobs instead of as blue-collar workers on the assembly line. But the relative pay of these jobs is falling further and further behind those of the college-educated. Contrary to popular perceptions, therefore, the jobs currently being created as a result of innovation are not low-paying but high-paying jobs. Because these jobs require a higher level of education, those without the requisite skills are shut out from the benefits.

Table 4.4. *Educational attainment of the population aged 25–64 years (%, 2000)*

	Below upper secondary	Upper secondary and post-secondary	Tertiary
Austria	24.3	61.8	13.9
Belgium	41.5	31.4	27.1
Denmark	19.8	53.7	26.5
Finland	26.2	41.5	32.3
France	36.1	40.6	23.0
Germany	17.4	59.4	23.2
Greece	48.6	33.6	17.8
Ireland	42.4	22.0	35.6
Italy	56.7	33.2	10.0
Luxembourg	47.3	34.6	18.1
Netherlands	45.0	32.0	22.2
Portugal	80.1	10.8	9.0
Spain	59.7	16.2	23.6
Sweden	19.4	49.0	31.6
UK	37.1	36.9	26.1
EU-15	38.9	37.3	23.8
USA	12.3	50.3	37.3

Source: OECD 'Education at a Glance'.

Table 4.5. *Total expenditure on tertiary education (% of GDP, 1999)*

	Public expenditure	Total expenditure
Austria	1.7	1.7
Belgium	1.5	n.a.
Denmark	2.4	2.5
Finland	2.1	2.2
France	1.1	1.3
Germany	1.1	1.2
Greece	1.1	1.1
Ireland	1.2	1.6
Italy	0.8	1.0
Netherlands	1.3	1.7
Portugal	1.0	1.1
Spain	0.9	1.2
Sweden	2.1	2.4
UK	1.1	1.7
EU	1.1	1.4
USA	1.4	3.0

Source: OECD 'Education at a Glance'.

When demand for labour shifts in favour of the higher educated, both employment and relative wages also shift in their favour. A rise in wage inequality is therefore to be expected under these conditions. If the supply of highly-educated labour increases in response to this situation then, this rise in wage inequality will be attenuated. Because higher education is a long-term investment, still largely undertaken while young, in the short term, the supply of the highly educated is somewhat inflexible. However, immigration can meet some of the needs. In Canada, it appears that the increase in the supply of skilled labour has been sufficient to meet demand so that income inequality has not increased, contrary to the United States (Murphy et al. 1998). A higher skill component of immigration would appear to be a major explanatory factor.

Along with skills, the key intangible impact on innovation clearly comes from research and development. As mentioned above, the model of centralised laboratory R&D prevalent in the period of mature technology has given way to a model in which R&D more often takes place in small firms and in universities and for which business/university research links become more important.

In the United States, the 1980 Bayh–Dole Act provided a much easier route for universities and other not-for-profit bodies to patent output from publicly financed programmes. The United States also introduced a system of R&D tax credits which has been regularly extended. Several EU countries have introduced similar systems but it remains very much a patchwork. Tax credits have a number of advantages over direct grants. They require less administration, they reward success because only profitable companies can use the credit, they are less liable to capture by lobbying on behalf of special interests, and they do not rely on bureaucrats to pick winners. The Institute of Fiscal Studies in the United Kingdom finds that R&D responds to changes in its user cost with a long-run elasticity of around unity (Bloom et al. 2002).

Deficiencies in the level of European R&D have led the European Council to set a target for R&D expenditure of 3 per cent of GDP. It is clear that, compared with the United States, Europe is investing less in R&D, and that the overall efficiency with which the current investment is converted into usable output is lower.

In 1999, total US expenditure on R&D at 2.6 per cent of GDP was over a third higher than that of the EU (Fig. 4.5). Nearly all of the difference can be attributed to a substantially higher investment in R&D by business (1.8 against 1.2 per cent). Within the EU, the low level of business R&D reflects a general north–south divide. Finland and Sweden have both overall and business-financed R&D expenditures exceeding those of the United States, while Germany is not far behind. At the other extreme, all EU Mediterranean countries have low overall and business-financed levels of R&D. Nor are trends in R&D expenditure favourable to Europe. The United States increased its lead in R&D expenditure by €95 billion between 1996 and 2000, of which

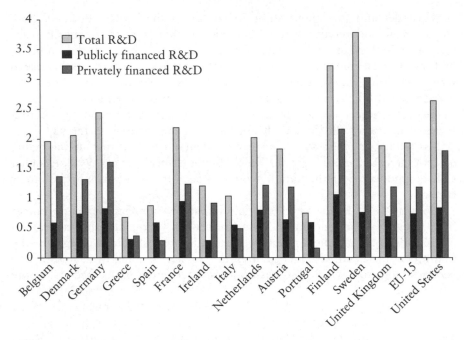

Figure 4.5. *R&D finance by source in 1999, as % of GDP*
Source: European Commission, New Cronos database.

€20 billion was publicly financed. Between 1991 and 2000, public research budgets in Europe declined from 0.91 to 0.73 per cent of GDP.

Patents provide one partial measure of R&D output. It is clear that Europe's output of international patents has not kept up with that of the United States. By the year 2000, even the best-performing EU Member States could only manage half the number of patents per million inhabitants as the United States, and the EU as a whole only a quarter. A recent study by the Technology Review and CHI Research Inc., which examined not only the number of patents but also the significance of patents through citations, indicated that Europe retains technological strengths in areas such as automotive, chemicals, consumer electronics, and telecommunications, but has a particular weakness in the field of computers and to a certain extent in biopharma. Furman et al. (2002) find decisive and robust effects on international patenting from:

- R&D manpower and spending;
- aggregate policy choices such as the extent of intellectual property protection and openness to international trade; and
- the share of research performed by the academic sector and the share funded by the private sector.

With regard to the organisation of research in public institutions, the higher share of research in specialised non-university institutions in Europe is to be remarked upon. A further structural difference covers the widespread recourse to peer review by the US National Science Foundation which guarantees a higher and more consistent level of quality of research and better evaluation procedures of programmes from inception to realisation than are common in Europe.

4.1.4. *New entry and product markets*

To the extent that new entrants more easily make innovations at the frontier, the shift to the new growth regime has increased the importance of entry and exit in the growth process (Geroski 2000). The threat of cannibalising or even destroying existing markets by radical innovation presents large established players with a dilemma. Avoiding innovation leaves them open to threat from innovators, while innovation undermines profits from traditional lines of business. Because of the greater degree of uncertainty stemming from radical innovation, a higher degree of turbulence ensues as the selection procedure weeds out those new firms that fail to make it in the market and those existing firms that fail to adapt in time.

Evidence of the rising importance of turbulence comes from regular surveys of large firms. In the 1950s and 1960s, it took two decades to replace one-third of the Fortune 500. In the 1970s, it took one decade. In the 1980s one-third of the Fortune 500 firms were replaced within five years and in the 1990s within less than three years. Stability among the largest firms is greater but, even there, at the end of the 1990s 12 per cent of the largest fifty US firms by market capitalisation had been founded less than twenty years previously against just 4 per cent in Europe.

Not only entry per se but also the growth performance of enterprises in the years after entry is important. The data on gross entry rates for the United States and Europe is ambiguous. Large numbers of firms are also being created in Europe (Scarpetta et al. 2002). However, the evidence on growth potential is unambiguous (Fig. 4.6). Employment growth in companies in the United States is much faster than in Europe. Immigration also makes a substantial contribution to high technology in the United States. According to Saxenian, nearly a quarter of high technology start-ups in Silicon Valley have been by entrepreneurs of Chinese or Indian origin (Saxenian 1999).

The type of regulatory environment required to encourage start-ups and new entry in a period of rapid change differs from that required in a stable environment dominated by large firms. First of all, the regulatory environment must be conducive to the creation of business opportunities and the challenging of existing established positions. Second, it must protect new entrants from anti-competitive attempts by incumbents to exclude them from the market instead of essentially limiting abuses of competition between existing players.

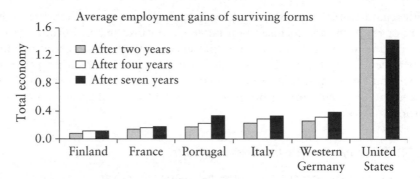

Figure 4.6. *Net employment gains among surviving firms at different lifetimes, 1990s*

Source: Scarpetta et al. (2002).

Beginning in the 1970s with the liberalisation of road haulage, the US embarked on a substantial rewriting of business regulation. This covered both individual industries such as network services and the general business environment, with, for example, the simplification of the corporate tax code and greater attention to regulatory process. In the EU, the Single Market Programme attempted to address similar issues.

Connecting previously separate national markets lies at the heart of the Single Market Programme. Removing discrimination between enterprises because of their national origin satisfies the legal requirement for a common market. It puts incumbent firms into competition and allows the economies of scale that were at the heart of the Cecchini Report (European Commission 1988) on the cost of non-Europe to come into play. These are essentially one-off gains. Both the macro and micro evidence from the early 1990s indicate such gains as being of a static equilibrium type. Restructuring leading to heavy employment loss, big productivity gains but low growth typified that period. Firms reorganised production, allowing multiple national markets to be supplied from fewer plants or plants that were specialised in just a few lines. The abolition of border controls meant that for the first time just-in-time production could be introduced using cross-border component suppliers, which also stimulated competition. Previously, frontier delays would have disrupted production schedules to an unacceptable extent.

However, to secure lasting effects on growth, the type of integration based on geographically contiguous markets is not sufficient. After restructuring, firms must invest in new capacity and enter new markets by developing new products as well as new export markets. Here the content of regulation can play a role. Harmonisation around existing levels of regulation may defend established incumbents instead of stimulating entry and exit. The record of the Single Market on this score appears at best mixed.

Telecommunications is one area in which market liberalisation has generally been accepted as successful in terms of growth and innovation. However, it is noticeable that success has been concentrated in the field of mobile telecommunications rather than fixed-line services. In mobile telecommunications, new entrants have made a major impact in both telecommunications equipment and in services.

In fixed-line telephony and other public utilities such as energy, market liberalisation has led to fewer new entrants, while incumbents have maintained a large share of the market. Incumbents who attempted to enter neighbouring markets have also to a large extent pulled back to concentrate on domestic territory. In other areas such as retail financial services (banking and insurance), incumbents also continue to maintain high market shares. Consumer inertia, switching costs, and unrealistic initial expectations about the pace of market integration may explain much of the current situation. The example of telecommunications would seem to indicate that truly innovative markets also seem to lead to much faster European market integration than traditional ones.

In measuring the impact of the Single Market, it is clear that effective competition and prices are related. The price of long-distance and international phone calls both fell by over 45 per cent during 1998–2002. Local phone call prices fell only marginally over the same period. Even though the difference can be attributed in part to the need to rebalance line rentals and local call tariffs, the fact that incumbent firms had a market share of over 80 per cent in the local telecommunications market in twelve Member States in 2000/2001 can be expected to have played a major role. Similarly, prices for industrial users of electricity have fallen by 9 per cent over the past five years (1997–2002) where a certain amount of competition has been introduced while prices for household users fell by only 5 per cent. Falling prices stimulate demand and in the case of telecommunications constitute an important input to innovatory processes in the information society. However, falling prices are quite compatible with a regulatory regime that allows competition between incumbents without encouraging entry. They do not, therefore, represent a good indicator of innovation.

National regulations also play a major role in facilitating or hindering entry. General business conditions are of particular importance for start-ups since they do not have the capacity to deal with very complex regulatory environments from the beginning. One area in which a major effort has been made is in the time cost involved in setting up a company. Nevertheless, administrative burdens remain high in Europe. For instance, authorisations for industrial investments have both very long lead times in certain Member States and also wide differences across projects. Since speed to market is an essential aspect of innovation where a large proportion of total profits are often made in the first months of commercialisation, such delays are likely to depress the returns on innovation.

Product markets of virtually all OECD countries have become more market friendly, justifying consistent efforts by governments of developed countries (Nicoletti and Scarpetta 2003). However, more diversity in the level of regulation has resulted from this process even—and surprisingly above all—within the EU. This is because the pace of reform has varied significantly across countries that already had very different policy approaches at the beginning of the period. Such differences within the EU can stem from a variety of sources: failure by some countries to adopt liberalisation at EU level while others forge ahead, failure to implement EU liberalisation measures, or differences in approach to areas which are not subject to EU liberalisation.

Nicoletti and Scarpetta found that the lower the entry barriers and state control, the faster the process of catching up with best-practice technologies in manufacturing industries. They also found that the process of privatisation involves additional direct productivity gains. However, efficiency gains may depend on whether privatisation is accompanied by adequate promotion of competition in the markets in which privatised companies operate.

4.1.5. *Infrastructure*

Adequate physical infrastructure to facilitate the free flow of people, goods, and ideas is required for the Single Market to function correctly. Although heavy investment has been made in the past, some of this investment is now showing its age. In addition, the new Member States still lag behind the most developed regions in their level of infrastructure provision. From the point of view of the Single Market, the most serious current deficiency lies in the fact that infrastructure has been built around national economic priorities. As a result, an integrated transport network for Europe is largely lacking, a weakness that will become much more evident after enlargement when east–west connections are likely to become as important as the currently dominant north–south routes.

4.1.6. *Finance for innovation*

The need for strong equity backing for start-ups in the risky business of radical innovation where future cash flows can only be uncertain has long been recognised. Venture capital was mobilised to meet the needs of such firms, with the potential for high returns compensating for high risk. Along with business angels, they represent the most important source of finance for high-tech start-ups in the United States. The conditions for the successful development of a venture capital industry are also well known by now:

- a deep pool of suitable projects to diversify risks
- an adequate exit route in the form of secondary stock markets so that investors can realise a profit

- very knowledgeable fund managers who provide a significant non-financial input for their clients; and
- a willingness on the part of founders of new businesses to accept a dilution of control in exchange for faster growth.

In addition to finance, high growth start-ups need experienced managers that they can only attract by offering stock options in the place of cash rewards. The financial environment for growth in a period of radical innovation needs to be supportive.

That the situation in Europe is insufficiently supportive has been recognised for some time, leading to the adoption of the Risk Capital Action Plan (European Commission 1998). Europe's main weakness lies in the provision of early-stage financing, and there was considerable development in the availability of funds in the second half of the 1990s. Even so, early-stage risk capital in the EU averaged only 0.05 per cent of GDP during the years 1999–2001 against 0.17 per cent in the United States. It is also the case that the profitability of such investments in Europe remains well below that of the United States. A 1997 pan-European venture capital performance survey found that the cumulative net internal rate of return (IRR) to 1996 was 18.6 per cent on a pooled basis, but for funds focussed on early stage investment it was 5.7 per cent. For general funds investing in a mix of investment stage situations, comparable US returns at 16.5 per cent were actually lower than in Europe in this period, but early stage returns at 14.2 per cent were two and a half times higher. As a result, the incentive to invest in innovatory start-ups is much lower in Europe than in the United States.

New growth theory tells us that the innovators' ability to appropriate at least a fraction of the revenues from their innovations is the key to sustaining innovation incentives and growth (Aghion and Howitt 1998). This also carries over to the case of venture capitalists, who finance innovations. If taxed too heavily, they will not have sufficient incentive to put funds into risky ventures.

It should be noted that we are dealing primarily with start-ups or small- and medium-sized enterprises (SMEs). Because they are less capital intensive than the large firms of the old economy, financed by venture capital and retained earnings and with limited managerial time, relatively simple corporate tax structures with low tax rates and broad tax bases are more appropriate for this type of firm than complex structures with high tax rates and narrow tax bases that tend to favour the large, capital intensive firms of the post-war period. Both the United States and the United Kingdom introduced corporation tax reforms in the 1980s that went in the direction of facilitating growth of start-ups and SMEs. Within Europe, there still remains a large degree of heterogeneity in corporate tax systems, largely due to the wide range of tax relief available (Table 4.6). Generally speaking, corporate tax rates have been coming down but without necessarily simplifying the system.

Table 4.6. *Effective average corporation tax rate by country, 1999 and 2001 by asset and source of finance*

| | 2001 | | 1999 | | | | | | | | | |
	Corporate tax rates[a]	Overall mean	Corporate tax rates[a]	Overall mean	Intangibles	Industrial buildings	Machinery	Financial assets	Inventories	Retained earnings	New equity	Debt
Austria	34.0	27.9	34.0	29.8	28.6	29.2	28.4	33.2	29.9	33.9	33.9	22.3
Belgium	40.2	34.5	40.2	34.5	30.7	36.1	31.0	39.2	35.3	39.1	39.1	25.8
Denmark	30.0	27.3	32.0	28.8	21.3	34.7	25.3	31.2	31.2	32.3	32.3	22.1
Finland	29.0	26.6	28.0	25.5	24.8	24.8	23.1	27.3	27.3	28.8	28.8	19.3
France	36.4	34.7	40.0	37.5	30.6	40.6	40.1	39.0	37.1	42.1	42.1	28.8
Germany	39.4	34.9	52.4	39.1	33.9	39.0	34.9	46.8	40.8	46.1	40.1	27.7
Greece	37.5	28.0	40.0	29.6	35.5	30.4	33.4	11.6	37.1	34.4	34.4	20.8
Ireland	10.0	10.5	10.0	10.5	8.9	15.8	8.2	9.8	9.8	11.7	11.7	8.2
Italy	40.3	27.6	41.3	29.8	24.9	29.8	27.4	36.1	31.1	31.8	31.8	26.1
Luxembourg	37.5	32.2	37.5	32.2	28.6	33.7	29.2	36.6	32.9	36.6	36.6	24.0
Netherlands	35.0	31.0	35.0	31.0	26.7	32.4	29.2	34.2	32.5	35.1	35.1	23.3
Portugal	35.2	37.0	37.4	32.6	33.2	31.8	28.6	36.5	32.8	37.0	37.0	24.5
Spain	35.0	31.0	35.0	31.0	31.1	31.8	27.4	34.2	30.7	35.2	35.2	23.3
Sweden	28.0	22.9	28.0	22.9	19.6	23.4	19.7	25.7	25.7	26.0	26.0	17.1
UK	30.0	28.3	30.0	28.2	24.2	33.7	24.7	29.3	29.3	31.8	31.8	21.6

Note: Each asset column represents an average across all three types of finance, with weights of 55% retained earnings, 10% new equity, and 35% debt. Each finance column represents an unweighted average across all five assets. The overall average is an average across all fifteen types of investment, with the same weights.

[a] Including surcharges and local taxes.

Source: European Commission (2001e).

4.1.6. *Labour markets*

As indicated previously, Europe's poor record of employment creation has been a major factor behind poor growth over the last three decades. One of the reasons has been the way in which the previously successful interaction between social protection and economic performance in the post-war period subsequently turned into a negative spiral (Blanchard and Wolfers 2000; Steinherr 2000). At a time of rising employment levels and large increases in productivity, social security financed by levies on payroll provided ever-increasing resources for the welfare state. However, with the decline in employment rates, lower productivity growth, and growing numbers of dependants, ever-higher charges were required to maintain existing levels of benefits. As a result, the tax wedge on labour became very high, further discouraging employment. By 2001, the tax wedge for a single worker with no children at the average production wage had risen to 43.1 per cent against 30 per cent in the United States, with a maximum of 55.6 per cent in Belgium (Table 4.7). The entire difference

Table 4.7. *Tax wedge in 1997 and 2001[a] for a single worker with no children at the average production wage*

	Personal income tax		Total social security contribution		Total tax wedge	
	2001 in %	Change 1997–2001	2001 in %	Change 1997–2001	2001 in %	Change 1997–2001
Austria	8.1	0.3	36.6	−1.3	44.7	−0.9
Belgium	21.1	0.6	34.5	−1.7	55.6	−1.0
Denmark	32.0	−3.1	12.2	2.1	44.2	−1.0
Finland	20.7	−1.6	25.2	−1.4	45.9	−3.1
France	9.5	2.1	38.3	−2.4	48.3	−0.4
Germany	16.8	−0.8	33.9	−0.9	50.7	−1.7
Greece	1.7	0.1	34.3	0.0	36.0	0.1
Ireland	10.7	−7.7	15.1	−0.5	25.8	−8.2
Italy	14.0	1.2	32.2	−6.5	46.2	−5.3
Luxembourg	9.5	−2.7	24.4	1.4	33.9	−1.3
Netherlands	7.6	1.6	34.7	−2.9	42.3	−1.3
Portugal	4.5	−1.4	28.1	0.0	32.5	−1.4
Spain	9.6	−1.0	28.3	−0.1	37.9	−1.1
Sweden	18.6	−2.8	30.0	0.7	48.6	−2.1
UK	14.3	−0.8	15.4	−1.4	29.7	−2.3
EU average[b]	13.3	−0.2	29.9	−1.9	43.1	−2.1
USA	15.7	−1.1	14.2	0.0	30.0	−1.1
Japan	5.7	−1.9	18.6	5.4	24.2	3.5

[a] Weighted average (weighted by no. of employees).
[b] Data for 2001 are preliminary.

Source: OECD, Taxing wages (for tax data), Eurostat (for weights).

between the United States and Europe is accounted for by social security contributions. Recently, the tax wedge has been falling in nearly every EU country but the relatively modest fall of 2.1 points between 1997 and 2001 has not been enough to reverse the previous increase.

With the increased importance of innovation and the increased pace of restructuring, the importance of labour market flexibility also increases. Part of the EU's growth deficit has been attributed to lack of labour market flexibility. While labour market flexibility is a generic term that covers many different institutional arrangements, one particular form of inflexibility, concerning the terms and conditions under which firms may employ or lay off labour (employment protection legislation), is particularly significant for growth. However, greater flexibility in this area comes at a cost in terms of more unstable employment trajectories.

Flexibility allows firms to match employment with output levels more closely. It also facilitates matching the skills and the abilities of the labour force with specific tasks, by enabling firms to redeploy (internal flexibility) or to change skill composition of the workforce through hiring and firing (external flexibility) more easily. However, at the same time, flexibility may discourage long-term investment in transferable skills by the employer since the worker may not stay with the firm. It also discourages investment in firm-specific skills by the worker since there may not be an adequate return for that investment in the absence of job security. Whether the advantages of flexibility outweigh the disadvantages depends very much on the economic environment within which firms operate. At a time of very rapid change and a need to adjust both production and skills quickly, flexibility comes at a premium.

Greater flexibility in both the United States and the United Kingdom has translated into greater income inequality both between and within groups (Gosling et al. 2000). Intragroup flexibility has mainly affected the temporary component of income with a clear relationship between intragroup inequality and variability in individual incomes over time (Blundell and Preston 1998). The question is how to deal with the negative effects of such variability on individual welfare.

4.2. Macroeconomic stability

4.2.1. *The European Union quest for macroeconomic stability*

Why macroeconomic stability is important
Macroeconomic stability has come to be regarded as a set of rules or behaviours aimed at guaranteeing monetary stability and fiscal discipline. In the Maastricht Treaty, the quest for nominal stability has been embodied in a single monetary policy entrusted to an independent central bank and in criteria on budget deficits and debt. Nominal stability is seen as being conducive to higher welfare and growth. It is also considered to be a precondition to ensure output stability (i.e. a smoother business cycle).

The official view on the benefits of price stability and fiscal discipline (the 'Brussels–Frankfurt consensus') is the following (Issing et al. 2001).

The maintenance of price stability—reflected in low rates of inflation—facilitates achieving higher rates of economic growth over the medium term and helps to reduce cyclical fluctuations. This shows up in a lower variability of output and inflation. In turn, sound public finances are necessary both to prevent imbalances in the policy mix, which negatively affect the variability of output and inflation, and also to contribute to national savings, thus helping to foster private investment and ultimately growth. The latter beneficial effect is magnified as low deficits and debt, by entailing a low interest burden, create the room for higher public investment, 'productive' public spending, and a low tax burden. Finally, the beneficial effects of price stability and fiscal discipline on economic performance reinforce each other in various ways. On the one hand, fiscal discipline supports the central bank in its task to maintain price stability. On the other hand, prudent monetary and fiscal policies avoid policy-induced shocks and their unfavourable impact on economic fluctuations while ensuring a higher room for manoeuvre to address other disturbances that increase cyclical instability.

Now, how much empirical support does the official view have?

Concerning inflation and growth, there is evidence of a negative relationship over the medium term. The much-quoted study by Barro (1996) finds a significant negative correlation between both variables on the basis of a panel of around 100 countries in the period 1960–1990. The costs of moderate inflation—say in single digits—are much disputed: economists disagree on whether at low levels, inflation puts 'sand' or 'grease' in the wheels of the price formation mechanism. Some authors claim that costs may be more important than usually thought. A recent study by Andrés et al. (2000) finds that industrial countries that enter into an inflationary process, even at moderate rates of inflation, never experience an improvement in their growth or per capita income prospects and are most likely to experience a deterioration. The national case studies contained in Feldstein (1999) conclude that industrial countries can enjoy significant permanent welfare gains when moving from moderate rates of inflation towards price stability, once the distorting effects of a nominalist tax system on resource allocation are taken into account. Other authors, however, conclude the opposite. Akerlof et al. (2000) argue that, in the presence of nominal rigidities in wage setting, the Phillips curve flattens at very low inflation rates. This implies that while aiming at a 'too high' inflation rate certainly entails costs, aiming at a 'too low' inflation rate would also entail a substantial loss of output and a permanent rise in unemployment, thus highlighting the importance of aiming at the 'right' inflation rate.

Another highly disputed issue is the link between policy behaviour and output volatility. The official view sees a credible discipline on both the fiscal and monetary sides as a precondition for using policies for stabilisation purposes. As to fiscal discipline, experience clearly shows that high deficits and debt limit the room for manoeuvre in the event of negative shocks and reduce the effectiveness of fiscal policy in dealing with cyclical fluctuations.

The literature, however, has pointed to a number of caveats concerning monetary discipline. Svensson (2002) argues that an excessive fixation on price stability on the part of the central bank can—in a context of nominal rigidities—reduce inflation and inflation volatility but at the cost of exacerbating output volatility. This practice, which Svensson terms 'strict inflation targeting', refers to the rather extreme case where the central bank only cares about keeping inflation low and disregards completely output behaviour.

In reality, however, even those central banks which firmly orient monetary policy towards price stability—with or without explicit inflation targeting strategies—also take into account the output consequences of their policy actions when deciding how soon and how much to adjust interest rates in the pursuit of price stability. Furthermore, when reviewing the relationship between inflation and output volatility, it has to be remembered that if monetary authorities are not sufficiently pre-emptive and let inflation get out of hand, they will have to step on the monetary brake later on, creating both higher output and inflation variability. Indeed, many post-war recessions in the United States and elsewhere have happened following inflation peaks and subsequent interest-rate hikes by monetary authorities.

What explains macroeconomic stability?

The degree of stability shown by inflation and output depends, in general, on three factors: the shocks affecting the economy, the structure of the economy, and the policy responses.

1. *The nature of shocks matters.* As is well known, the price and output effects of demand and supply shocks differ. While both demand and supply shocks increase the variance of inflation and output, under supply shocks—like cost-push shocks—there is a policy trade-off between inflation and output variability. The degree of persistence of the shock also matters. Demand shocks are seen as short-lived in most instances, while supply shocks may be temporary or long lasting. In the latter case, stabilisation around the former level of potential output, by preventing output from adjusting to its new equilibrium level, would actually be destabilising.

A feature of shocks that is particularly important in the euro area is the extent to which they are common or country-specific. Clearly, the former can be addressed by the single monetary policy, while this is not the case with country-specific shocks. Thus, the more asymmetric the shocks, the more national economic situations will tend to differ unless the appropriate national non-monetary policy measures are implemented to deal with such shocks.

An important issue in the European context has to do with the changes in the sources of shocks derived from the establishment of EMU. In the euro area, given the strong orientation of the single monetary policy towards stability, monetary policy shocks are less likely. On the fiscal policy side, the normative framework of the SGP also reduces the likelihood of fiscal shocks in the Union. In both cases, however, policy shocks do not disappear altogether in EMU. On the monetary side, the one-size-fits-all monetary policy may be regarded as a policy shock for diverging countries.[2] On the fiscal side, low budget deficits, by recreating room for fiscal discretion, may strengthen the 'temptation' to run politically-motivated fiscal policies.

2. *The structure of the economy affects both exposure and adaptability to shocks.* In an economy that is less diversified, the likelihood of sectoral shocks having widespread macroeconomic effects is higher. The structure of goods and labour markets is also important in shaping the effects of shocks. More flexible markets guaranteeing speedier adjustments in relative prices and wages improve the ability of the economy to absorb shocks, rendering the system more resilient and reducing the magnitude and persistence of cyclical fluctuations.

The structural changes implied by EMU have important implications for the ability of the euro economies to absorb shocks. The risk highlighted by some authors that EMU will lead to productive specialisation thus rendering it more exposed to asymmetric shocks has so far not materialised. Instead, what is already apparent is that EMU has led to a rapid integration of financial markets across borders (like money markets) which will hopefully be accompanied in the future by significant progress in the integration of capital markets. This process is important, among other things, because it allows a better inter-temporal and international dispersion of risks within the euro area that helps absorb shocks.

3. *Monetary and fiscal policies may act to stabilise output and prices in the event of shocks.* Macroeconomic policy is the right instrument to stabilise output and inflation in the event of shocks. In the case of demand shocks, a well-timed counter-cyclical demand policy may succeed in reducing both the output gap and the deviation of inflation relative to its objective. In the case of supply shocks like cost-push shocks—the task of policy-makers tends to be more difficult as they face a trade-off between output and inflation stabilisation and, in the case of permanent shocks—like technology shocks—it has to decide how quickly to let the economy converge to the new level of potential output (Gali et al. 2000; Viñals 2001).

Concerning the changes implied by EMU for the role of monetary and fiscal policies, the single monetary policy has to address the above-mentioned trade-offs between output and inflation variability when faced with common supply shocks. Nevertheless, in the presence of country-specific demand or supply

[2] This effect is strengthened if national transmission mechanisms of monetary policy differ across EMU members. Recent research conducted at the Eurosystem (European Central Bank 2002) has concluded, however, that the available empirical evidence does not show statistically significant differences between euro-area countries in policy transmission that are robust across different studies and methodologies.

disturbances which lead to differences in national economic situations, it is
the national authorities that have to react by using the policy tools at their
disposal.

Of course, in case of inaction or constrained policy instruments at national
level, there are adjustment mechanisms through the market within the euro
area that will help re-establish equilibrium over time. The problem, however,
is that such a process may be lengthy, especially if rigidities hamper the
functioning of product and labour markets.

All of the above point towards the importance of accompanying the stability-
oriented single monetary policy with the appropriate national policies aimed
at dealing with different national economic situations within the euro area.
Well-functioning product and labour markets are critical in providing the
degree of wage and price flexibility that is required to effect the necessary
relative price adjustments when the exchange rate is no longer available to
facilitate them. Moreover, the SGP needs to be run in a symmetric manner so
as to guarantee that national fiscal policies can adequately contribute to sta-
bilising the economy in periods of both economic expansion and contraction.

4.2.2. *Output and price stability: Stylised facts and explanations*

Macroeconomic stability across the Atlantic
Table 4.8 summarises the EU and US behaviour of real GDP and inflation in
the past four decades in terms of both level and variability.

Table 4.8. *Output and inflation stability in the United States and the EU*

	1961–1970	1971–1980	1981–1990	1992–2000
US				
Real GDP Growth				
Average of annual rates	4.2	3.3	3.2	3.6
Standard deviation	2.0	2.5	2.2	0.6
Inflation				
Average inflation	2.8	7.9	4.7	2.6
Standard deviation of inflation	1.7	3.1	2.2	0.5
EU-15				
Real GDP Growth				
Average of annual rates	4.8	3.0	2.4	2.1
Standard deviation	0.9	1.7	1.2	1.1
Inflation				
Average inflation	3.9	10.8	6.7	2.4
Standard deviation of inflation	0.8	2.8	2.9	0.9

Note: GDP of the unified Germany was first recorded in 1991, this is reflected in the last column.
Source: European Commission, AMECO database.

A cursory look at the table points to two stylised facts. First, in Europe and the United States, inflation, having increased sharply in the 1970s, fell considerably in both level and volatility during the two subsequent decades, and especially in the 1990s. Second, real GDP growth has shown a sharply different behaviour across the Atlantic. In the United States, average growth has remained broadly stable since the 1970s while output volatility has declined since the mid-1980s, particularly during the 1990s. In contrast, Europe's growth performance has constantly deteriorated, while output volatility has declined more modestly. Towards the end of the period, output volatility was quite close in the United States and the EU. All in all, the dynamism of the US economy has been increasingly combined with higher stability of output and prices. In Europe, lower and more stable inflation has gone hand-in-hand with stable output but lower growth.

The difference between the United States and Europe is striking. In the United States, the maintenance of significantly high growth rates over the past thirty years has been accompanied by a reduction in output and inflation variability relative not only to the 'unstable decade' (the 1970s), but also compared to the 1960s. So, no trade-off seems to emerge in the medium to long term between growth and stability (output or inflation) in the United States. In the EU, on the other hand, not only is growth lower than in the United States, but it has been falling gradually in each of the decades since the 1960s. Furthermore, while macroeconomic stability improved in the EU in the 1990s relative to the previous two decades—in the price dimension, but less so in the output dimension—it is still lower on both counts compared to the 1960s.[3]

Due to higher growth, coupled with a substantial reduction in inflation, the United States went back in the second half of the 1990s to a 1960s-type of performance, as shown by the joint behaviour of unemployment and inflation in Fig. 4.7. In contrast, the reduction in European inflation took place at broadly constant, historically high rates of unemployment. *Prima facie*, in the case of the United States, the evidence in the figures is consistent with an underlying outward shift in the short-run Phillips curve in the 1970s and the first half of the 1980s followed by a shift in the opposite direction which would have brought the curve back to its initial position in the second half of the 1990s. In Europe, the picture is more consistent with a rise in the natural rate of unemployment (meaning an outward shift in the long-run Phillips curve) until the first half of the 1980s followed by a downward shift of the short-run curve in subsequent years and only a limited shift to the left in the 1990s. By the end of the 1990s, inflation was at the level of, or even lower than, the 1960s, but at an unemployment rate almost four times higher. The downward shift in the short-run Phillips curve in the last fifteen years appears to be consistent with a stronger anti-inflationary commitment and credibility

---

[3] The picture of a less performing economy in Europe compared to the United States is confirmed if one looks at other 'real' variables such as unemployment and the output gap.

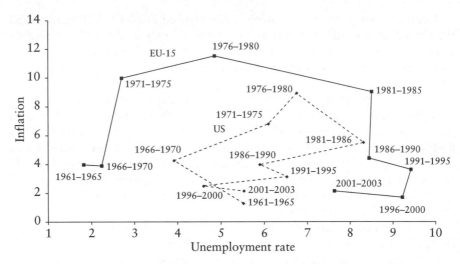

Figure 4.7. *Inflation and unemployment in the EU and US*

Source: European Commission, AMECO database.

of European monetary policies. Only in the most recent years, may we be witnessing a reduction in the natural rate of unemployment.

The picture of Europe compared to the United States that emerges from the above analysis is that of high inertia, low reward. While practically all EU countries experienced lower and less volatile inflation, on the 'real' side of the economy the picture is not uniform across Europe.

A relative majority of countries—Belgium, Germany, Greece, Spain, Italy, Austria, and Portugal—behaved similarly to the EU average in the 1990s, by experiencing lower growth compared to the 1970s coupled with unchanged or slightly lower output variability. France, Sweden, and Finland had a worse performance, namely real growth that was not only lower, but also more variable. However, in the case of Sweden and Finland, such unfavourable performance is essentially explained by the deep recession at the beginning of the 1990s. Finally, five countries—Denmark, Ireland, The Netherlands, the United Kingdom, and Luxembourg—did better than average in that they experienced an unchanged or even higher growth accompanied by broadly constant or lower output variability. Interestingly, several of these countries are amongst those usually identified with bolder efforts to reform their welfare system and improve market functioning.

All in all, and in spite of the country differentiation highlighted above, the picture in Europe compared to the United States is bleak. Loosely speaking, while the United States has traditionally been a 'higher return-higher risk' economy relative to the EU, in the second half of the 1990s it became a more preferable 'asset': its gap in output variability with the EU has narrowed significantly, while its average return has increased, as differentials in potential growth are now higher.[4]

Greater macroeconomic stability: Good practices, good policies, or good luck?

A growing body of literature has focussed on the causes of greater US macro-economic stability in the past two decades. Three views have been put forward to explain the lower volatility: the higher output and inflation stability can be due to 'good practices', 'good policies', or 'good luck'. However, the debate has focused mainly on the United States, while the evidence on Europe is scant.

'Good practices' usually refer to just-in-time management of inventories, fostered by ICT. As found by several studies, the importance of this factor is consistent with the finding that the higher output stability in the US stems essentially from a decline in the volatility of output (in particular of durables) compared to that of sales.

'Good policies' appear to underpin the stronger macroeconomic stability in both Europe and the United States. The macroeconomic policy framework has considerably improved on both sides of the Atlantic, although the macro-economic policy 'philosophies' continue to differ: the commitment to rules-based policies is stronger in Europe than in the United States where monetary and fiscal policy discretion appears to be stronger. A clear anti-inflationary commitment by central banks has helped to anchor inflation expectations, thus contributing to lower and more stable inflation. As to fiscal policy, over the 1990s and until very recently, enhanced budgetary discipline both in Europe and the United States has contributed to macroeconomic stability. On a more specific basis, the effectiveness of automatic stabilisers appears to be stronger in Europe than in the United States, given its more extended tax and welfare system.[5] As to discretionary policy, there is evidence that it may have become more counter-cyclical in OECD countries, but its effectiveness may have decreased over time (Perotti 2002).

The 'good luck' view posits that lower output and inflation volatility may simply stem from the drop in variance of exogenous disturbances hitting the economy. In the last two decades, Europe has been subject to the shock of German reunification and the creation of EMU, which can also be seen as a shock. The United States has been subject to the rise (and fall) of the technology bubble at the end of the 1990s. However, both economies have been spared the very adverse supply shocks of the 1970s (the two oil price hikes) which created a conflict between output and inflation stabilisation.

---

[4] However, the large macroeconomic imbalances accumulated by the US economy are a source of concern for its future development.

[5] Studies show that automatic stabilisers in the EU offset between 10% and 30% of the shock depending on the country and the type of shock. See Brunila et al. (2003). Auerbach (2002) finds that the smoothing power of automatic stabilisers has changed little over the past decades in the United States.

On the whole, better monetary policy appears to be behind the lower and more stable inflation in Europe and the United States while a combination of better practices, better policies, and less adverse shocks has helped reduce output volatility in the United States towards the levels traditionally prevailing in Europe.

4.2.3. *Macroeconomic policies in the European Union in the 1990s: 'Cleaning up the balance sheet'*

The Maastricht convergence process

Macroeconomic policies in Europe in the last decade were geared to nominal consolidation. European countries had entered the 1990s with relatively high inflation rates and growing fiscal imbalances. Prompted by the need to re-establish basic conditions of macroeconomic stability, budget deficits, and inflation were reduced substantially. Meeting the EMU macroeconomic requirements was instrumental in bringing about a regime shift. The nominal adjustment worked: between 1993 and 1998 (the so-called 'stage two' of EMU), inflation and budget deficits were reduced dramatically and their dispersion throughout the EU decreased substantially.

Bringing down inflation was the explicit goal of monetary policy. Until 1997–1998, the stance of monetary policy in many European countries—especially those belonging to the Exchange Rate Mechanism of the European Monetary System—reflected to a significant extent that of the Bundesbank (with a risk premium incorporated in non-German interest rates) and remained restrictive (see Fig. 4.8).[6] This contributed to reducing average inflation from 4 per cent in 1993 to around 1.5 per cent in 1998. The monetary stance, however, became gradually less tight. As documented in European Commission (2000), for the euro area as a whole, easier monetary conditions accompanied the fiscal retrenchment in most years. Therefore, while remaining restrictive to bring down inflation, monetary policy appears to have been broadly supportive of fiscal consolidation.

Faced with the inevitable need to put public finances on a sounder footing and under pressure from the Maastricht calendar for joining EMU, policymakers carried out a strong adjustment (Fatás and Mihov 2003). As shown in Table 4.9, between 1993 and 1998,[7] the actual and cyclically-adjusted deficit fell by over 3 percentage points in the countries now comprising the euro area.

Viewed from Member State level, some spectacular turnarounds in fiscal performance occurred. Italy and Greece managed to bring back their public finances from the brink of unsustainability. Finland and Sweden quickly regained control of their public finances after the crises of the early 1990s.

---

[6] Interestingly, as Fig. 4.8 shows, most countries now in the euro area experienced something very close to a one-size-fits-all monetary policy well before the euro was actually launched.

[7] Notice, however, that the period 1993–1998 may not be the most appropriate for all EU countries as several started the consolidation well before 1993.

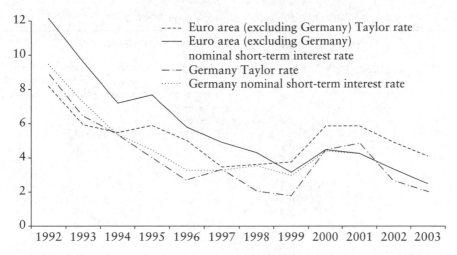

Figure 4.8. *Monetary policy in the 1990s: actual versus Taylor interest rates*

Note: The Euro area is taken to refer before 1999 to the twelve countries now belonging to it. The Taylor rates were calculated with the formula: $i_t^T = r + \pi^{ob} + 1.5(\pi_t - \pi^{ob}) + 0.5ygap_t$. The equilibrium short-term real interest rate was assumed constant at 2%. The inflation objective is taken as 2% throughout the period. The output gap is estimated with the production function of European Commission services.

Source: European Commission, AMECO database and own calculations.

A strong improvement also occurred in the United Kingdom after the 1992 Exchange Rate Mechanism (ERM) crisis. On the contrary, countries such as Germany and France, traditional bastions of fiscal prudence, struggled to keep control of budget deficits that were fuelled, respectively, by the costs of unification and subdued economic performance.

Overall, the fiscal adjustment over the 1990s appears to be not only impressive in size, but also of 'good quality': on average, the contribution of current expenditure retrenchment was considerably larger than that of tax increases or cuts in capital spending.[8] While it is true that public investment was reduced somewhat, research shows that the reduction was lower in the 1990s than in previous years and was smaller in the EU than in other OECD countries.

What was the impact of the budgetary consolidation on economic growth? Answering this question is not easy as the 'counterfactual' is not evident: what would have been the implications of failure by some countries to come to grips with mounting debt and deficits? Hence, one cannot exclude an outright financial crisis taking an even bigger toll on output. This caveat notwithstanding, it is likely that budgetary consolidations contributed to the

---

[8] As an expenditure-based adjustment signals a stronger political commitment to budgetary consolidation, it is more likely to be successful and trigger so-called 'non-Keynesian' effects (European Commission 2003d).

Table 4.9. *Budgetary consolidation 1993–1998*

	Level of structural deficit 1993	Change structural deficit	Change in structural expenditure				
			Total	Change fixed investment	Change other expenditure	Change debt service	Change structural revenue
Austria	4.3	−1.8	−3.1	−1.4	−1.6	−0.4	1.7
Belgium	6.2	−5.7	−1.3	−0.4	−0.9	−3.5	−0.9
Denmark	−0.3	−0.2	−1.0	−0.2	−0.8	−2.0	2.8
Finland	1.6	−1.8	−9.1	0.0	−9.1	−0.9	8.2
France	5.6	−3.3	−1.5	−0.6	−0.8	0.1	−1.9
Germany	3.4	−1.6	−0.8	−1.0	0.2	0.3	−1.0
Greece	12.9	−10.1	0.5	0.3	0.2	−4.8	−5.8
Ireland	0.8	−2.9	−6.1	0.4	−6.5	−3.3	6.5
Italy	9.4	−6.5	−3.0	−0.3	−2.7	−4.7	1.2
Luxembourg	−1.7	−1.2	−4.3	−0.8	−3.5	0.0	3.1
Netherlands	2.1	−0.7	−6.7	−0.1	−6.6	−1.3	7.3
Portugal	5.3	−2.8	3.8	0.0	3.8	−2.6	−4.1
Spain	6.1	−3.6	−5.2	−0.8	−4.5	−0.7	2.4
Sweden	8.5	−11.1	−11.2	−0.5	−10.7	−0.3	0.5
UK	6.5	−6.4	−6.0	−0.8	−5.2	0.5	−0.9
Euro area	5.2	−3.2	−1.8	−0.4	−1.3	−0.8	−0.6
EU-15	5.4	−3.8	−2.4	−0.4	−2.0	−0.6	−0.8

Source: European Commission, AMECO database.

disappointing growth performance of Europe in the middle years of the last decade. However, the prevailing evidence points to lower output costs of fiscal retrenchment in the 1990s, compared to fiscal consolidations in previous decades.[9] In some countries, favourable impact on expectations and good composition may have tempered the direct impact of lower deficits on aggregate demand.[10]

In any case, in view of the deteriorated fiscal situation of the early 1990s, the temporary adverse effects on economic activity were the necessary price to pay for restoring budgetary discipline, itself a very favourable factor for medium-term growth.

Why did Maastricht work?

As argued above, the adjustment process that took place in the 1990s allowed EU countries to 'clean-up their macroeconomic balance sheet'. The nominal adjustment cannot be attributed exclusively to the Maastricht norms as a similar process also took place outside Europe. Nevertheless, Maastricht

---

[9] This is the conclusion by von Hagen et al. (2002). It is consistent with conclusions of Perotti (2002) who, although covering a different sample of countries, finds evidence of lower multipliers in the last decade. See also Mélitz (2000), and for the 1980s Giavazzi and Pagano (1990).

[10] European Commission (1999) found evidence that Italy benefited from non-Keynesian effects, which reduced the direct cost of the fiscal retrenchment.

undoubtedly played a role in the policy turnaround in the 1990s, especially in countries traditionally characterised by large nominal imbalances.

The literature has identified a number of key factors that were at the basis of the Maastricht success:[11]

1. *Public visibility*. The objective of meeting the Maastricht convergence criteria became the centrepiece of government strategy in many EU countries. The objective of reducing inflation was followed by concrete reforms of the central bank status and was explicitly factored into wage negotiations. In the public finance area, public visibility was greatly facilitated by the simplicity of the 3 per cent of GDP deficit criterion which provided a clear signpost for economic policies regardless of political colour of national governments, especially in countries which entered the 1990s with very high deficits and looming threats of unsustainability.

2. *Clear structure of incentives*. Reward and penalty linked with the Maastricht requirements were very clearly laid out. Politically, meeting the convergence criteria would allow countries characterised traditionally by unstable macroeconomic conditions to join their virtuous partners in the new policy regime, while failing to comply carried the penalty of exclusion from the euro area. This was considered too hard a political sanction especially for countries traditionally at the forefront of the process of European integration.

3. *Political ownership*. The whole debate on nominal convergence reflected Germany's concern with monetary and fiscal discipline: both the Maastricht inflation and fiscal criteria and the SGP clearly bear Germany's fingerprints. Strong macroeconomic stability came to be regarded as an essential precondition for Germany to accept merging monetary sovereignty into a single currency.

4. *Constraining calendar*. The Maastricht Treaty set very clear deadlines for moving to the final stage of EMU. Countries willing to join with the first wave had no choice but to make the required effort to meet the convergence requirements.

5. *Effective monitoring*. The simplicity and the unambiguous definition of the convergence requirements—especially those concerning the budget deficit and inflation—allowed an effective monitoring on the part of the European Commission which played the role of external agent commonly entrusted with the correct interpretation and implementation of the Treaty criteria.

6. *Collegial culture*. The process of convergence contributed to the progressive building of a collegial culture of stability through personal contact amongst policy-makers and national and EU officials. This new climate contributed to peer pressure between national authorities and enhanced the role and authority of the European institutions.

---

[11] See Buti and Giudice (2002). The analysis in their paper focuses on fiscal consolidation, but it can be extended also to the disinflationary process.

If these factors were at the basis of the political drive that made Maastricht a success, a fundamental question is the extent to which they are still at work in EMU. We will come back to this question after examining the macroeconomic experience of the euro area in the early years of EMU.

4.2.4. *The early years of European Monetary Union: A mixed picture*

The policy mix: Euro area versus national economies

Since 1999, monetary policy for the euro area has been set by the European Central Bank (ECB) and the fiscal rules of the SGP have applied fully to the countries belonging to EMU. As shown in Table 4.10, economic growth was buoyant in 1999 and 2000 while it slowed down substantially in subsequent years. Annual inflation hovered just above 2 per cent in the past three years.

Performance within the euro area was, however, varied: at one end of the spectrum, Ireland achieved for most years the strongest growth level combined with the highest inflation, while, at the opposite end, Germany recorded the slowest growth rate associated with the lowest inflation.

Evidence of divergent behaviour is particularly clear in the case of inflation. Figure 4.9 presents evidence on the behaviour of inflation for the DM area[12] and the euro area since the mid-1990s. It provides an indication of the degree of convergence of inflation and the way inflation changes were correlated between members of the group: a position high and to the left in the figure indicates that the inflation rate in these countries is not only very similar, but tends to go up or down in parallel; on the other hand, a low position to the right indicates that inflation rates are very different and poorly correlated.

The graph shows firstly that there was a strong inflation convergence in the 1990s within the group of countries who now make up the euro area, attaining a maximum in 1999–2000. In the same period, the differences of inflation rates within the former DM area did not change appreciably. Since then, the gap has reopened somewhat. The second point to note is how the correlation of inflation rates, after having increased in both groups between 1995–1996 and 1999–2000, has been reduced markedly. This provides prima facie evidence that euro-area countries experienced largely common shocks during the period 1999–2000.[13] However, in more recent years, the re-emergence of inflation differentials may signal some 'artificial' compression of the relative inflation rates achieved during the run-up to EMU. This, coupled with cross-country adjustments within the euro area, may have implied a more dispersed pattern of national inflation rates.

---

[12] Germany, France, Austria, and the Benelux countries. These countries have been often identified in the literature as a de facto currency area.

[13] On the contrary, the relatively low correlation for the DM area at the beginning of the period may be linked to the asymmetric implications of the post-German reunification adjustment.

Table 4.10. *Growth and inflation in the early years of EMU*

	Euro area	Standard deviation	Min.	(Country)	Max.	(Country)
Growth						
1999	2.8	2.4	1.7	(Italy)	11.1	(Ireland)
2000	3.5	2.2	2.9	(Germany)	10.0	(Ireland)
2001	1.4	1.5	0.6	(Germany)	5.7	(Ireland)
2002	0.8	1.7	0.2	(Germany)	6.0	(Ireland)
2003 (p)	0.4	1.3	− 0.9	(Netherlands)	4.1	(Greece)
Inflation						
1999	1.1	0.7	0.5	(Austria)	2.5	(Ireland)
2000	2.1	1.0	1.5	(Germany)	5.3	(Ireland)
2001	2.4	1.0	1.8	(France)	5.1	(Netherlands)
2002	2.2	1.1	1.3	(Germany)	4.7	(Ireland)
2003 (p)	2.1	1.0	1.1	(Germany)	4.1	(Ireland)

Note: For 2003, projections by the European Commission of Autumn 2003.

Source: European Commission, AMECO database.

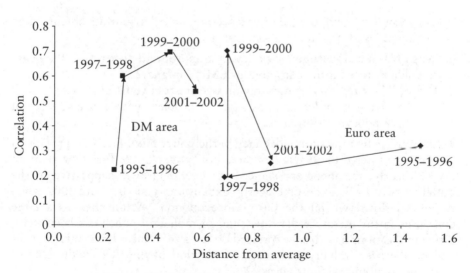

Figure 4.9. *Inflation convergence and correlation*

Note: X-axis: average of the absolute value of the distance of national inflation from the group average; Y-axis: average correlation of inflation within the two groups of countries.

Source: European Commission, AMECO database and own calculations.

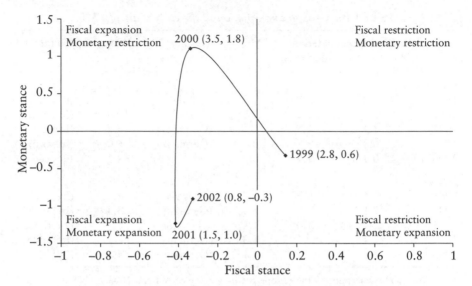

Figure 4.10. *Euro area policy mix: 1999–2002*

Note: Fiscal stance: change in the cyclically-adjusted primary balance; monetary stance: change in the short term real interest rate. In brackets, beside each year, is the real GDP growth and the estimated euro area output gap.

Source: European Commission, AMECO database and own calculations.

From a policy standpoint, the macroeconomic behaviour at the euro area and national levels begs three questions:

1. Was EMU's macroeconomic policy mix appropriate to fend off the negative shocks that hit the euro area in EMU's infancy?
2. Did EMU's budgetary rules imply an over-restrictive fiscal stance?
3. Do the divergent inflation rates signal a problem with a one-size-fits-all monetary policy?

To answer the first question (adequacy of the policy mix), Fig. 4.10 provides a synthetic picture of the macroeconomic policy mix in the first four years of EMU. Clearly, the monetary stance was overall growth-supportive in the initial years of EMU to become overtly expansionary in 2001 and 2002 when the global slowdown hit the European economy.[14] While there is a large consensus in the literature that the 'sign' of monetary policy has been right, different positions have been expressed on the size of the interest rate changes and on the predictability and speed of reaction of the ECB in the face of changing economic circumstances.[15]

[14] Notice that this conclusion would be reinforced had the measure of the monetary stance included the movements in the exchange rate (e.g. by using the Monetary Conditions Index).

[15] While Allsopp (2002) finds that the ECB has quite active, Begg et al. (2002) conclude that, while the ECB's behaviour is captured well by a standard Taylor-rule reaction function, the interest-rate changes tend to be delayed.

On fiscal policy, the graph shows that, after a modest restriction in 1999—the first year of EMU—fiscal policy turned expansionary in the subsequent years. While from a cyclical standpoint such policy stance may be regarded as appropriate in the face of the global slowdown which started in 2001, the fiscal expansion was clearly inappropriate in the year 2000 when buoyant economic growth (3.5 per cent for the euro area as a whole) was coupled with inflationary pressures fuelled by rising oil prices. This policy error prevented budgetary policy from playing its stabilisation role in full during the subsequent downturn (especially in 2003).

Coming to the second question (fiscal stance at the national level), evidence shows that, even in countries still featuring large imbalances, structural deficits rose in 2001 and 2002, thereby supporting aggregate demand. However, in these countries, fiscal policy became increasingly inconsistent with the fiscal discipline requirements of the Treaty. The 'original sin' can be found in failure by countries with high deficits to seize the opportunity to reduce their fiscal imbalances in the previous years of sustained growth. In particular, the fiscal out-turn of Germany, France, and Italy in 2000 was worse than the already timid efforts embodied in their stability programmes. This contrasts sharply with most of the other countries whose budgetary out-turn was better than planned. The experience of the early years of EMU also suggests that, with an extended period of below-potential growth, budget deficits tend to deteriorate sharply. This strengthens the requirement to move into surplus in cyclical upswings so as to have a sufficient room for manoeuvre in the subsequent downturn.

Another, less obvious factor that compounded the fiscal difficulties was the fact that countries continued to project public spending and revenue on the basis of very optimistic growth forecasts. However, a lower potential growth implies that the spending programmes which countries can afford at a given tax ratio are correspondingly lower. *Ex post*, this resulted in stubbornly high structural deficits.[16]

As to the third question (problems with a one-size-fits-all monetary policy), one has to trace the origin of the inflation differentials: these can be benign or malign. Within the euro area, differences among national inflation rates are worrying only to the extent that they lead to divergence of the real exchange rate from its equilibrium level. On the contrary, to the extent that they are driven by different rates of productivity growth (the so-called Balassa–Samuelson effect), or result from the correction of initial real exchange rate disequilibria, or reflect the adjustment to country-specific shocks, they are a natural phenomenon (and are indeed welcome). Part of the inflation differentials

---

[16] Establishing the annual budget laws on the basis of over-optimistic assumptions on GDP growth is one way in which governments free up resources for higher spending in pre-electoral periods. Buti and van den Noord (2003) find evidence of this type of behaviour in the early years of EMU.

is certainly explained by these three effects. In the case of some countries—notably Ireland—the divergent behaviour has also been compounded by different exposure to the devaluation of the euro exchange rate and to the bursting of the technology bubble (Honohan and Lane 2003). Therefore, exchange rate stability at or around appropriate levels should contribute to reduce inflation differentials.

Nevertheless, the reopening of inflation differentials is also related to the one-size-fits-all monetary policy. As pointed out earlier in this chapter, the single monetary policy can result in the low inflation-low activity countries experiencing higher real interest rates while the high inflation-high activity countries have lower real interest rates, thus exacerbating initial divergences among national economic situations. As Fig. 4.11 shows, this effect was particularly evident in the early years of EMU when Germany and Ireland—the two countries at the opposite ends of the growth-inflation league—faced real interest rates that were probably inappropriate from a purely domestic standpoint.

Correcting the macroeconomic imbalances fuelled by an inappropriate monetary stance requires activating other channels of adjustment. Here there is a clear interplay between the ECB monetary strategy, real exchange rate changes within the euro area, and fiscal policy changes. If the overall area-wide inflation rate is set too low, a potentially dangerous spiral can set in for low-growth countries. With the budget balances burdened by sluggish growth, these countries need to boost demand by devaluing their real exchange rate. However, doing so while the euro area's average inflation is kept very low is

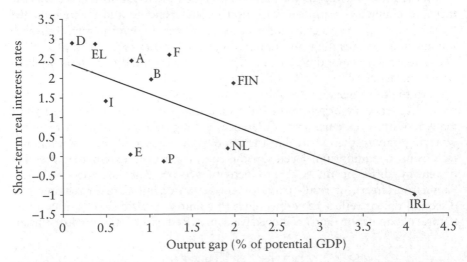

Figure 4.11. *A pro-cyclical monetary stance in the euro area? (average figures 1999–2002)*

Source: European Commission, AMECO database.

problematic and risks of a particular country ending up in deflation cannot be ruled out. While the ECB's definition of price stability appears adequate to prevent deflation to take hold at the euro-area level, attempting to keep the area-wide inflation rate much below its upper bound (2 per cent) may be risky in a period of protracted slowdown and downward pressure on prices in so far as it increases the probability of deflation occurring in a particular country. Such a risk is probably higher in EMU's infancy when other channels of adjustment are still underdeveloped.[17]

Adapting to the new policy regime

The picture emerging from the foregoing analysis of the economic and policy behaviour in the early years of EMU is mixed. In the monetary area, price stability has been assured and monetary policy has generally been supportive of economic activity since the downturn in activity began. But in an environment of downward pressure on prices it needs to be sufficiently forward-looking. In the public finance area, budgetary policies have not reverted to those of the pre-Maastricht era, but several countries (notably the largest members of the euro area) failed to create the necessary room for manoeuvre under the 3 per cent of GDP deficit ceiling during favourable growth conditions. As a result, they found their fiscal policy increasingly constrained in a situation of protracted economic sluggishness.

There is a large consensus that the ECB did a good job in an eventful period where it had to operate with less-than-perfect statistical information and knowledge of the functioning of the euro-area economy. Before the euro was launched, observers pointed to the risk of an over-restrictive monetary policy given the need of the newly-created central bank to build up its anti-inflationary reputation. This risk has not materialised and price stability has been achieved while maintaining a growth-supporting monetary stance. Nonetheless, according to a number of observers, the 'newness' of the ECB has played a role by reinforcing the natural caution of central bankers and implying a somewhat slow reaction of monetary policy in the face of rapidly changing economic circumstances. Attaining the optimal timeliness of policy actions by the ECB remains an important matter.

On fiscal policy, the picture is quite unsatisfactory. Evidently, some political economy factors which underpinned the success of Maastricht have not carried over into EMU: diminished political ownership of EU fiscal rules and the limited incentives to run prudent policies in good times are at the root of the current difficulties with the SGP. Several Member States failed to abide by the 'fiscal philosophy' of the SGP which implies attaining close to balanced structural positions and let automatic stabilisers play freely. Since exceeding the 3 per cent of GDP deficit ceiling still carries a political cost, high-deficit countries came to face an increasingly difficult dilemma between

---

[17] See IMF (2003) for an empirical evaluation of deflationary risks.

sticking to the rules and sustaining demand in a situation of protracted economic sluggishness.

The need to attain more symmetry in the functioning of the Pact led the Commission to propose a number of changes in November 2002 (European Commission 2002c), which were broadly endorsed by the Council in March 2003: definition of the medium-term budgetary targets in structural terms, some more flexibility for countries with sound public finances, and enhanced surveillance in cyclical upswings. These changes, coupled with the repeated call for enhancing microeconomic adjustment mechanisms (improving the functioning of labour and product markets), clearly go in the right direction. However, it remains to be seen whether, also in the light of enlargement, they go far enough to improve cyclical stabilisation while ensuring long-term sustainability. Another issue is whether the current mechanisms of EU governance are effective to ensure ownership and compliance at the national level (Beetsma and Uhlig 1999; Wyplosz 2003).

4.3. Cohesion

Article 2 of the Treaty on European Union states that one of the objectives of the EU is: '*to promote economic and social progress and a high level of employment... in particular... through the strengthening of economic and social cohesion*'. Article 158 contains a more explicit definition: '*In order to promote its overall harmonious development, the Community shall develop and pursue its actions leading to the strengthening of its economic and social cohesion. In particular, the Community shall aim at reducing disparities between the levels of development of the various regions and the backwardness of the least favoured regions or islands, including rural areas.*'

Concern with 'cohesion' is strong on the part of both national and supranational political processes in Europe, where intense interpersonal redistribution is implemented by taxes, subsidies, and regulations. The relevant instruments are essentially left to the Member States and lower levels of government, but distribution-oriented policies influence in an important way the nature of cross-boundary economic relationships, and are in turn constrained in some respects by supranational policies meant to safeguard undistorted international trade. In addition, a small layer of supranational redistribution-oriented policy instruments exists in the form of EU cohesion policy directly motivated by the effects on regional and national income inequality of the European economic integration process.

In what follows, we review the theoretical motivation and effects of European redistribution policies, as well as empirical evidence regarding the evolution of regional and interpersonal inequality in the last few decades. Section 4.3.1 focuses on the convergence issues in both a country and a region dimension, and Section 4.3.2 reviews pre- and post-tax inequality trends at the personal (and household) level. The two dimensions are interrelated, of course, and both sets of theoretical mechanisms and empirical findings are key to assessing the overall cohesion performance of the EU system of economic policies. Both sections also outline the extent to which observed inequality trends may be ascribed to market forces (influenced in turn by internationalisation of economic relationships) or to specific national and supranational policy intervention.

4.3.1. *Countries and regions: Convergence policies and trends*

Economic theory suggests that investment and savings should foster percapita income convergence when technological conditions are (or become) uniform across geographical entities characterised by constant returns to scale.[18] Economic integration introduces further convergence forces in that setting, as unfettered factor and goods flows should enforce equality of marginal productivity, and of income, throughout an integrated area. If income differences reflect different initial conditions, over time production should grow faster in initially low-income regions and countries than in initially high-income ones, as capital flows into the latter and out of the former, and trade allows each to specialise in the sectors where its comparative advantage lies.

In reality, however, economic activity does not diffuse uniformly across integrated territories: within each Member State, and within each region, production 'agglomerates' in cities and industrial districts (Krugman 1991; Martin and Ottaviano 2001). Agglomeration tendencies reflect locally increasing returns to scale, that is, a tendency for unit costs to fall as more economic activity concentrates in a given region. In the EU economic integration context, such phenomena can endanger cohesion objectives. If relatively advanced regions attract an even larger share of the overall economic activity, an increase in the scale and intensity of continent-wide economic interaction could well cause relatively backward regions to lag further behind, rather than catch up with, the more advanced portions of the integrated economic area. More generally, initially low-income areas may develop in a non-uniform way, thus generating 'polarisation' effects within each region.

From this economic geography perspective, not only initial levels of economic activity matter for the development prospects of regions but also their size relative to, and distance from, the centres of gravity of the integrated area's economic activity. If the advantages of economic integration reflect new and more intense linkages across geographical entities, in fact, 'core' regions enjoy many more such new linkages than 'peripheral' ones, which might experience economic decline rather than growth when their isolation is broken by dismantling of barriers to trade and factor flows.

European Union cohesion policy
Enlargement of the EU to low-income and peripheral countries in the 1980s gave prominence to geographic development concerns and prompted the

---

[18] As in the neoclassical growth model. See Barro and Sala-i-Martin (1991).

implementation of a complex set of supranational policies as described briefly in Box 4.3. These cohesion-oriented policy instruments aim at fostering income equality across Europe's geographic units, but they do not simply transfer resources to low-income regions (as an explicit redistributive policy

Box 4.3. *The EU cohesion policy in brief*

European Union cohesion policy is the second largest item in the EU budget, making up about 35 per cent of total expenditure. Cohesion policy is translated into financial disbursements through its two main instruments: the Structural Funds and the Cohesion Fund, with the former accounting for roughly 90 per cent and the latter for 10 per cent of the total. Prior to 1989, EU cohesion policy was relatively unstructured and financially much smaller. Cohesion policy 'proper' began with the introduction of the EU's pluri-annual spending guidelines or Financial Perspectives, as they are called. These were the so-called Delors I package for the period 1989–1993, the Delors II package for the period 1994–1999 and the Agenda 2000 package for the period 2000–2006.

During the period 1994–1999, Structural Funds allocated money to regions on the basis of six 'objectives' (all data from European Commission (2001a: 122–58) unless otherwise indicated):

1. Supporting development and structural adjustment of regions whose development is lagging behind. They received 68 per cent of the funds. In 1999, 24.6 per cent of the EU population lived in regions that received objective 1 funding from the EU.
2. Helping frontier regions or parts of regions seriously affected by industrial decline.
3. Combating long-term unemployment and facilitating the integration into working life of young people and of persons exposed to exclusion from the labour market.
4. Facilitating the adaptation of workers to structural change.
5. Speeding up the adjustment of agricultural structures as part of Common Agricultural Policy (CAP) reform (objective 5a), facilitating the development and structural adjustment of rural areas (objective 5b).
6. Promoting (since 1995) the development and structural adjustment of regions with low population density.

The Cohesion Fund as such, which only exists since 1993, has a national rather than regional focus and targets those Member States (Greece, Spain, Ireland, and Portugal) whose GDP per capita is lower than 90 per cent of the EU average and that are following a programme of economic convergence. It is reserved for environment and transport infrastructure.

As for the period 2000–2006, the Agenda 2000 package allocates a total of €213 billion to cohesion policy. Of this, about €195 billion (European Commission 2002d: 226) are allocated to the Structural Funds and €18 billion to the Cohesion Fund which still targets Greece, Spain, Ireland (only till 2003) and Portugal. If one adds in the €22 billion earmarked for new Member States in the period 2004–2006, the total cohesion effort comes to €236 billion for the whole period, or about 34 per cent of the total EU expenditure.

Agenda 2000 made a major effort to simplify the Structural Funds, which for the period 2000–2006 are divided into just three objectives (instead of six as previously):

(1) development and structural adjustment of regions lagging behind (formerly objectives 1, 5a, 5b, and 6): about 70 per cent of the Structural Funds;
(2) development of border regions and regions in industrial decline (formerly objective 2);
(3) adaptation and modernisation of education and training systems (formerly objectives 3 and 4).

For the sake of the analysis, cohesion policy can be disaggregated in three main parts:

(1) objective 1 funds, which have a clear regional focus, which target the low-income EU regions across Member States and which represent about 65 per cent of the total cohesion policy;
(2) other objectives, which have a horizontal focus and which represent about 25 per cent of total cohesion spending;
(3) cohesion funds, which have a clear national focus, which target the low-income Member States and which represent about 10 per cent of the total cohesion policy;

The predominantly regional focus of cohesion policy generates two results which are worth mentioning: (a) all Member States, except Luxembourg and Denmark (and Belgium and Netherlands from 2007) have at least one region receiving financial aid under objective 1; (b) countries with a similar level of per capita GDP, may receive very different shares of EU funds. For example, Sweden and Italy have comparable levels of per capita GDP, but since the latter suffers from much wider regional inequalities it receives considerably greater support from EU cohesion policy.

---

would). Low GDP levels are an important criterion for making EU funds accessible to specific countries and regions, both on the basis of the formal qualification criteria and in practice. A negative correlation between GDP per capita and funds received under the EU cohesion policy is observed.[19] The disbursement of funds, furthermore, is conditional on formally clear, if economically debatable, indicators of industrial structure, a peripheral geographic position, and other regional characteristics that are presumed to endanger regional development in the absence of policy interventions. 'Additionality'

---

[19] The simple correlation between Community cohesion policy disbursement and GDP levels per head across the seventeen macro-regions ranges from − 0.5 (in 1991 and 1995) to − 0.6 (in 2000). These seventeen macro-regions are Austria, Belgium, Denmark, Finland, France, Germany eastern *Länder*, Germany western *Länder*, Greece, Ireland, Italy Mezzogiorno, the Rest of Italy, Luxembourg, Netherlands, Portugal, Spain, Sweden, and the United Kingdom. Germany and Italy have very wide regional differences in GDP per capita which imply that EU cohesion policy focuses mostly on the poorest part of the country. For our analysis, it is therefore more significant to split each country in two subsets.

criteria are meant to avoid any risk of crowding out local investments and to ensure that cohesion policy finances investments that otherwise would not have been undertaken.[20]

It is no surprise that EU-level policy aiming at fostering cohesion should transfer funds with important strings attached. The Treaty itself refers to a reduction in 'disparities between the levels of development', not in disposable income levels. Indeed, agreement on unconditional transfers to low-income regions would hardly be politically feasible: transparent transfers of funds across the borders from Member States' redistribution schemes would create obvious winners and losers and would be difficult to agree upon at the Community level. Furthermore, political processes also indicate that the extent of intracountry redistribution varies substantially within the EU (see Section 4.3.2 below).

The overall picture of EU regional subsidies is further complicated in three respects. First of all, the link between Community fund disbursement and genuine regional development needs is weakened by a politically unavoidable tendency to balance transfers across Member States (almost all of which, no matter how rich, claim at least some underdeveloped regions to obtain highly visible, if small, Structural Fund allocations). This is reinforced by the fact that the unanimity rule in decision-taking, which regulates the planning of cohesion policy funds, gives every country a considerable amount of leverage. Second, Member States have a tendency to trade cohesion policy funds against other financial flows,[21] such as those under the CAP and other internal spending programmes which have fewer strings attached. The negative correlation between GDP per capita of the beneficiary countries and regions and EU expenditure towards them is lost once the CAP and the other internal programmes are added to cohesion policy.[22] Indeed, the CAP and the other internal programmes, which represent slightly more than half the EU budget, compared with 35 per cent for cohesion policy, tend to be positively correlated to incomes. Third, Member States pursue their own active regional development

---

[20] Additionality is targeted by (a) the requirement that '[f]or each objective, the Community aid given to each Member State concerned during the programming period may not lead to a reduction in its public or equivalent cohesion policy compared with the previous programming period' (European Commission 2002d: 232); and (b) by 'co-financing' requirements: the Community contributes between 50% and 75% of objective 1 operations, less for other objectives, and national matching funds need to be available for the rest. In 1999, the total of national matching funds in objective 1 regions amounted to almost €82 billion, much larger than the €30 billion from EU funds.

[21] The enlargement negotiations produced the latest evidence of this kind of trade-off: the final deal was struck when the Council accepted that part of the funds destined for new members come from the CAP rather than cohesion policy because of the different strings attached.

[22] Adding CAP and the other internal spending programme funds to cohesion policy disbursement, the simple correlation between total Community fund disbursement and GDP levels per head across the seventeen macro-regions (see footnote 2) drops to −0.4 (in 1991) and to −0.2 (in 1995 and in 2000).

policies, which are in turn constrained by supranational guidelines meant to prevent trade distortions. Interestingly enough, when considering together the national and the EU intervention in favour of areas lagging behind, one observes that a significant negative correlation with the GDP per capita of the receiving areas is respected.[23] This means that the national (but subject to EU authorisation) state aids do not undo the overall cohesion effort pursued by the EU central budget.[24]

The evidence

The available empirical data on economic convergence in the EU give a very different picture depending on whether one looks at the fifteen Member States or at the 211 administrative regions across the Union. On the one hand, in the period 1980–2000, a tendency of per capita GDP to converge can be observed at the Member State level. Initially low-income countries grew faster, on average, than high-income ones whose disappointing growth performance was reviewed in Section 4.1 above. On the other hand, within each country, GDP per capita (and unemployment rates) has tended to diverge across regions, increasing inequalities. Inequality within each country accounted for roughly half of total EU regional inequality in the early 1980s, but this rose to about two thirds by the mid-1990s, while inequality between countries fell by about a third during that period.[25]

In fact, by looking at the intermediate aggregate of macro-regions one may refine the 'country convergence' and 'region divergence' findings. The bulk of the structural and cohesion funds flows into six macro-regions (Greece, Spain, Ireland, Portugal, the six eastern German *Länder*, the Mezzogiorno in Italy) which receive on average about 68 per cent of the total.[26] When convergence of these macro-regions is assessed, one finds that their average GDP did

---

[23] Articles 87(3)a and 87(3)c TEU allow Member States to grant state aid to economic areas: the first applies a criterion of regional under-performance; the second requires the aid to be non-distorting with respect to the Single Market. Such state aid is generally a smaller amount than the national matching funds since the latter also comprises big infrastructure projects. In 2000, state aid under Article 87 totalled about €85 billion across the EU, of which €14 billion went to the six low-income macro-regions (eastern Germany, Greece, Ireland, south of Italy, Portugal, and Spain). Adding national matching funds and state aid to cohesion funds, a very significant correlation with GDP per head across the seventeen southern macro-regions is still observed. This correlation is equal to −0.5 (in 1991, 1995, and 2000).

[24] Member States also implement regional redistribution through schemes that do not fall under Article 87, ranging from lump-sum transfer schemes between regional budgets in some federal Member States to concentration of public expenditure and employment in low-income regions and other very specific measures. It is difficult to assess quantitatively this type of redistribution, because of its many different forms. Project loans granted by the European Investment Bank also have a regional orientation, but only a small percentage of the funds represent a subsidy (e.g. in terms of softer interest rates).

[25] See the next section, Puga (2002), Neven and Gouyette (1995) and references therein.

[26] Considering that objective 1 regions are, by definition excluded from some 25% of the cohesion policy (money allocated to other objectives) these six macro-regions are the beneficiaries of about 90% of cohesion and objective 1 funds.

Table 4.11. *Growth differences between seventeen macro-regions for GDP growth rates (in %)*

	1980–1990	1991–2000	1991–1995	1995–2000
6 macro-regions	2.6	3.3	2.8	3.7
Rest of Europe	2.3	1.9	1.3	2.4
EU-15	2.4	2.1	1.5	2.6

Table 4.12. *Growth differences between seventeen macro-regions for Index per head (GDP/head in PPS)*

	1980	1990	1995	2000
6 macro-regions	69.3	70.7	73.5	76.8
Rest of Europe	109.5	109.1	109.9	108.7
EU-15	100	100	100	100

Source: AMECO and New Cronos databases.

converge. This is true both in terms of *sigma* convergence (lower dispersion of the income distribution) and of *beta* convergence (stronger tendency for low-income macro-regions to grow faster than high-income ones). The six macro-regions displayed annual growth of 3.3 per cent between 1991 and 2000, while the rest of the EU produced annual growth of 1.9 per cent (Table 4.11 and 4.12).

However, within the broad macro-region convergence picture there are wide differences across the six areas considered. The Italian Mezzogiorno showed no sign of convergence, while Spain, Portugal, and Greece grew only slightly faster than the EU average. Ireland and eastern Germany have driven the convergence of the six macro-regions. The impressive performance of Ireland is such that in only fifteen years it has moved from the bottom group of the poorest four EU countries to become one of the top four (in terms of GDP per capita).

A provisional conclusion to be drawn from the available macroeconomic evidence is that convergence is observed both at the level of Member States and at the level of macro-regions. However, at the level of administrative regions across the EU, the evidence is mixed: low-income regions have displayed a faster growth, but GDP per capita of the regions is becoming more widely dispersed across the EU.

Link between policies and evidence
This evidence is, at least superficially, consistent with the agglomeration-based concerns which motivate EU cohesion policy. It is much harder, however, to

ascertain whether such policies have had an impact, that is, whether regional divergence would have been more pronounced in their absence.

Many studies have analysed the dynamics of EU regional GDPs, and their relationship to EU structural policies. Low-power statistical methods based on poor data sets can easily fail to discern any effect of EU cohesion policy.[27] But it is also not difficult to provide some statistical evidence of favourable convergence effects in less prosperous regions: for example, the negative relationship between initial low per capita GDP and faster subsequent growth is stronger for regions with objective 1 status.[28]

In practice, however, there is simply not enough relevant regional GDP data for statistical procedures to distinguish the effects of cohesion policies in the absence of data on other regional characteristics, such as initial income, human capital, local industrial structures, quality of local administration, the peripheral nature of the region, and of random influences. The net result is that it is not possible to establish conclusively what the relative performance of these regions would have been in the absence of EU cohesion policy and other policies.

For example, the quality of local administration and policies may not only determine a region's economic development directly, but also interact with EU policies, insofar as regions with low-quality local institutions also find it difficult to spend Community funds allocated to them.[29] The classical indicator of performance for managing EU cohesion policy is the so-called disbursement ratio—the difference between the amount of money allocated to a given country and the actual amount paid out to it. For example, for objective 1, the EU average ratio for the period 1994–1999, was 79 per cent, but it varied from a minimum of 67 per cent in Italy to a maximum of 90 per cent in Portugal. The same indicator for Germany, Spain, and Ireland ranged from 81 to 87 per cent.[30] Figure 4.12 points to a positive correlation between GDP growth and the disbursement ratio during the period 1994–1999.

In addition to local characteristics, national conditions, such as macro-economic stability and sound public finances, are also likely to affect the convergence pattern of the regions. Greece and Ireland showed little sign of convergence until both countries undertook a policy of macroeconomic stabilisation combined with structural reform. Stability and macroeconomic reform have been instrumental in attracting foreign direct investment, which for both countries has been a primary factor of convergence.[31]

Furthermore, when assessing the economic impact of EU policies exchange rate fluctuations pollute all income data prior to the creation of the euro, and

[27] Boldrin and Canova (2001).

[28] Leonardi (2003). Of course, this might be due to nonlinearity of the overall relationship or to characteristics of those regions other than initial GDP. This point is well explained by Davies and Hallet (2002).

[29] See Hurst et al. (2000), Mairate and Hall (2000), and Hallet (2002).

[30] There seems to be a high inverse correlation between the disbursement ratio and measures of corruption such as the 'Corruption Perception Index' (an index collected from several surveys by Transparency International (www.transparency.org)).

[31] See Martin et al. (2001).

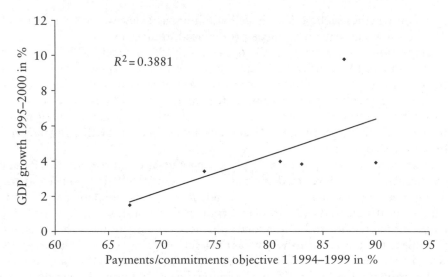

Figure 4.12. *Use of funds and growth for the six low-income macro-regions*
Source: European Commission, New Cronos database, and European Commission (2001*a*).

purchasing-power adjustments are inevitably imprecise. It would be interesting and useful to compare the performance of Ireland in moving from a low-income to a high-income country with that of Greece and Portugal by assessing the impact of the structural funds on the development of each of them. Greece, Portugal, and other countries and regions may have been different in terms of initial income and subsequent development of income as well as in terms of the incidence of EU cohesion policy. But they were also very different in terms of language, geographic position, national policies, and a host of other national and regional characteristics.

Empirical analysis based on industry-level data can offer more insight, both because it can be focused on the structural mechanisms at the root of agglomeration effects, and because it can better monitor other policy influences (chiefly state aid to industry).[32] As predicted by theory, European regions do appear to have become more specialised in the aftermath of economic integration, reflecting both their comparative advantages (especially in terms of the population's skill endowment, a key regional characteristic in a low-mobility environment) and incipient agglomeration effects due to local economies of scale. EU policies do appear to interfere with this process. This is not surprising, since Structural and Cohesion Funds were indeed tasked to prevent agglomeration of 'desirable' technologically-advanced industries in the core regions. In terms of regional GDP, however, the impact of structural policies oriented to foster the development of such industries is positive only

---

[32] Midelfart-Knarvik and Overman (2002).

when the resulting sectoral orientation is consistent with the region's comparative advantage. Again, Ireland provides a good example of a country which invested EU funds in industries where it enjoyed a comparative advantage. Conversely, EU and state funding of R&D-intensive industries seems to have failed to stimulate economic growth in those countries and regions, which combine general development-hindering structural features with a level of population skills unsuited for employment in those sectors.

As experienced by the current Member States, the quality of local administration can be a binding constraint on the effectiveness of EU cohesion policy and on the convergence process as a whole. For the new member countries the picture should be brighter. From the outset of the enlargement process, the Copenhagen criteria provided a *fil rouge* to guide the creation of legal and administrative capacity. Around one half of the pre-accession funds was targeted at institution-building, both at national and local level, and a number of twinning programmes between current and new members have been implemented. This effort must continue and the quality of the legal and administrative environment must be recognised as a crucial element of a convergence policy. In Part III, this report will argue in favour of measures aimed at ensuring that the legal and administrative capacity of countries receiving EU cohesion funds is sound and apt to make the best use of those funds.

Box 4.4, which compares the situation of Ireland with that of the Mezzogiorno, can offer some more intuition into the determinants of economic convergence and the relative importance of different factors.

Box 4.4. *Ireland and Mezzogiorno: similar EU policy, contrasting economic performance*

> The Mezzogiorno (South of Italy) is a large macro-region of about 20.9 million inhabitants (36 per cent of Italy) with a GDP of €220.2 billion (24 per cent of Italy). Ireland is a much smaller region, of 3.8 million inhabitant and a GDP of €82 billion.[33] Between 1991 and 2000, Ireland grew on average by about 8 per cent a year, while the Mezzogiorno grew by about only 1 per cent. As a result, the per capita GDP of Ireland moved over the ten years from 77 to 116 per cent of the EU average, while that of the Mezzogiorno remained between 74 and 69 per cent. The income of an Irish resident in 2000 is about 168 per cent of the income of a resident in the south of Italy while, back in 1991, it was only 4 per cent greater. According also to other economic and social indicators (unemployment, poverty, etc.), Ireland is often among the top performers with the Mezzogiorno often the weakest performer (e.g. see European Commission 2001a, 2003c). Funds per head effectively
> *Continued*

[33] AMECO Database for the year 2000 at 1995 prices. The regional split for Italy is obtained by using Eurostat New Cronos data.

Box 4.3. *Continued*

paid out by the EU cohesion policy were four times higher for Ireland than for the Mezzogiorno in 1991, 40 per cent higher in 2000 and 25 per cent lower in the period 2000–2006.

The radically different economic performance of the two areas cannot be simply explained by the different level and trend of EU cohesion policy. The economic literature has stressed a set of reasons why the performance of the two areas might have been so different.

First, and (arguably) foremost, Ireland revealed an impressive capacity to attract foreign direct investment. This seems to be the result of the Irish strategy aimed at developing human capital, by investing in education, training, life-long learning so as to provide investors with a good business climate. Furthermore, the investment inflows seem to have concentrated in sectors and fields where the Irish initial endowment of R&D and human resources was already good, thus developing a cluster of growth poles which largely contributed to the overall positive effect.[34] Also, as indicated in the section above, Ireland has been able to maintain good standards of administrative capacity and in general a favourable investment climate. This resulted in improved competitiveness and greater capacity of traded sectors to conquer market share. Finally, the macroeconomic environment is crucial for a small open economy such as Ireland. Indeed, Ireland witnessed a dramatic improvement in public finance: debt was slashed from 97.3 per cent of GDP in 1991 to 38.6 per cent of GDP in 2000 and a deficit of 2.9 per cent in 1991 become a surplus of 4.4 per cent in 2000. Due to its high growth, regaining control of public finance certainly proved less painful and less harmful for short-term growth than in other countries.

The Mezzogiorno, on the contrary, did not show a particular capacity of attracting investment inflows, because of a mixture of factors. Low quality of public administration both in dealing with business needs and in providing public services (energy supply, transport, link to networks, etc.) have deterred investors from entering the area. Furthermore the lower productivity of the south of Italy, compared with the north of the country, was not reflected in lower wages due the centralised wage bargaining system. Administrative capacity in the Mezzogiorno did not rise to the challenge in two respects. First, the Mezzogiorno has the lowest ratio of funds spent/funds allocated as documented above.[35] Second, the administrative authorities proved unable to channel EU funds towards activities, which could build upon the local industrial structures, and/or the local endowment, and/or the local human resources' skills. Finally, the persisting presence of organised crime has been a major obstacle to development. It has been calculated

---

[34] Davies and Hallet (2002) point out that although all Irish regions have converged towards the EU average the high growth rate of some of them (the Dublin area, namely) has led to a widening of regional disparities within Ireland.

[35] This seems to run against the intuition that economic agents, in regions with weak governance, would take all the allocated funds and waste them on activities of private, rather than public relevance. One possible explanation as to why those regions make so little use of the funds allocated is because of the conditionality attached to EU funds.

that, for the year 2001, the impact of local criminality on the growth of Mezzogiorno was equivalent to some 2.7 per cent of its GDP, rising to 5–6 per cent in some sectors.[36]

In this respect, the data and the signals of the last few years provide some hope.[37] The trend away from convergence seems to be reversing. Since 1996, the Mezzogiorno has had a growth rate greater than or equal to the rest of Italy, due to the emergence of growth poles, and external demand for both goods and tourism. Statistics also show that this trend is accompanied by a reduction in the degree of control over the local economy by organised crime.

4.3.2. *Interpersonal inequality*

Total inequality in disposable income between citizens in the current EU has decreased somewhat over the last thirty years. The reduction of the total inequality is measured here by three indicators: the ratio of the income held by the top 5 per cent over the income of the bottom 20 per cent,[38] the Gini coefficient and the Theil index.[39] They confirm that income inequality mildly decreased over the whole period. It reached its minimum in 1980 before rising again (see Table 4.13).

It is interesting to decompose the total inequality in the EU into 'inequality within countries' and 'inequality between countries'. One can see that the former accounts for some 90–95 per cent of the total inequality. While inequality within countries first fell from 1970 to 1980, and subsequently rose back to the 1970s levels by the late 1990s, inequality across countries fell by half between 1970 and 1998, with a particularly sharp decrease starting in the 1980s (see Table 4.13). The ability to reduce 'inequality within countries' seems directly linked to growth: it was high in the periods of high growth (1960–1980) and much lower, if not non-existent, in the period of moderate growth (such as 1980–1998). This does not imply that growth automatically reduces inequality, but it means that it is easier to reduce inequality in period of high growth than in periods of sluggish growth. Symmetrically, the

---

[36] See Fondazione BNC-Censis (2003).

[37] See Ministero dell'Economia e delle Finanze (2003).

[38] For example, a value of two means that the richest 5% of the population commands twice the income of the poorest 20% of the population. Since the latter group is four times greater than the former, it means that, in per capita terms, the income of the richest is eight times the income of the poorest.

[39] The Gini coefficient ranges from 0 to 1 and indicates the distribution of income across population. A totally egalitarian income distribution (where each 1% of population commands 1% of income) implies a Gini coefficient of zero, while a totally inegalitarian distribution (where 1 individual commands 100% of income and all the other individuals command no income at all) implies a Gini coefficient of 1. Gini coefficients below 0.25 are usually regarded as 'low' (e.g. Sweden with a Gini of 0.228 is regarded as a low inequality society), while coefficients around or above 0.5 are regarded as 'high' (e.g. Turkey with a Gini of 0.49 is regarded as a high inequality society). Gini coefficients in EU in 1998 ranged from 0.211 (Finland) to 0.361 (Portugal).

Table 4.13. *Distribution of disposable income within the EU, inequality indices*

	1970	1980	1990	1995	1998
Income shares: top 5%/bottom 20%	2.01	1.73	1.77	1.73	1.86
Gini coefficient	0.320	0.299	0.301	0.303	0.309
Theil index					
'Within' countries	0.152	0.130	0.142	0.142	0.152
'Between' countries	0.017	0.016	0.012	0.008	0.008
Total inequality	0.169	0.146	0.154	0.150	0.160

Source: Morrisson and Murtin (2003).

reduction of the 'inequality between countries' depends on the implementation of EU-wide policies, such as the Single Market or the cohesion policies.

This confirms the result of the previous section: convergence across member countries did take place. The EU has been and remains a remarkably equal high-income entity, while the rest of the world witnesses a much higher and perhaps increasing inequality.[40] However, the strong European concern with economic and social cohesion, which emerged after the Second World War, is now challenged by the increasing interpersonal inequality of the last 10–15 years. Hence, it is interesting to review briefly the possible role of EU policies (chiefly economic integration itself) and national redistribution policies in determining the empirical outcome.

Integration and inequality
Economic integration may or may not lead to convergence of regional average incomes, depending on the strength of agglomeration effects. But geographic entities are not populated by identical 'representative' individuals, and new trade and factor-mobility opportunities generally tend to alter personal income distribution within each region or country.[41]

Trade makes it possible for consumers to obtain goods which are produced more efficiently, hence more cheaply. But since trade affects factor incomes as well as goods prices, economic integration makes *all* individuals better off only in rather special circumstances. When trade opportunities arise from

---

[40] Morrisson and Murtin (2003) estimate total inequality of the EU to be about 10% lower than in the United States and 50% lower than world inequality. This is of course due to an incomparably lower inequality between countries within the EU but also to a much lower inequality within EU countries. They also find global income inequality to be slightly increasing in recent decades (see also Bourguignon and Morrisson 2002). However, there is no consensus as to whether relatively mild increases in global within-country inequality offset broad convergence patterns between some groups of countries (Sala-i-Martin 2002).   [41] Bean et al. (1998: ch. 2).

differences in technologies, all workers would gain from trade if they were identical and could freely move from one industry to another. The identity of each worker would then be completely immaterial, and with access to the technological possibilities of the other country everyone would necessarily enjoy higher consumption. But units of labour and other factors of production are in practice not alike, and economic integration tends to affect not only the total amount of economic welfare, but also how it is shared out. Trade can also be motivated by factor endowments rather than technology, and will generally raise (lower) the relative income of factors that are in relatively abundant (scarce) supply within each country. But trade liberalisation effects are not only more complex than simple theories make them, but also mixed with the effects of technological innovation and institutional changes that tend to raise demand for skilled labour. However, economic integration among countries at increasingly different levels of economic development—such as that implied by the EU's past and coming enlargements—may well make such distributional effects more important in relation to efficiency-enhancing effects of trade among countries producing differentiated goods using similar technologies and factor bundles.

National systems of redistribution

Within each European country, redistribution of income through tax policy and other interference with laissez-faire market interactions plays a very important role. To see the impact on total inequality of the different national system of redistribution one should compare inequality in market income (pre-tax income)[42] and in disposable income (post-tax income)[43] in the EU and in the United States. Table 4.14 gives estimates for inequality in market income and in disposable income in the EU and in the United States, for 1985 and 1995.[44] They show that inequality in market income is higher in the United States than in the EU and also that the tax and welfare system corrects less in the United States than in the EU. In the EU, the system reduces inequality by about 25 to 30 per cent, while in the US the reduction is at most 20 per cent. Morrisson and Murtin (2003) also show that the EU system basically doubles the income share of the bottom 20 per cent of the population, while the US system increases it by about 70 per cent. Both the EU and the US systems increase the income share of the bottom 80 per cent of the population, by decreasing the income share of the top 20 per cent of the population.

Beneath this broad picture, important differences exist across EU countries as regards the impact of redistribution on families and individuals of different

[42] It includes income from labour and capital. Unemployed persons are included as persons with a zero income from the labour market.

[43] Disposable income underestimates the actual size of redistribution as transfers in kind are not considered.

[44] Market income includes labour income (zero for non-employed persons) and capital incomes. Disposable income accounts for taxes and monetary transfers; it may underestimate actual redistribution, as transfers in kind are not considered.

Table 4.14. *EU versus US distribution of pre-tax and post-tax income*[45]

	1985		1995	
	Pre-tax	Post-tax	Pre-tax	Post-tax
Income shares: top 5%/bottom 20%				
EU	3.49	1.51	4.14	1.66
US	5.12	2.42	4.97	2.43
Gini coefficient				
EU	0.381	0.279	0.408	0.294
US	0.415	0.337	0.421	0.342

Source: Morrisson and Murtin (2003).

ages.[46] First of all, it is clear that richer and more productive countries carry out more extensive redistribution within the EU. The direction of causality is not easy to ascertain. The fact that the US redistributes much less than European countries at similar levels of development, however, indicates that social cohesion concerns are typically stronger in Europe. The fact that similar concerns lead to lower expenditure in low-income countries indicates that political processes are importantly constrained by income level. Further, across EU countries different policy instruments are tasked to the various goals of redistribution policy (combating social exclusion, reducing overall inequality, and fostering labour market fairness), and are funded in different ways. The Scandinavian model of universal social protection as a right of citizenship coexists with the Anglo-Saxon model of the United Kingdom and Ireland as well as with the 'Bismarckian' employment-based model of Germany, France, Austria, and the Benelux countries. In the remaining southern Member States, state-sponsored systems of redistribution are less mature, more fragmented, and highly idiosyncratic: much of social expenditure accrues to retirees, and family relationships play a relatively important role in smoothing interpersonal income disparities.

Of course redistribution—whether meant to foster *ex ante* equality, or to remedy market failures in the provision of insurance against *ex post* shocks—has costs in terms of productive efficiency. Transfers to *ex ante* low-income individuals must be financed by taxes that reduce overall efficiency by introducing wedges between market demand and supply outcomes. Income-support policy instruments targeted at unlucky individuals receiving negative shocks face much the same information constraints that prevent insurance markets from functioning well: workers have no less incentive to decrease their effort when covered by social instead of private insurance. Efficiency costs are

---

[45] EU data refer to Belgium, Denmark, Finland, France, Germany, Ireland, Italy, The Netherlands, Sweden, and the United Kingdom.   [46] Bertola et al. (2001).

apparent along regional as well as other dimensions in the EU. In the less developed regions of large and heterogeneous countries (Germany, Italy, Spain) uniform national systems of labour market regulation and income-support lead to persistent unemployment, and permanent fiscal flows.

Systems of redistribution, therefore, have to balance efficiency and equity considerations, and in practice need to accept a degree of both *ex ante* and *ex post* inequality even in the presence of strong political cohesion concerns. The welfare systems in the Member States were designed before EU integration and are very slowly evolving in response to that and other challenges. Social expenditure has remained essentially stable, since the 1980s, as a fraction of total income, and its composition has remained highly heterogeneous across groups of countries. In the last few decades, however, each system of redistribution has been encountering increasing difficulties in fulfilling its objectives. The Anglo-Saxon model based on means-tested and in-work benefits has proved unable to stem the tide of increasing wage inequality. The continental model of employment-based instruments and wage compression has led to long-term unemployment. And the Scandinavian model, which tries to break out of the trade-off between social protection and employment by 'active' labour market policies, has encountered budgetary problems in the face of recent developments.[47]

Thus, the efficiency costs of redistribution are becoming more evident on the one hand, fostering limited reforms, while on the other hand higher disposable-income inequality[48] appears to result from largely unchanged systems of redistribution. The source of these difficulties need not be solely, or even primarily, the increased intensity of market pressure resulting from European economic integration. However, tensions are apparent between member countries' cohesion concerns and the continental scale of EU integration. In particular, the national character of redistribution processes interferes with labour mobility, especially as regards pension portability and other rights. And while little concerted supranational action is observed as regards taxation and labour market regulation, supranational constraints are to some extent binding as regards entitlement of European citizens to social services.

---

[47] See Bertola et al. (2001) for some discussion.
[48] In most countries the disposable income inequality was higher in 1998 than in 1980, but lower than in 1970. In the United Kingdom it is also higher than in 1970.

5

Economic trade-offs

Over the past fifteen years the European Union (EU) has witnessed a big leap forward in its integration process which led to the establishment of the Single Internal Market in 1993, to the creation of an Economic Monetary Union (EMU) in 1999, and to the most recent agreement to welcome ten new members into the EU in 2004. Judged by the progress made in the integration process, there is no doubt that this period has been a considerable institutional success. Nevertheless, the verdict is more mixed from the economic viewpoint: while macroeconomic stability has significantly improved overall—as reflected, for example, in the marked reduction in inflation rates and budget deficits—and a high degree of cohesion has been preserved, *the EU has underperformed in economic growth*.

This underperformance is all the more remarkable since it is relative not only to expectations but also to past European performance and to that of the United States. Indeed, in the EU there has been a gradual lowering of the average growth rates decade after decade with per capita GDP stagnating at about 70 per cent of the US level since the early 1980s. Furthermore, given that the United States has achieved higher per capita growth relative to the EU through both higher levels of productivity and higher employment, this implies that the EU is actually operating inside the production possibility frontier or, in other words, is not using its resources to the full extent of their capacity.

The main purpose of this chapter is twofold. On the one hand, to identify and analyse the trade-offs, or complementarities, underlying the relationship between the EU's three main economic objectives: growth, stability, and cohesion. And, on the other, to examine how trade-offs can be improved upon and complementarities better exploited in the future to achieve higher sustained growth in a macroeconomically stable and cohesive enlarged Union.

5.1. Trade-offs among objectives

In principle, there may be both trade-offs and complementarities among the objectives of growth, stability, and cohesion. The analysis presented in Chapter 4 makes it possible to be more specific concerning the type of trade-offs or complementarities that arise and the key factors shaping them. In what follows, the relationships between each pair of objectives are examined.

5.1.1. *Growth and stability*

When looking at the past economic performance of the EU since the 1970s, there seems to be an apparent overall medium-term trade-off between growth and stability since there has been considerable progress in improving macro-economic stability, particularly over the 1990s, while average growth rates have been gradually declining decade after decade. This is in sharp contrast to what has happened in the United States, which has been able to achieve greater macroeconomic stability over time while maintaining growth at relatively high rates.

Should this lead us to conclude that the EU's growth underperformance is in some way or another linked to the improvements made in the degree of macroeconomic stability reflected, say, into lower budget deficits and lower rates of inflation? Is therefore the 'apparent' European trade-off a 'real' one? What makes such a trade-off appear in the EU but not in the United States?

When addressing the above questions concerning the relationship between growth and macroeconomic stability it is worth recalling three things. First, since our definition of macroeconomic stability is rather broad, 'more stability' means lower budget deficits, lower and less volatile rates of inflation, and smaller cyclical fluctuations. Second, given the stickiness of wages and prices over shorter horizons, it is important to distinguish between the short-term and the medium-term. And finally, the creation of EMU has implied such significant changes to macroeconomic policies that the relationship between stability and growth should be seen in a different light. These various aspects of the relationship between growth and stability are discussed in what follows.

Before EMU

As mentioned in Chapter 4, the process of *fiscal consolidation* followed in the EU in the 1990s on the road to EMU implied a significant reduction of budget deficits as well as a reversal of potentially explosive debt dynamics. Is it thus likely that the process of fiscal adjustment may have hurt growth?

Over the short term, budgetary retrenchment tends to lead directly to a demand contraction that could depress growth temporarily. Nevertheless, by improving the debt dynamics budgetary consolidation may also have positive credibility effects, reflected in lower longer-term interest rates, which in turn exert an expansionary impact on private demand thus countering the direct contractionary effects of fiscal consolidation. The European experience suggests that both effects may have been present to some degree, the latter being more intense in those countries with initially higher long-term interest rates. Yet the available evidence (e.g. see Perotti 2002; von Hagen et al. 2002) would point overall towards a somewhat net contractionary effect from fiscal consolidation over the short term, which also squares well with the traditional wisdom on the macroeconomic role of fiscal policy.

What about the medium-term effects on growth which are the more important ones for ascertaining the 'real' existence of any medium-term trade-off like the one 'apparent' in EU experience? In principle, it may be thought that in so far as fiscal consolidation results in higher tax rates or lower government investment there would be a negative impact on growth. However, this is not what seems to have happened in the EU since most of the reduction in deficits during the 1990s on the road towards EMU came from lower debt service (linked to lower interest rates) and lower current spending. As a result, the reduction in government investment accounted in most cases for only a small fraction of the total deficit reduction. On average, it amounted to 0.4 percentage points out of a total reduction of nearly 4 percentage points of GDP in structural deficits. In turn, fiscal consolidation should have exerted downward pressures on interest rates thus crowding in private investment. Finally, when assessing the medium-term effects of fiscal consolidation, we should take into account the highly beneficial impact on growth of avoiding eventual debt crises, which, as history shows, are severely disruptive and damaging to a country's economic prospects.

All in all, it seems that the improvement in the budgetary situation of EU countries did not lead to any significant deterioration in medium-term growth prospects, even if there may have been negative short-term effects in a number of countries. In this regard, it is also worth recalling that the deterioration of growth performance in the EU started during the period of higher budget deficits in the 1970s and 1980s, confirming that other major forces must have been behind this sub-par growth performance during the last thirty years. Indeed, growth is highly likely to have benefited more recently from the absence of debt crises made possible by the significant progress made in fiscal consolidation in the 1990s.

Coming now to the relationship between *inflation* and growth performance, the implementation of stronger anti-inflationary monetary policies since the 1980s is likely to have led—particularly in the earlier years—to temporary costs in terms of activity in an environment of imperfect credibility of such policies and sticky wages and prices, as is well documented in the literature. Nevertheless, the weight of the international evidence is that monetary policies aimed at achieving and maintaining price stability facilitate achieving higher growth in the medium term (Viñals 1998, 2001).

Lastly, regarding the relationship between *output volatility* and growth over the medium term, although the international evidence is rather controversial, it points if anywhere towards lower output volatility and higher growth coming together, other things being equal. In this regard, it is hard to understand why the low and decreasing degree of output variability observed in the EU since the beginning of the 1980s may have resulted in lower growth rates.

To sum up, while there may be reasons to think that the achievement of a higher degree of macroeconomic stability in the EU may have resulted in some temporary negative effects on economic activity (as a result of disinflation and fiscal consolidation), there are no convincing reasons to think that this may have compromised growth performance over the medium term. On the contrary, the success on the stability front has established the conditions for faster growth to be achieved in the future. Therefore, the 'apparent' medium-term trade-off between stability and growth is not 'really' there, while the complementarity between stability and growth needs to be acknowledged. *In other words, our analysis suggests that the sub-par growth we have had over the past thirty years is not the consequence of the higher degree of macroeconomic stability achieved.*

Inside Economic Monetary Union

The above notwithstanding, and thinking forward with the help of the short experience of the Stability and Growth Pact (SGP) and the Single Monetary Policy, there may be several grounds to revise certain features of the design of macroeconomic policies within EMU to improve growth prospects without compromising the degree of stability achieved. This is so because the very significant changes implied by the creation of EMU could lead, unlike in the past, to certain tensions between stability and growth or even between several of the dimensions of stability reviewed above—like nominal and output stability.

The existence of the Single Monetary Policy means by definition that the authorities of the countries belonging to the euro area should resort to differentiated national fiscal and structural policies to counter the effects of idiosyncratic shocks which lead to different national evolutions. Yet the experience of the past years suggests that, in addition to the lack of progress in instrumenting structural reforms aimed at increasing economic flexibility, the way the SGP has been run has not provided several countries with enough room for manoeuvre to carry out sufficiently counter-cyclical fiscal policies in the downward phase of the cycle. It may thus be necessary to rethink certain features concerning the SGP to avoid the tension between the requirements of prudent fiscal policies and the desire not to exacerbate cyclical fluctuations.

Given that the primary goal of the Single Monetary Policy is to maintain price stability, the precise definition of 'price stability' carries an enormous importance. At present, as stated by the ECB, price stability is defined as a year-on-year increase of harmonised consumer prices for the euro area as a whole of below 2 per cent, to be maintained over the medium term. As modern monetary theory makes clear, the choice of the appropriate definition for what constitutes price stability depends on a number of factors like the cost-of-living measurement bias in consumer price indexes, the need to balance 'sand and grease in the wheels' arguments concerning how inflation affects the workings of the price system, and the dangers posed by the zero bound on nominal interest rates. In addition, experience inside EMU suggests that one would have to take into account also the impact that a chosen definition of price stability has on the probability of specific countries eventually entering into serious deflation in the presence of significant persistent national inflation differentials.

Consequently, while choosing an inflation rate that is too high might certainly hurt medium-term growth prospects, choosing too low a rate might impose an unnecessary degree of tension for the workings of EMU. In particular, in the latter case it would be necessary for some countries to have negative rates of inflation for an extended period of time—with the ensuing risks of falling into a deflation spiral—in order to achieve the necessary adjustments in real exchange rates vis-à-vis other member countries. In this case, not only cyclical instability may be exacerbated but growth prospects compromised for, at least, part of the euro area (Calmfors et al. 2003).

5.1.2. *Growth and cohesion*

Is it possible that one of the reasons for the past growth underperformance of the EU is the emphasis put on cohesion? If so, what would be the key linkages?

In principle, the relationships between growth and cohesion are bidirectional (Herce et al. 2001; Scharpf and Schmidt 2000). Integration processes like the one undergone by the EU lead to gains from trade and efficiency gains which—if coupled with policies which allow the re-employment of the resources freed from rationalisation and which preserve a suitable economic and regulatory environment—translate into higher growth. Yet the gains from trade arising from market liberalisation and integration may spread unevenly across nations, regions, and/or individuals.

Precisely for those reasons, policies oriented towards maintaining what is socially regarded as an adequate degree of cohesion may reduce the efficiency and growth benefits arising from market liberalisation and integration. As our analysis makes clear, policies carried out at the EU level have in a number of cases interfered with the specialisation of regions in the aftermath of economic integration, and quite deliberately so since such policies were aimed at preventing agglomeration effects in the first place.

In addition, policies carried out at the national level with the aim of strengthening intracountry cohesion have also had detrimental side-effects in terms of efficiency and growth. A particularly important case has to do with policies concerning the portability of pensions and other rights. Since they exemplify the national character of redistribution processes, such measures interfere with labour mobility across EU countries, thus reducing the degree of integration of national labour markets. In the same vein, national labour market regulations which limit the effective degree of intracountry labour mobility across regions, sectors, and/or firms in an attempt to reduce interpersonal inequalities tend to run counter to the requirements for a dynamic economy and thus reduce growth potential.

In political economy terms, achieving a socially acceptable minimum degree of cohesion at the European level is necessary for the harmonious functioning not just of the EU's economic system but of the EU as a whole, thus permitting agreements to be reached that permit advances in the integration process. Similarly, at the national level interpersonal cohesion fosters social peace and removes a source of uncertainty that could otherwise negatively affect innovation and investment. However, the European experience suggests that *some specific instruments chosen to preserve cohesion in the course of the process of market liberalisation and integration may have exerted too high a toll in terms of growth*. This has been both through limiting the deepening of such processes and through trying to counter the unequal spreading of the resulting gains from trade in a distorting manner at both the European and national levels.

5.1.3. *Stability and cohesion*

In the EU system, the linkages between stability and cohesion result mainly from the policy decisions made at the national level. In this regard, fiscal consolidation may lead—as has been the case in many EU countries—to lowering current spending, thereby reducing the room for carrying out social policies oriented towards interpersonal cohesion. Yet it must also be recognised that the budgetary retrenchment observed in the EU over the 1990s and the stronger anti-inflationary commitment of monetary policy—first through the Exchange Rate Mechanism (ERM) and more recently through the European Central Bank (ECB)—has resulted in lower and less volatile inflation rates. This should have benefited the interpersonal distribution of income since the poorer segments of the population are precisely those who are the least able to protect themselves against the cost of inflation. Finally, the lower degree of output volatility exhibited in the EU over time implies a lower intensity of economic fluctuations and reduces the need to provide social safety nets to help cushion the impact of recessions on the interpersonal income distribution.

Overall it seems that the progress made in the various dimensions of macroeconomic stability in the EU—most notably during the 1990s—should not have significantly affected the ability to carry out cohesion policies.

5.2. Growth and the trade-offs

The analysis of European economic performance clearly shows that, in spite of the enormous progress made along the road to economic and monetary integration, the EU economic system has been unable to deliver a satisfactory growth performance. As noted, however, a high degree of cohesion has been maintained and considerable advances have been made overall in achieving a high degree of macroeconomic stability.

From the examination carried out in the previous section, it appears that the design of some cohesion policies both at the EU and national levels has run counter to growth, and that while growth performance has benefited from the progress made in stability there are concerns that following the establishment of EMU there may be some elements of European macroeconomic policies which may reduce cyclical stability and dent growth prospects.

Nevertheless, *the main reason behind the poor growth performance of the EU in the past seems to be related to the supply side of the economy.* In particular, the significant obstacles which still remain to complete the integration of markets—most notably of labour markets and of certain segments of financial markets—as well as the failure to improve the regulatory framework and to carry out the structural reforms needed for a competitive, dynamic, and innovative economy.

It could be argued that, given European preferences for having wider and thicker social safety-nets, the above growth performance is nothing but the natural consequence of such choice. However, this fails to take into account that the sustainability of the so-called European model is called into question more and more in a low growth context. Indeed, the unappealing consequences of low growth rates for unemployment put significant strains on public finances which are incompatible with the fiscal rectitude that a growing economy requires, thus further lowering growth prospects and compounding the problem. Consequently, there is a need to give higher priority to growth, not just because it is the means to achieve higher per capita incomes but because a growing, competitive, and dynamic economy is needed to finance a certain degree of cohesion in a durable manner.

Similarly, the establishment of an economic and regulatory environment which enhances competition and innovation may also have important beneficial side-effects for the consolidation, and even improvement, of macroeconomic stability in various ways. A more integrated, competitive, and flexible European economy will show greater resilience in coping with shocks. In turn, this self-stabilising behaviour will reduce the need for fiscal policies to incur the otherwise very large deficits in such cases, thus making it easier to comply with the SGP. And finally, a more flexible and resilient economy will also lessen the risks posed by the proximity to the zero bound on nominal interest rates and the need to operate around higher inflation rates to achieve the relative price adjustments within countries—and the relative price level adjustments across countries—which are required.

While it would be important to redesign cohesion policies at both the EU and national levels to address better the adverse consequences of such policies for growth, and while some features of the current macroeconomic policy setting in EMU should be revised to favour growth while maintaining stability, these measures would achieve only limited results if not complemented by decisive microeconomic policies aimed at expanding growth potential.

These latter policies, which are directed at the supply side of the economy, must reverse the present state of affairs, where the EU economy mainly operates inside the production possibility frontier. As a comparison of the past performance of the US and EU economies reveals, it should be possible for the EU to grow faster through the assimilation of existing technology and organisational practices. This change in the growth pattern, which involves continuously pushing out the production possibility frontier, would allow reversing the unfavourable trade-offs between employment creation and advances in labour productivity, which—unlike in the United States—have been a predominant feature of past European economic performance.

Last, but not least, for the EU to achieve higher sustained growth in a macroeconomically stable and cohesive Union it is not only necessary to reassess carefully the trade-offs and complementarities among the various objectives and efficiently align the various policy instruments towards the pursuit of such goals. In addition, as explained in our discussion of economic governance issues in Chapter 6 of this Report, it will be necessary to revise the methods of governance to ensure both that the various instruments are allocated to the appropriate decision levels and that the latter behave coherently with the ultimate aims of the EU economic system.

6

Economic governance in the European Union

6.1. The issue

How economic policies are managed in the European Union (EU) has become a key issue in recent years. There has been a growing sense that improved economic governance is critical to the chances of the European economy performing better, that institutional and management deficits impede economic performance, and that getting the governance right will be even more important as the Union enlarges. This concern as regards economic policy-making is part of a wider debate about reforms to the institutions and processes of the EU, which were the focus of the Convention on the Future of the EU. In addition, the increasing use of the term 'governance' conveys an emphasis on broad processes of policy-making across public institutions and also private actors as being relevant to how policies are developed and how markets operate. Moreover, as enlargement will increase significantly the heterogeneity of the Union, the question arises as to whether a uniform system of rules and procedures can be applied in the face of more and more diverse situations.

Governance as such was much less of a preoccupation ten or fifteen years ago. In that pre-Economic and Monetary Union (EMU) period what seemed the most important was to agree on a set of policies that would make European integration efficient, robust, and sustainable. On the implementation side, the focus was on enabling the Council to agree more easily on legislation to regulate the Single Market. The debate on governance has evolved since the late 1980s in conjunction with a series of important developments.

First, the poor economic performance of the EU in the past decade suggests that the Union and its Member States lack the capacities to address systematically many areas of shared concern, with the implication that approaches to economic governance may be partly at fault.

Second, the drive to intensify integration, launched in the 1980s with the Single Market project, produced as could have been expected an anti-centralisation backlash. The delimitation of powers between the EU and the Member States (or sub-national entities) has increasingly become an issue which the rather ambiguous references to subsidiarity introduced into the Treaties have not solved.

Third, as integration within the EU deepens and its stated ambitions are rising, it is deploying a wider set of methods than originally envisaged. Member States have been reluctant simply to delegate additional competences and powers to the Union and have relied on forms of parallel policy-making, principally coordination, and introduced further variants, notably bench-marking. This has led to a discussion about the effectiveness and mutual compatibility of those methods.

Fourth, there was (and still is) a discussion on the approach to governance required by the euro. French insistence first on the notion of an 'economic government' (a concept whose precise meaning was never spelled out) and later on economic policy coordination epitomised the discussion, but the issue is broader.

Hence, it has become vital to review the inherited approaches to economic governance and to explore how these might be improved.

6.2. Current patterns of economic governance within the European Union

What we currently find in place in the EU is a patchwork of different arrangements for managing economic policies. Four basic approaches can be distinguished:

1. *Delegation.* Some policies are fully delegated to the Union, that is, are decided and operated at the EU level. This obviously applies to the Union's areas of exclusive competence, but also to an array of policies belonging to shared competences. Examples include trade policy (completely in goods, partially for services), competition policy, for much of market regulation and—more recently—monetary policy. Patterns of delegation vary: delegation is most often to the European Commission, but policies are also sometimes attributed to another independent European body, such as the European Central Bank (ECB), as stated in the Maastricht Treaty.

2. *Commitment.* For some policies, Member States retain ultimate respons-ibility but have subscribed to binding commitments, are subject to EU surveillance and can be subject to sanctions if they do not meet their obligations. The prime example is budgetary policy in the macro field. Another example is state aids (which are subject to Commission oversight).

3. *Coordination.* Important areas of macroeconomic policy, but also many microeconomic policies and those that lie at the interface between eco-nomic and social policy, are largely decided and implemented at the level of Member States, but subject to an EU process of (usually soft) coordination. The difference from (2) is that no enforceable commitment exists in those areas. However, multilateral surveillance, dialogue and benchmarking, an increasingly attempted technique, may substantively influence policy decisions. Examples include those aspects of macroeconomic policies that

do not fall under the jurisdiction of Article 104 of the Maastricht Treaty (the excessive deficit procedure), structural reform and employment policies.
4. *Autonomy*. Many policies are decided and implemented autonomously 'within' Member States, with no involvement of the EU level except sometimes by policy dialogue. In many respects, this can be regarded as a regime of policy competition. Examples include direct taxation policy, education, and social protection.

Table 6.1. *A schematic representation of the EU governance regimes*

	Micro	Macro
Delegation	Common Agricultural Policy (CAP) Trade (goods) Competition (most) Product market rules Regional development (some) R&D (EU)	Monetary policy[a]
Commitment	Value added tax (VAT) State aids Greenhouse emissions control	Fiscal policy (Article 104)[a]
Coordination	Labour markets Financial supervision Service and utility markets Regional development	Fiscal policy (Article 99)
Autonomy	Direct taxation National public spending Education Welfare R&D (national)	

[a] These headings apply only to members of the euro area.

This characterisation is obviously a simplification. Even for delegated policies, the modes of decision and implementation may vary a great deal. Hence, trade policy is decided upon by the Council and implemented by the Commission (i.e. the Council is the principal and the Commission is the agent—although there is still a reluctance to delegate fully trade in services), while competition policy is decided upon and implemented by the Commission without Council involvement (although here too we should note the introduction of a network approach with national authorities).

Commitment enforcement procedures also vary both as regards their nature (appeal to the European Court of Justice versus financial sanctions) and their strength.

Coordination involves very different channels. It can:

1. be through explicit guidelines to which Member States are expected to conform, and subject to multilateral surveillance (this is the role of the Broad Economic Policy Guidelines based on Article 99);

2. be based on a collective rule, amenable to agreement by qualified majority voting (Single Market regulations);
3. take the form of a permanent, informal high-level dialogue (within the Eurogroup); or
4. rely on mutual information and assessment (the so-called Open Method of Coordination (OMC) introduced in 2000).

Generally, implementation relies on cooperation between Union and Member States' authorities. The EU administrative apparatus relies heavily on those of the Member States for implementing decisions. Table 6.1 provides an illustration of the EU system in the early 2000s.

Not only are there these different approaches, but many different instruments are used to execute policy, from hard collective rules to milder instruments of persuasion and soft procedures for cooperation and dialogue.

1. *European legislation.* This instrument is most extensively used to govern the Single Market and to set the framework for those measures agreed by Member States that shall apply across the Union.
2. *Strong European rules.* These govern the single currency partly in treaty form, and partly by Council decision.
3. *Decisions.* These deal with specific situations (in one country or in one sector) or specific cases (as in the instance of competition policy).
4. *Collective negotiation mandates.* These are agreed tightly for most of trade policy and more loosely in the case of, for example, greenhouse gas emissions.
5. *Sanctions.* Enforcement of common rules can rely on pecuniary sanctions (examples are state aids and the Stability and Growth Pact (SGP)).
6. *Financial incentives.* These are provided from the Community budget, both for the structural and cohesion policies or to develop some collective programmes, as in the case of R&D policy.
7. *Agreed targets, benchmarks or indicators.* In a number of areas, especially under the Broad Economic Policy Guidelines and by so-called Lisbon Strategy (see Section 6.3.3.), the Member States increasingly agree to establish similar approaches and objectives and a shared methodology for reporting and assessing performance.
8. *'Voluntary' alignment and policy transfer.* Some forms of convergence take place to the extent that Member States choose to move towards a shared policy template, by imitating each other.
9. *Networks.* The Union has always depended to some extent on forms of networked governance, sometimes as a tool for developing the basis for a more collective regime, and sometimes as an instrument in its own right.

Thus, it is quite misleading to suggest that the choice for the EU lies between 'the' Community method and forms of 'intergovernmental' cooperation. Already we can observe a great variety of Community methods and a great variety of forms of cross-country cooperation, with the former shading into the latter and vice-versa, and with a range of different roles and responsibilities for European and national institutions within as well as between areas of economic policy.

Table 6.2. *EU legal acts adopted by policy domain in the early 2000s*
(number of individual legal acts adopted)

	Regulations	Directives	Decisions
Micro integration	*134*	*1004*	*2551*
Common market	48	890	184
Competition and company law	73	38	2309
Taxation	13	76	58
EMU	*45*	*1*	*80*
Sectoral policies	*3915*	*650*	*2738*
Agriculture	3733	484	2245
Other sectoral policies	182	166	493
Education, social, and environment	*336*	*447*	*773*
Environment	66	193	188
Education, research, culture	13	76	58
Citizens and social protection	257	178	527
International	*1790*	*21*	*1474*
International trade	1568	20	1216
Other international relations	222	1	258

Source: Adapted from Alesina et al. (2002).

A quantitative examination of existing legislation and individual case decisions (including those of the Court of Justice) provides a complementary view (Table 6.2). Several features stand out:

1. quantitatively, the bulk of EU legislative activity is concentrated in three fields, the Single Market, the CAP and the common trade policy, which are major EU competences.[1]
2. the instruments for implementing sectoral policies, competition policy, and the common trade policy are primarily uniform EU-wide regulations and product- or case-specific decisions, while the basic instrument for the Single Market is the directive, which leaves some room for adaptation to the national context.
3. EMU-related legislation is essentially limited to setting the framework of macroeconomic policy and to introducing the single currency, as one would expect of a field that is also subject historically to very little

---

[1] We should note that in the case of the CAP many of the legal acts are short-lived market management rules.

national legislation. This confirms the change in character introduced by EMU.

4. the role of the EU in implementing competition and trade policy is apparent in the high number of individual decisions (e.g. on merger controls or anti-dumping cases). Here, the role of the EU is not only to set the rules, but also to implement them, like a government; and

5. there is very little legislative EU activity in the fields of innovation, education, and research, all of which are meant to represent common priorities for the Lisbon Strategy.

Another criterion is public spending. Table 6.3 disaggregates the spending side of the EU budget. The familiar picture emerges: the bulk of EU budgetary expenditures are concentrated on agriculture and regional development. In spite of Lisbon, research, and technology only account for 4 per cent of total expenditures.

Table 6.3. *Breakdown of the EU 2002 budget (commitments)*

Subsection	Euro mio	%
B1: EAGGF Guarantee Section	44,505.1	45.2
B2: Structural operations, structural and cohesion funds: financial mechanism, other agricultural and regional operations, transport, and fisheries	34,002.5	34.5
B3: Training, youth, culture, audio–visual media, information, social dimension, and employment	918.7	0.9
B4: Energy, euratom nuclear safeguards and environment	246.7	0.3
B5: Consumer protection, internal market, industry, and Trans-European networks	1,172.9	1.2
B6: Research and technological development	4,055.0	4.1
B7: External action	8,314.0	8.4
B8: Common foreign and security policy	30.0	0.0
B0: Guarantees and reserves	213.0	0.2
DA: Administrative expenditure (of all of the institutions)	5,176.8	5.2
Total	98,634.7	100

Source: European Commission, DG Budget.

However, neither the legislative nor the quantitative data reveal the variety of roles played by the Union. Table 6.4 presents schematically EU competences, roles, and methods. The EU can act as a rule-maker, a policy-maker, a regulator, a supervisor, or a facilitator. Those are very different roles and it should be no surprise that having the same institution(s) perform such a variety of tasks creates perplexity.

In short, the picture that emerges is one of confusion and tension. Confusion is created by the complexity of the EU system and the diversity of the roles

Table 6.4. *EU competences, roles, and governance methods: a schematic presentation*

Competence	EU role	Governance method	Examples
EU competences	*Rule-maker*	Delegation of legislative powers to the EU	Single Market
	Policy-maker	Delegation of executive powers to a EU institution	CAP, trade, monetary policy in the euro area
	Regulator	Delegation of judicial or regulatory powers to EU institution	Merger control
Shared competences	*Rule-maker*	Partial delegation of legislative powers to the EU (through framework laws, directives)	Single Market
	Policy-maker	Partial delegation of budgetary functions to the EU budget	Cohesion policy
	Supervisor	Enforcement of commitments, possibly through sanctions	State aids SGP
	Facilitator	Coordination of national policies, possibly through incentives	Labour markets

performed by the Union in its relationships with Member States, sub-national entities and private agents. Tension comes from the gap between goals and means. It is hard to reconcile the view 'from above'—the goals enshrined in the Treaty and announced by the European Council—and the view 'from below'—the nitty-gritty of legal acts and budgetary choices. This gap is a natural consequence of the political character of the EU. To bridge it would require hard choices—either to give up on some of the common ambitions or to make a decisive step in the direction of integration. But this should be no reason for letting it becoming ever wider.

6.3. Economic governance: An evolving agenda[2]

Ten or fifteen years ago the focus of the EU economic debate was on policies rather than methods. Broadly speaking, all Member States participated in all Community policies; the delegation model was predominant; there was a simple institutional set up; and the primary role of the Community was to set rules, not to make recurrent policy decisions. As the Community seemed equipped with a strong model of governance and able to take on new

---

[2] Some of the discussion in this section is based on case studies prepared as background material for the Report.

responsibilities, the—fierce—debate was about which additional economic policy powers could or should be assigned to the European Community. Nowadays, however, economic governance as such has become a primary preoccupation. Hence we offer here an outline assessment of the state of affairs across the main areas of economic policy.

6.3.1. *The impact of the Single Market*

The Single Market was based on straightforward principles but it has turned out to be harder to implement than originally anticipated.

First, the development of the Single Market shows considerable variation in the positions of Member States. In some sectors, notably financial services, progress was impeded by persistent differences of approach and of regulatory cultures. In other sectors, such as food safety and animal welfare as well as biological science, societal concerns cut across economic and business innovation. Differing social preferences and locally-negotiated welfare state institutions also impeded cross-border labour mobility.

Second, the Union's ambition to develop a single regulatory apparatus has increasingly been subject to criticism. To be sure there is evidence that incumbents reluctant to face market opening often shelter behind claims of cultural or social difference, but there are also deeply-embedded differences of preference revealed by consumers and citizens with impacts on economic policy options. Subsidiarity was offered as a solution to the trade-off between the requirements of the Single Market and the need to adapt to preference heterogeneity, but without an agreement on how this principle could be made operational.

Third, the relationship between the EU institutions, Member States and private players is changing. Whereas the removal of trade and non-trade barriers could rely on the integration of markets by private actors seeking out economic opportunities, regulation involves a constant tension between market-opening and the interests of national incumbents, especially in markets which require continuous regulation to ensure access to physical networks (as in telecommunications or energy). Furthermore, new patterns of independent regulation and of entrepreneurial behaviour made the classical EU processes of cooperation between the Member States and the Commission hard to operate in some areas. The proliferation of new, often autonomous, regulatory bodies within the Member States, as well as the emergence of forms of self-regulation by stakeholders, made it harder for the Commission to develop its policy surveillance responsibilities. The new framework for telecommunications regulation provides an example of the institutional and legal complexity involved (Box 6.1).

Fourth, from a political economy standpoint, a perverse evolution has been at work since the 1980s: national governments had every incentive to blame 'Brussels' for decisions that could hurt domestic interest groups. The EU thus

Box 6.1. *Partnerships of national authorities as agents of European integration: the example of telecommunications regulation*

In telecommunications regulation, the Commission is trying to use a network of national authorities as a promoter of European integration but in contrast to competition policy, the immediate legal basis for regulatory intervention is provided by national law, guided by various European directives, rather than the Treaty. The system created by Directives 2002/19–22 of the European Parliament and the Council was designed in response to the observation that in some Member States the opening of national telecommunications markets was not proceeding at a satisfactory pace.

Under the new system, the Commission draws up a list of telecommunications markets that are in principle candidates for regulation. Each national regulatory authority considers whether competition is 'effective' in these markets. 'Effectiveness' of competition is identified with the absence of players with significant market power. A market without effective competition is subject to regulation. Which regulatory regime is being used is up to the national regulatory authority, which can go all the way from the simple imposition of transparency rules to a full regime of *ex ante* access and price regulation. There is however a proviso that the more intense mode of intervention shall be imposed only if less intense modes are ineffective in furthering the development of competition.

In this setting, the national regulatory authorities' assessments of which markets are to be regulated and which are not, as well as the imposition of obligations concerning the granting of access to essential facilities, have to be developed in agreement with the European Commission and with the other national regulators. National regulators present the results of their considerations to the Commission and to their peers. They are obliged to 'take the utmost account' of the latter's comments. Individual national regulators are also obliged to provide the Commission and the other national regulators with whatever information is needed to ensure coherence of telecommunications regulation across the EU.

The Commission's position in this area is weaker than in competition policy because it is based on directives rather than the Treaty. One source of foreseeable conflict is in the question as to whether the Commission's list of markets that are in principle candidates for regulation is binding on national authorities. Can the national regulator expand this list? If so, by what criteria? Can it shorten it? If so, by what criteria? Moreover, what happens if the national regulator and the Commission disagree about the results of the market analysis?

Involvement of multiple national regulators in the assessment of market analyses also raises the issue of extraterritorial effects of the pronouncement of foreign national institutions. What happens if the results presented by one national regulator are objected to by another? What constitutional basis is there for say a Dutch regulatory authority to make pronouncements on German telecommunications markets of which the German regulatory authority must 'take the utmost account'?

Answers to all these questions are uncertain because the formulation of the European directives binding national institutions to 'take the utmost account' seems to leave some leeway for national autonomy, which is bound to be tested in practice. As these questions will be resolved through the development of a suitable legal routine, much of the burden will lie with the courts.

However, the legal uncertainty that prevails until these matters are resolved is itself a major impediment to economic activity, in particular to market entry by new companies. Paradoxically, the legal uncertainties associated with the creation of the new regulatory framework for telecommunications works against the very aim of the framework itself, which is to foster market opening and competition. Removal of this uncertainty must therefore be a matter of first priority.

became the easy scapegoat, as well as a target for the attacks of well-organised lobbies. The Union's legitimacy was weakened by its lack of visibility as regards the public goods it was supposed to provide, while national governments could claim responsibility for security, public order, health, education, social justice, and so on. Economic prosperity through the setting up of efficient market infrastructures, arguably a European public good, was too abstract to grasp the attention of public opinion.

That the Single Market had a quantitatively significant impact on EU governance is apparent in Fig. 6.1, which gives for the 1971–2000 period the evolution of EU legislative activity (flow data) in three categories: regulations, directives, and (individual cases) decisions. The level of EU activity grew strongly in the 1980s as the implementation of the Single Market gathered pace. More recently, the rate has slowed to decisions, that is, enforcement of existing legislation, or occasional amending or updating directives. This suggests some degree of maturing of the legal apparatus (Wallace and Wallace 2000; Young and Wallace 2000).

The speed of implementation of EU directives has been a matter for controversy. Nevertheless, in May 2003, of the nearly 1500 directives related to the Single Market Programme, 2.4 per cent had not yet been transposed by all Member States—a figure below the 1.5 per cent target set by the European Council in 2000. The main problem, however, is not so much the failure to transpose (which is regrettable)—but the failure to implement directives. Each year, some 2000 infringement cases are examined by the Commission (especially in the environment and Single Market fields) approximately half of which lead to a formal infringement procedure, with 150–200 being eventually referred to the Court of Justice after persistent non-compliance by a Member State.[3] Implementation of Community law is thus not as mechanical and smooth as could be wished.

In short, the transition from a model combining shallow integration with a limited set of common policies to a model involving comprehensive legislation, continuous regulation, and recurrent EU supervision of Member State behaviour was already creating strains within the system.

[3] European Commission (2002*a*).

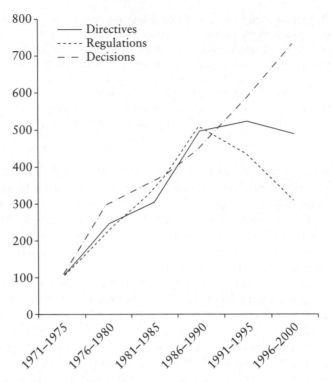

Figure 6.1. *Indicators of EU legislative activity, 1971–2000,*
base 1971–1975 = 100

Source: Alesina et al. (2002).

6.3.2. *The impact of Economic and Monetary Union*

The Maastricht Treaty and especially EMU introduced major changes in all
four dimensions of the Community system:

1. *Variable geometry.* For the first time, participation in common policies was
   effectively limited to a subset of EU members.[4] Britain and Denmark were
   legally given an unconditional right to opt out of the single currency (and a
   conditional right to opt in). Sweden was *de facto* given the same status.
   Even if Britain, Sweden, and Denmark join the euro in the coming years,
   which is far from certain, variable geometry will persist as enlargement will

---

[4] In addition the Social Chapter was developed initially without the United Kingdom and
outside the usual EU arrangements, but this exception was removed once the British Government
lifted its opt-out in 1997.

increase the number of Member States that are not immediately involved in the single currency.

2. *Complexity in the management of shared competences.* While monetary policy responsibility was attributed to the ECB by the Treaty, fiscal policy was neither delegated nor left entirely at the discretion of Member States. Though the responsibility for fiscal policies belongs to national governments and parliaments, they are committed to avoiding excessive deficits and to coordinating their policies with the other EU members under a surveillance procedure. In other words, there was a 'thickening' of the intermediate layer between Community and national competence.

3. *Institutional differentiation.* The creation of the ECB was a departure from the standard Community model, as a major policy responsibility was assigned to an institution independent of the Commission, the ECB. This was a very conscious choice, but which had the effect of introducing a new player in an already complex game.

4. *EU involvement in major discretionary policy decisions.* In the regulation of the Single Market, it could be said that the EU was setting the rules while discretionary decisions were left to the (democratically elected) governments of the Member States. The EU certainly had to exercise discretion in certain areas (e.g. when making decision on competition policy cases). But the bulk of its activity was of a rule-setting nature. With the creation of the ECB, this is no more the case: the EU has entered the domain of discretionary decisions.

EMU thus represented a step change in the governance methods of the EU system and while successful, it has raised new challenges, which have not been fully surmounted.

6.3.3. *The impact of Lisbon*

During the mid-1990s there was a broadening of the ambitions and potential responsibilities of the EU system. At the Lisbon European Council of March 2000 the EU took on wider goals to achieve 'growth, stability, and cohesion'. However, in the absence of EU competences and instruments to develop directly some of the relevant policies, more and more emphasis was placed on coordinating national policies. This new emphasis built on the so-called processes of Luxembourg, Cardiff, and Cologne, dealing respectively with employment policies, product markets, and the links between macro and microeconomic policies. In March 2000, these 'processes' were brought together under the umbrella of the 'Lisbon Strategy'. A new policy instrument, the OMC, was also introduced. It consists of four ingredients:

- fixing common guidelines for national policies;
- developing indicators of national performance to compare best practice;

- asking countries to adopt national action plans to implement the guidelines;
- joint monitoring and review of results.

The Lisbon Strategy identifies a large number of policy objectives that are
more or less shared by all the EU countries. It also acknowledges both that
many of the relevant policy responsibilities remain with the Member States
and that many of the actions needed depend on the behaviour of economic
agents and stakeholders. It was agreed that each spring session of the European
Council should be devoted to taking forward the Lisbon Strategy, backed by a
monitoring process through which to assess the performance of individual
members in achieving certain agreed targets. The Strategy applies to topics
previously outside the remit of European integration such as education,
research, innovation and enterprise creation, labour markets, and welfare
where there is great variation between national preferences and policies.[5]

The Open Method of Coordination (Hodson and Maher 2001; Rodrigues
2002) is the chosen instrument for drawing together policymakers from across
the Member States into a process of comparing national approaches to the
common policy goals. These policy-makers are supposed over time to build up
a fruitful dialogue of interchange and policy learning, using techniques
imported from the Organisation for Economic Cooperation and Development
(OECD) and business practices (peer review, target and trajectory setting,
definition of indicators, benchmarking of best practices). The process is
described as coordination, but with open outcomes, rather than necessarily
leading to a single template. The broad aim is of course improved economic
dynamism over the medium term, but many of the specific outcomes were
expected to be localised (often at the very microlevel) and behavioural.

The Lisbon approach has attracted support from opposite quarters. Some of
its supporters see it as bringing the coordination process into areas which are
important for growth, but should not be part of the Union's competences; their
hope is that the OMC will foster policy action at national level, and, if successful, provide an alternative to the tighter collective rules. Already, some
fields that were supposed to come under the delegation technique as part of the
Single Market have somehow slipped into the Lisbon soft-coordination category. Other supporters of OMC, however, aim at progressively bringing new
policies (e.g. social policies) within the orbit of the Union as an eventual
counterweight to the liberalisation agenda pursued by the Union with the Single
Market and EMU. Their hope is that the OMC might become an antechamber
to the Community method. The changes brought by this new approach are best
illustrated by a comparison between the 2000 Lisbon Strategy and the 1985

---

[5] A recent account on the implementation of the Lisbon Strategy can be found in European
Commission (2003*a*, *b*).

Table 6.5. *A tale of two strategies: the Single Market and Lisbon compared*

	Single Market	Lisbon
Ultimate aim	Integration and growth	Growth, social cohesion, employment
Intermediate objectives	Cuts on cost of cross-border transactions for products and services	Advances in education and innovation, Increase in R&D spending Liberalisation of service industries, Increase in labour force participation and employment rates, etc.
Means	Elimination of border controls Harmonisation and approximation of laws	Definition of common targets Performance reporting and benchmarking Joint monitoring
Instruments	EU directives Enforcement by case law of courts	Mostly national (spending, taxation, regulation)

Single Market Programme. Narrow intermediate objectives, precisely defined means and effective instruments have been replaced by broader objectives, softer means, and weaker instruments (Table 6.5).

Resistance to further transfers of competence has thus resulted in new models of voluntary cooperation, networking, and other forms of soft coordination. This is a significant departure from the traditional choice between delegation and autonomy. To the extent that the Lisbon Strategy might require forms of intervention by incentives (rather than prohibitions) and the application of discretion across space and time, these depend on parallel actions by national authorities. As a result, more and more is expected from the intermediate layers of governance methods—commitment and coordination.

But can this strategy be successful—or is it only a temporary, politically expedient solution? Substantive outcomes are so far meagre, but only three years into the process may be early days for judging this. In any case, to make a success of OMC requires a more sustained investment in developing effective methodologies. One frequent criticism is that the Commission has not got a grip on what is needed to make OMC work—a discussion reminiscent of the debate about the Single Market in the early 1980s.

6.3.4. *The impact of regulatory innovations*

Instead of reliance on common EU rules and regulation to prohibit deviant or diverse national regulation, new forms of joint regulation have recently emerged, especially in services and utilities where progress towards common regulation has been slow. The liberalisation of formerly state-dominated network industries, such as transport, electricity, and telecommunications, has seen the emergence of national regulators, independent of Member State governments, rather than of EU authorities. Many of these national regulators, affected by a common legal framework and with similar concerns, have begun to liaise through loose regulatory partnerships. As these partnerships develop, they may become carriers of integration.

The evolution of financial services supervision provides the clearest example of the partnership approach. Instead of the creation of a either a single European supervisory agency or a series of specialised agencies, national regulators, and central banks retain their responsibility for supervision, following the principle of 'home country control' and rely on coordination committees (Lamfalussy et al. 2001). The basic argument is that decentralised regulators have better access to information than a centralised one and that network-based regulation is thus better equipped for crisis prevention.[6] However, the effectiveness of this approach in a context of increasing integration through market opening and—so far limited—cross-border mergers remains to be tested.

In the area of telecommunications, recently introduced new directives harden the coordination provided by the network by giving the Commission and the other national regulators veto power over important decisions of national regulators such as which markets to regulate, what kinds of access regulation to impose, and the like (as we saw in Box 6.1). In the area of competition policy, the new Council Regulation 01/2003 relies on the network of national competition authorities as a framework for decentralising decisions under the Treaty that hitherto had been in the exclusive domain of the Commission (Box 6.2).

Developments in various fields thus raise questions concerning not only the delimitation of competences between EU and Member States, but also the extra-territorial competences of different national regulators. That this question arises is a reflection of the increasing interpenetration of markets and it illustrates that the appropriate level of regulation is a function of the degree of market integration. Spontaneous groupings of national institutions should not be regarded as the springboard for active intervention by the Commission. In most cases, the trade-off is between, on the one hand, the advantages of having national institutions close to the relevant markets and, on the other hand, the advantages of limiting assignment uncertainty and of avoiding regulatory capture through centralisation. In any event, it is important that legal uncertainties be kept as low as possible.

---

[6] A similar argument has led to the creation of the Financial Stability Forum (FSF) which relies on the cooperation of international financial institutions, ministries of finance, central banks, financial supervisors, and international supervisory and regulatory standard-setting bodies.

Box 6.2. *Networks of national authorities as agents of European integration: the example of competition policy*

Since the very beginning of the European Communities, competition policy has been a key area of Commission activity. Articles 81–89 (previously 85–94) of the Treaty lay down rules to restrict anti-competitive practices and abuses by firms and to restrict state aid contravening the Common Market. For a long time, the application of these rules has been the sole domain of the Commission. Current developments aim at decentralising the task through delegation to national competition authorities. Formation of a centrally steered network of these authorities is intended to ensure coherence in competition policy across the EU.

In many Member States, competition authorities were created only in the late 1980s and early 1990s, contemporaneously with the introduction of the Merger Control Regulation, which explicitly provides for the possibility of delegating a merger case to the competition authority of a Member State if the latter applies for this. In practice, such delegation has taken place in cases that primarily concerned the Member State in question, even though the conditions for the case to be of Community-wide importance were formally fulfilled. In such cases, the competition authority involved was applying national law.

The recently-enacted Regulation 01/2003 aims to also decentralise the application of Article 81 of the Treaty. Under sections 1 and 2 of this article, agreements between firms that restrict competition are illegal and void; however, under section 3 of the article, this provision can be declared inapplicable if the agreement in question provides for efficiency gains, technical and economic progress, which benefit consumers as well as the firms in question. Regulation 01/2003 abolishes the previously-used procedure whereby the application of section 3 to an agreement requires notification to, and prior approval by, the Commission. Now, the inapplicability clause of section 3 is deemed to hold unless it is refuted in a formal administrative or legal procedure, in which case the agreement in question is deemed to have been invalid from the very beginning. Procedures challenging the legality of an agreement can be initiated by national competition authorities as well as the Commission; private parties can also take the initiative, either by going to court and suing for damages, or by asking a competition authority to look into the matter. The assessment of whether Article 81 section 1 is to be declared inapplicable under section 3 of this article is thus delegated to the national courts and national competition authorities. However the Commission reserves the right to take any given case into its own hands.

Regulation 01/2003 raises serious issues of governance of European competition policy. First, what mechanisms ensure consistency of decisions across jurisdictions? To be sure, the Commission can eliminate inconsistencies simply by taking over cases and imposing its own will. However, this would run counter to the very intent of the reform, to decentralise the application of Article 81 section 3. Much hope is placed on the network of competition authorities and the Commission ensuring the exchange of information as well as mutual assistance. The Commission itself is in the process of preparing several notices on criteria for the application of Article 81 section 3, on cooperation between the Commission and the

Continued

Box 6.2. *Continued*

national courts, on complaints, on opinion letters of the Commission in individual cases... However, to the extent that national authorities, and the national courts, are independent in their decisions—rather than acting as agents of the EU—there is a risk that in practice the assessments of the benefits of agreements that are required for Article 81 section 3 will differ across Member States. The risk is all the greater because tools such as opinion letters in individual cases, which the Commission envisages using to guide Member State institutions, are not legally binding upon the courts handling these cases. Moreover, the application of the criteria of Article 81 section 3 requires political evaluations that pose a major challenge for judicial consistency.

The issue of consistency across jurisdictions is particularly important for cases involving several Member States. Consider an agreement between transportation companies. Suppose the Dutch competition authority or a Dutch court declares this agreement to satisfy the conditions of Article 81 section 3 and thus to be deemed compatible with the Common Market. What is the impact of this declaration by a Dutch institution on the legality of clauses in the agreement concerning transportation in Germany? After all, national constitutional law typically does not provide for the delegation of authority to foreign national—as opposed to Community—institutions. Without such delegation though, parties will be burdened with the costs of multiple parallel proceedings. The problem is diffused if cases involving several Member States are mainly treated by the Commission. However, the line is sometimes hard to draw. Therefore the conflict between the avoidance of extra-territorial effects of decisions by national authorities and the need to avoid multiple procedures is likely to be a recurrent theme under the new regime.

6.4. Where are the governance fault lines?

A key question is whether the economic shortcomings of the EU can be traced back to fault lines in its patterns of governance. These may be of three major types:

(1) a policy may be *inappropriately allocated* between the EU and the Member State levels with respect to the objective that is being pursued (either inappropriate centralisation or decentralisation) or despite being appropriately allocated, it may not reach its objectives because of *spillovers from failures in another policy field*;

(2) a policy may be appropriately allocated, but its *design or implementation may be deficient* because of an institutional failure or of the lack of appropriate instruments. For intermediate levels (commitment and co-ordination), this includes failures arising from the procedures that organise coordination;

(3) the failure can be entirely internal to a policy domain, because either the goals, or the strategy, or the policy instruments are not appropriate.

All three reasons can be invoked to account for a shortcoming in perform-ance,[7] but the first two are systemic in nature and regard the functioning of the governance regime.

On the issue of the allocation of policy responsibility, it remains a matter of discussion whether the current assignment of competences can be considered optimal (Sinn 2003). The two main costs we see in the present assignment of competences are those of confusion in allocating policy responsibility and inertia in responding to changing circumstances.

1. Confusion is economically costly if it stifles policy competition or prevents coordinated responses when required. In addition it complicates account-ability. We fear that the complexity of the EU system has reached a stage where these costs can no longer be considered as secondary.
2. The risk of inertia arises because the EU's institutions and rules are enshrined in a treaty that can be modified only by unanimity. Even amendments to some secondary legislation may require as much consensus and political capital as a constitutional reform in a unitary state. Also the rules and institutions of the EU tend to embody the policy thinking of the period in which they were defined and to 'lock in' a particular policy philosophy.[8] We should beware of falling into the same trap again, that is, we should not simply replace yesterday's paradigm with today's paradigm, but rather look for a way forward that has some built-in elasticity for responding to tomorrow's challenges.

As for issues of institutional design, there are reasons for concern. Case studies prepared as background for the report suggest that, while shortcomings can be diagnosed across the policy range, problems are more severe for those dependent on commitment than for those based on delegation. They are also more severe for cases based on coordination than for commitment.

1. The methodology used for the Single Market has not yielded the expected benefits in the cases of financial services and utilities.
2. For EMU, it is hard to escape the conclusion that the EU has been facing more difficulties than expected in implementing the commitment approach to fiscal policy and that it has not yet found an organising concept for the design and the operation of economic policy coordination. Also the respective roles of the Council(s) and the Commission have not yet stabilised.

---

[7] Taking innovation policy as an example, it could be argued that fault lines arise from (*a*) the wrong choice in the allocation of responsibilities between the EU and the Member States in fields such as research and development or spillovers from, say, failures in the Member States to build first-class universities; or (*b*) a deficient EU management of R&D funds allocated to the Com-munity budget; or (*c*) wrong sectoral priorities.

[8] For example, the CAP has embodied (and still does to a large extent) the interventionist and productivist policy philosophy of the post-war period.

3. As regards the Lisbon Strategy and more specifically the European Employment Strategy, there is value in organising benchmarking and coordination, but incentives to cooperate effectively, let alone to change policy decisions, are weak.
4. Finally, the combination of centralised action and decentralised initiatives that characterises innovation policy has not yielded satisfactory results.

6.5. Conclusions

We have identified four key weaknesses in the governance of the EU:

Institutional complexity. The virtue of EU governance has never been its simplicity, but rather its ability to balance national and Community perspectives and to evolve as the integration process advances. It has, however, reached a stage of excessive complexity and sometimes confusion. Responsibilities not only overlap, but the same institutions (Council, Commission) also play different roles depending on the domain. Lack of clarity in the core functions of the institutions is detrimental to both efficiency and legitimacy. The emergence of variable geometry, especially in the monetary field, adds to institutional complexity.

A tension between responsibilities and instruments. The Community of the early decades had its responsibilities focused in the areas for which it had direct competence. Since the 1980s, it has increasingly taken on new responsibilities, either through extended competence (EMU) or as a result of a collective commitment vis-à-vis European public opinion by the heads of state and government (Lisbon). The scope of what are now explicitly or implicitly regarded as 'European public goods' has thus increased dramatically. Even before enlargement, the Union's ability to deliver on its commitments (and associated expectations) is increasingly at stake.

A persistent difficulty in making commitment and coordination methods deliver. In its early decades, EU governance essentially operated through a combination of common, uniform rules and delegation of specified policy functions. As its increased responsibilities have not—with the exception of monetary policy—been matched by the assignment of new policy instruments to the EU level, it has increasingly relied on cooperation between governments through commitment and coordination techniques. While these methods have had some effectiveness, they have not provided what was expected and necessary for the EU to deliver on economic growth and cohesion. Careful examination reveals instability in the guiding principles, weaknesses in the incentive structure, and uncertainty as regards the role of the various players.

Uneven implementation and enforcement. Whenever the implementation of a Union policy depends on the cooperation between different levels of government, it risks being diluted either because of administrative deficiencies or because the incentives to cooperate effectively are weak or absent. This problem may have been secondary in a smaller EU of relatively homogeneous states.

These weaknesses impair the economic performance of the current EU with fifteen members. They risk becoming even more damaging in a Union with twenty-five members.

PART II

CHALLENGES

7

Is the European model sustainable?

7.1. A good start

During the '*trente glorieuses*', the thirty years between 1945 and 1975, Europe witnessed an unprecedented period of growth, stability, and social cohesion. The post-war reconstruction created an economic and social environment, which ensured that the three sides of this 'magic triangle' operated in a mutually-reinforcing manner. The post-war settlement reflected a wide political consensus, which was broadly shared across western Europe. Business was guaranteed a stable economic, industrial, and social environment for sustained growth that reflected an implicit social contract with the people that the creation of new wealth would be fairly distributed. This commitment was enshrined in new features of the post-war consensus: a universal standard of social protection together with equal opportunity of education and in employment regardless of birth.

While economic stability and social cohesion were no doubt crucial conditions for European growth during the *trente glorieuses*, rapid economic growth was equally crucial to ensure the sustainability of economic stability and the social protection system.

The economic and social conditions in western Europe during the years 1950–1973 were truly remarkable. The current EU-15 enjoyed average annual growth rates of 4.6 per cent for GDP and 3.8 per cent for GDP per capita (growth accounting exercises typically ascribe around one-third of this per capita GDP growth to capital accumulation and two-thirds to growth in total factor productivity). As a result, the standard of living in the EU-15 witnessed a rapid catching-up with the United States: compared to a benchmark of 100 for the United States, GDP per capita (measured at purchasing power parity (PPP)) in the EU-15 rose from around forty in 1950 to a slightly above seventy in 1973. At the same time, both inflation (measured by the deflator of private consumption) and unemployment remained fairly low (with an average of 4 and 2 per cent, respectively).

Under those conditions, the cost of the welfare state remained fairly manageable. Although it had risen considerably over the years, the share of total government expenditure in GDP in the EU-15 was still a relatively modest 36 per cent in 1970. Three items accounted for nearly all public expenditures: government consumption (15 per cent), transfers (14 per cent, including

12 per cent in social transfers and 2 per cent in subsidies), and public investment (4 per cent).

The magic triangle started to unravel in the 1970s with the two oil shocks.
Since then the pressure has further mounted as a result of three profound and
interconnected changes in the socio-economic environment taking place across
Europe and the world: demographic patterns, technological breakthroughs,
and globalisation.

Whereas rapid growth, macroeconomic stability and the welfare state had
been mutually supportive during the *trente glorieuses*, the mixture of slow
growth, macroeconomic instability, and a welfare system conceived in a different set of circumstances proved difficult to manage in the years after 1973.

During the period 1974–1985, the average annual growth rate in EU-15
slowed down to barely 2 per cent for GDP and 1.7 per cent for GDP per
capita. As a result, the convergence of living standards between the EU-15 and
the United States achieved earlier on not only stopped but even reversed
somewhat. At the same time, average inflation jumped to 11 per cent and
unemployment rose steadily from less than 3 per cent in 1974 to 10 per cent in
1985—a level that had been unthinkable only a few years earlier.

The combination of slow growth and high unemployment resulted in
increased demands for social protection that were met in the EU-15 with
severe consequences for public finances. The share of total government
expenditure in GDP grew rapidly after 1973, reaching 46 per cent in 1980
and 49 per cent in 1985—an increase of 13 percentage points compared to
1970. This increase mainly involved two items: government consumption
(which rose by four points of GDP between 1970 and 1985) and transfers
(which rose by seven points, six for social transfers and one for subsidies). On
the other hand, public investment was actually reduced (by one GDP point).
This spectacular increase in public expenditure was financed partly by
additional public revenue (which rose by eight points of GDP) and partly by
public borrowing (which increased by five points of GDP between 1970 and
1985).

By the mid-1980s, Europe was stuck in a negative spiral: lower GDP growth
and employment rates meant increasing public expenditure, which required
increasing public revenue, which in turn implied higher social contributions
(these increased by nearly five points of GDP between 1970 and 1985) and
higher direct taxes (with an increase of nearly three points of GDP between
1970 and 1985), thereby reducing the incentive to work and to invest, hence
further reducing the prospects for output and employment growth.

7.2. New challenges

The reason why Europe seemed durably trapped in this spiral was twofold. First, the shocks to the system were long lasting. After the two oil shocks
of 1973 and 1979, Europe was confronted with population ageing, the

information technology revolution and globalisation, all of which substantially increased the demand for social protection. Second, the system seemed politically unable to reform itself and to establish a new social contract aimed at increasing growth and preserving social welfare. The problem was to find a way out of the following dilemma: preserving the costly European social model required higher GDP growth, but increasing growth also required adapting the social model to the new socio-economic environment (Drèze et al. 1987).

During the period 1986–2000, Europe made some progress. The EU-15 succeeded in bringing back inflation to pre-1973 levels. Average inflation during the period stood at 3.5 per cent and never exceeded 3 per cent after 1994. On the other hand, the unemployment rate remained far above pre-1973 levels, with an average rate of 9 per cent for the period. The progress on the growth front was equally meagre. During the period 1986–2000, the average annual growth rate in EU-15 was 2.5 per cent for GDP and 2.2 per cent for GDP per capita. This was just sufficient to keep GDP per capita in the EU-15 at 70 per cent of the level prevailing in the United States. Hence, the pre-1973 convergence of living standards between the EU-15 and the United States seemed to be no more than a relic of the past.

Sustained slow growth and high unemployment resulted in sustained demands for social protection in the EU-15 and a sustained deterioration of public finances. In 1993, total government expenditure in the EU-15 reached its highest-ever peak at 51 per cent of GDP. With public revenue at 45 per cent of GDP, this meant that 1993 was also the year when public borrowing reached its highest-ever peak—6 per cent of GDP. The Maastricht fiscal consolidation process, launched in 1993, was to put an end to the deterioration of public finances in the EU-15 that had started twenty years earlier. By 1999, the year the euro was introduced, public borrowing was down to less than 1 per cent. The turnaround was achieved by a combination of reduced government expenditure and increased government revenue. In 1999, total government expenditure had come down to 48 per cent of GDP—three points below the peak of 1993, but still twelve points above the 1970 level. At the same time, total government revenue had reached 47 per cent of GDP, its highest-ever peak and ten points above the 1970 level.

By the year 2000, it seemed that fiscal consolidation in the EU-15 had been achieved. For the first time since 1970, the consolidated budget of the EU-15 countries posted a positive balance. Government expenditure also seemed to be under control. In 2000, its share in GDP for the EU-15 was less than 46 per cent, the lowest level since 1981. In reality, however, the spiral of low growth and high public expenditure was still fairly intact. The year 2000 had been an exceptional year, with a growth rate of GDP in the EU-15 at 3.5 per cent, one full point above the trend for the period 1986–2000. When the downturn hit in 2001, public expenditure and public borrowing went back on the rise. By 2002, total government expenditure was again nearing 48 per cent of GDP and public borrowing was close to 2 per cent of GDP.

7.3. The road ahead

In 2003, as one looks to the future, one cannot help feeling that in spite of two important macroeconomic achievements of the run-up to the euro in the 1990s—the return to price stability and fiscal consolidation—Europe is still struggling with the spiral of low growth and high public expenditure. As in the 1980s, the reason is twofold: shocks produced by long-lasting trends in demography, technology, and globalisation; and the difficulty to reform the European social model in a way that combines higher growth and continued social protection.

Demographic trends are a matter of serious concern for Europe (Siebert 2002). Its population aged considerably after 1960. Between 1960 and 2000, the average dependency ratio (defined as the number of persons aged above sixty years per 100 persons aged 15–59 years) for the EU-15 rose from 26 to 35. At the same time, the dependency ratio for the United States remained almost constant at around 25.

The greying of Europe owed most to low and declining population growth. The average annual population growth in the EU-15 dropped from 0.8 per cent during the period 1950–1975 to 0.3 per cent during the period 1975–2000 (leaving aside the jump due to German reunification). During the same sub-periods, population grew by 1.3 and 1 per cent, respectively, in the United States. The underlying factors for the contrasting situation between the two sides of the Atlantic were differences in fertility and migration rates. In the EU-15, the fertility rate dropped below 2.1 children per woman, the natural replacement level, in the mid-1970s and declined steadily thereafter. By contrast, the fertility rate in the United States was still hovering around 2.1 at the beginning of the twenty-first century. A similar trend occurred with migration rates.

The combination of population ageing and early retirement schemes, instituted across Europe to cope with rising unemployment, was clearly one of the main drivers behind the rise in public expenditure that took off in the 1970s. Unfortunately, the outlook on the demographic front for the coming decades is even grimmer than the previous trend. According to the United Nations Population Division (2002), the dependency ratio in the EU-15 is expected to reach forty-seven in 2020 and seventy in 2050. The European Commission (2002*b*) estimates that the pure demographic effect of ageing would be an increase in public expenditure (related to pensions and health care) of eight points of GDP between 2000 and 2050.

Technological trends are no less crucial for Europe. There is general agreement that Europe has lagged behind the United States in developing and adopting information and communication technologies (ICT) (van Ark et al. 2002). As discussed in Chapter 4, this is viewed as the prime explanation for the slower growth of Europe during the second part of the 1990s in comparison with the United States. Even though the adoption of ICT has been somewhat slower than in the United States, it has greatly changed the workplace in Europe as well. The introduction of ICT throughout the economy in the

1980s and 1990s raised both fears and hopes about its effect on employment, wages, and income distribution. Pessimists worried that ICT would result in downsizing, stagnant wages, and/or unemployment, and growing income inequality; while optimists claimed that it was bound to raise wages and reduce unemployment.

There is a broad consensus in the economics literature that the diffusion of ICT led to skill-biased technological change and reduced the demand for unskilled workers. The resulting deterioration in the labour market for unskilled workers in the United States and in Europe during the 1980s and 1990s has been amply documented. It is important to note, however, that this major development has taken a radically different form on the two sides of the Atlantic.

In the United States, where labour markets are generally flexible, skill-biased technical change resulted in stagnant (or even decreasing) real wages for unskilled workers and rising incomes for (certain categories of) skilled manpower. The result was a great surge in income inequality. In Europe, where labour markets are more rigid and wage floors are more binding, skill-biased technological change tended to produce instead long-term unemployment among unskilled workers. At the same time, redistributive mechanisms prevented significant increases in income inequality.

Hence, differences in labour market and social security institutions between the United States and Europe seemed to interact in two important ways with the information revolution. First, together with barriers in product and financial markets, impediments in labour markets probably slowed down the diffusion of ICT in Europe. Second, the lower pace in the process of 'creative destruction' generated by a slower diffusion of ICT, on one hand, and the more rigid pay-scale and more generous redistribution schemes, on the other, largely insulated Europe from sharp rises in income inequality—despite severe increases in unemployment.

7.4. Facing the dilemma

The intensity of the dilemma faced by European policy-makers is likely to increase in the years ahead, when the pace of technological change will probably accelerate. Innovation and change will continue to open the prospect of higher productivity, higher wages, and improved living standards. But they will also continue to be disruptive, displacing workers, making some skills obsolete, and possibly creating more pressure towards income inequality. Moreover, these costs will continue to be concentrated in the short run, while the benefits will take a longer time span to materialise. But postponing inevitable changes would not be a real option since it would only delay the benefits and increase the eventual costs.

The third major shaping trend is *globalisation*. In the early 1970s, the world economy entered into a period of unprecedented free trade and capital mobility. Although the world had already witnessed a similar phenomenon during the period 1870–1914, when not only products and capital, but also labour, moved freely throughout the globe, the new phase of globalisation was radically different from the earlier one. The previous phase had set up a pattern of trade between the industrialised North and the developing South, whereby the South exported raw materials to the North in exchange for manufactured products. This traditional division of labour between the North and South lasted until well into the second part of the twentieth century. In 1970, the share of (extra) EU-15 imports of manufactured goods supplied by the South was still barely 10 per cent. This share nearly quadrupled during the next thirty years: it was already above 20 per cent in 1985 and reached 36 per cent in 2000. Most of this rise came from East Asia. The involvement of China came relatively late but was extremely dramatic. The share of EU manufactured imports supplied by China rose from less than 1 per cent in 1970 to only 2 per cent in 1985, but jumped to 10 per cent in 2000.

The emergence of the South as a major producer and exporter of manufactured products obviously raised questions about its effect on employment, wages, and income distribution in the industrialised countries with which the South was now competing. The issues were essentially the same as those raised by the ICT revolution since increased competition with the unskilled-labour-intensive South tended to reduce the demand for unskilled labour in the North in the same way as skill-biased technological change. This led to intense debate about whether trade and capital movements or technological change was the main 'culprit' behind the waning fortune of labour. In the end, however, the debate proved rather futile since globalisation is precisely the combination of trade and capital movement liberalisation on the one hand and technological change on the other.

Globalisation, therefore, produced the same effects as the ICT revolution. In the United States, where markets operate efficiently, it generated more wealth but also more income inequality. By contrast, in Europe, where the welfare state is more generous and markets less efficient, globalisation generated less additional wealth but also less income inequality (Sapir, 2001).

Looking ahead, the key policy issue for Europe is how to enjoy the benefits of globalisation while continuing to mitigate its costs. The problem is likely to become more acute than it already is because the trend towards more globalisation is likely to continue, notwithstanding the consequences of 11 September 2001. Increasing globalisation will come not only from the continuation of the ICT revolution, but even more importantly, from two important trends in North–South economic relations. The first is the demographic balance. The relative weight of the North (Europe, North America, Oceania, and Japan) in the global population is predicted to decrease from 20 per cent in 2000, to 16 per cent in 2020 and 13 per cent in 2050. The second trend is the economic transformation of the South. The rise of China as a leading producer and exporter of manufactured goods was long overdue, and is likely to continue. The same may be happening with India, the second most populous country in the world, which only started to open up its economy in the early 1990s. Size and history are certainly on their side. In 1820, the combined weight of China and India in world GDP (measured at PPPs) was more than 50 per cent and it was still around 25 per cent in 1890, in the midst of the second industrial revolution. It reached a low of less than 10 per cent around 1950 and had climbed back to 17 per cent by 2000.

Along with Chapter 6, this chapter has argued that since the 1980s the sustainability of the 'European model' has become more and more questionable. The combination of low growth rates and high unemployment rates have put significant strains on public finances which proved incompatible with the fiscal rectitude that a growing economy requires, thus further lowering growth prospects and compounding the problem. Hence, the need to give higher priority to growth, not just because it is the means to achieve higher per capita incomes but because a growing, competitive, and dynamic economy is required to finance a certain degree of cohesion in a durable manner.

This chapter further argued that Europe's failure to preserve the magic triangle reached during the *trente glorieuses* was the result of the combination of two elements: new trends in demography, technology, and globalisation, and the incapacity to invent a new social contract. It also made the case that these new trends are long lasting and are likely to further increase the demands for social protection, which will endanger even more the sustainability of the European model.

8

Making a bigger Europe work

Accession negotiations with ten candidate countries (eight from central and eastern Europe plus Cyprus and Malta) were finalised at the European Council in Copenhagen in December 2002. The summit decisions paved the way for admission of the new Member States on 1 May 2004.

Of course, the Copenhagen European Council did not answer all the questions pertaining to enlargement. What will be the impact of final elimination of remaining barriers to trade and the flow of resources on the economies of current and new members? How should the enlarged European Union (EU) respond to potentially negative implications of economic liberalisation and increased competition on labour markets and sensitive sectors? Are the new member countries really able to enforce effectively the *acquis communautaire* that they have formally adopted into their legal systems? Are they ready to absorb structural funds that will be put at their disposal? How will the EU institutions in practice accommodate the newcomers? And are the newcomers prepared to play a constructive role in the decision-making process within the EU? How to ensure effective economic governance in an enlarged EU encompassing a much more diversified economic area, and involving countries with distinctively lower levels of economic development? How and when should the new members join European Monetary Union (EMU)? These and other issues will soon have to be confronted and addressed.

The EU must not wait until the new challenges emerge. It is necessary to identify them in advance and to consider possible policy responses. Enlargement is not an uncontroversial process. It involves hopes but also worries. Both the incumbents and the new members have to prepare themselves for enlargement in terms of necessary institutional changes and policy adjustments in order to ensure that enlargement will not entail unnecessary costs and will indeed bring about much hoped-for benefits.

The purpose of this chapter is to identify these challenges and to discuss their possible implications. In what follows, the various challenges are classified in three broad categories: (*a*) implications for growth and cohesion, (*b*) implication for macroeconomic stability, and (*c*) implications for EU governance.

8.1. Implications for growth and cohesion

A number of studies already exist on possible economic implications of enlargement (e.g. Baldwin et al. 1997; Keuschnigg and Kohler 1999; Breuss 2001; European Commission 2001c; Boeri et al. 2002; Landesmann 2003). Two main findings emerge from this literature. First, it is argued that enlargement is likely to produce economic benefits, to both current members and the accession countries, provided adequate and coherent accompanying national policies are pursued. Depending on the methodology used, estimates of economic gains from enlargement in terms of cumulative increases of GDP vary between 0.5 and 0.7 per cent for EU-15 as a whole and between 6 and 19 per cent for the new Member States for the period 2000–2010. These gains include both static and dynamic effects of integration. Though these estimates are obviously sensitive to underlying assumptions concerning, *inter alia*, the level of actual financial transfers to new members and the degree of labour market flexibility, the general finding of significant economic gains from enlargement is quite robust. Part of those gains have already materialised with the development of integration between the accession countries and the current members. In particular, the EU-15 have benefited significantly from the opening of new markets in central and eastern Europe.

Second, the studies address a number of fears raised in the political debate on the enlargement process. Among those most frequently raised is the risk of mass migration after opening up borders with the new Member States, involving increased pressure on labour markets and national welfare systems of current members, a high cost of transfers from the EU budget to new members, the risk of industrial relocation to new members (including foreign direct investment (FDI) diversion), and the probability of a sharp reduction of structural transfers to the 'old' cohesion countries in EU-15 as a result of re-channelling those funds to newcomers.

These potential problems typically arise either as a consequence of the complete elimination of still remaining barriers to the free flow of goods, services, and production factors within the enlarged Europe (the extension of the 'four freedoms' of the European Single Market), or from including the new members in EU-wide common policies, mostly the Common Agricultural Policy (CAP) and structural/regional policies and—at a later stage—in the single monetary policy within EMU. As most of these problems are speculative and would materialise—if at all—only after enlargement takes place in 2004, the relevant studies differ widely as to the scope and level of risks involved as well as to the nature and design of recommended policies.

The various economic implications of enlargement are not independent of each other. Actually, they can be shown to represent various aspects of, or to be inferred from, one core problem—the existence of large per capita income differentials between EU-15 and the new Member States. Migration pressures are feared because it is assumed that it is chiefly much higher wages and higher levels of social welfare that would induce workers from the new members to migrate to EU-15. Likewise, the expected increase in FDI flows to the new EU countries can be assumed to be at least partly explained by their relatively low labour costs.

Of course, these income differentials entail various implications that would call for different policy reactions in different areas. Hence, it is important to realise that in order to cope effectively with various risks and challenges of enlargement it is essential to address first and foremost this primary cause. This means that policies aimed at ensuring as rapid income convergence as possible of the new members to EU-15 levels should become a key priority in designing a post-enlargement economic strategy for the EU. In what follows the issue of income convergence will be discussed first. Later, the two other most-debated issues—migration and regional policies—will be taken up.

8.1.1. *Income inequality and convergence*

The existing income disparities between current and new members are substantial. At purchasing power parities (PPP), the average per capita income in the ten candidate states in 2001 was at 45 per cent of the EU-15 level. This average masks important differences between individual countries, with income levels varying from 34 per cent of the EU-15 average in Latvia to around 70 per cent in Slovenia and Cyprus (see Table 8.1). These disparities are larger than those for the three Mediterranean countries (Greece, Portugal, and Spain) whose income levels were around 65 per cent of the old EU-10 average when they joined in the 1980s.

As we saw in Chapter 4, there was a slight increase in total income inequality in the EU-15 between 1980 and 1998. This was the result of two trends going in opposite directions: an increase of inequality within countries (i.e. a worsening of personal income distribution) and a decrease of inequality between countries (i.e. convergence). With the forthcoming enlargement, income inequality for the EU-27 will drastically increase compared to EU-15 (see Table 8.2).[1] However the entire effect will be due to the rise of inequality between countries, which means that successful convergence is the most straightforward response to the problem.

Neither theory nor the experience of earlier enlargements convincingly supports a hypothesis of automatic convergence. As discussed in Chapter 4, convergence only occurs in the presence of certain key growth factors. Identification of these factors and assessing to what extent they are present in the new Member States is necessary to answer the question as to whether these countries are well equipped for rapid and sustained growth. Mainstream growth theory has traditionally concentrated on physical and human capital

---

[1] The EU-27 comprises of the EU-15 and the ten new members joining in 2004 plus Bulgaria and Romania, which may join the EU in 2007.

Table 8.1. *Income disparities in the enlarged EU*

	GDP per capita in old and new members (in PPP), 2001 (EU-25 = 100)
Austria	122
Belgium	119
Denmark	126
Finland	114
France	114
Germany	113
Greece	71
Ireland	129
Italy	113
Luxembourg	215
Netherlands	126
Portugal	76
Spain	92
Sweden	112
UK	111
EU-15	110
Cyprus	81
Czech Republic	65
Estonia	44
Hungary	58
Latvia	37
Lithuania	42
Malta	60
Poland	43
Slovakia	52
Slovenia	79
Total new Member States	50
EU-25	100

Source: European Commission, AMECO database.

accumulation, labour, and technological progress. More recent contributions emphasise the role of non-standard factors, such as institutions and the rule of law. It may be useful to have a quick glance at all these factors.

The stock of physical capital in the new member countries is still inadequate with respect to the needs of economies that are opening up to international competition. Investment rates are relatively high at 24–25 per cent on average, above the EU-15 average of 18 per cent. At the same time, however, they have higher depreciation rates due to obsolete capital stock inherited from the old system. In addition, their investment structure is still more concentrated in

Table 8.2. *Inequality within and between countries before and after enlargement (Theil indices)*

	Within countries	Between countries	Total
EU-15	0.152	0.008	0.160
EU-27[a]	0.149	0.064	0.213
EU-27[b]	0.156	0.064	0.220

[a] Assuming a Gini-coefficient for the new Member States of 0.27, the value in Poland in 1989.
[b] Assuming a Gini-coefficient for the new Member States of 0.34, the value in Italy in 1998.

Source: Morrisson and Murtin (2003), data from 1998.

low- and medium-tech sectors. Furthermore, public investment in areas such as infrastructure is still inadequate. To ensure rapid GDP growth, investment rates will therefore need to remain at relatively high levels.

One important segment of capital endowment, which is particularly underdeveloped, is physical infrastructure, especially in transport. Progress in this area is urgently needed and resources spent from future convergence funds can be expected to yield very high external benefits. It is important, however, to make sure that the additionality and the co-financing principles are strictly observed so that crowding out of domestic investment by EU funds is avoided.

Investment efficiency and levels are strongly enhanced by FDI, which is commonly considered an important factor of growth and of technological progress in catching-up countries (affecting growth through increases in capital endowments and in TFP). FDI inflows to the new Member States in recent years have been very high compared the levels in the new Mediterranean members in the 1980s (3–6 per cent of GDP versus 1–3 per cent), though the geographic pattern has not been uniform and part of the inflows has been simply acquisitions under privatisation programmes to be phased out soon. But after the peak in 2000, FDI inflows substantially declined, reflecting changing worldwide patterns of FDI and less intensive privatisation. Can FDI inflows recover and increase even further? Some authors are quite sanguine about these prospects (e.g. Boeri et al. 2002 predict a doubling of FDI after accession), but will this expansion come as a result of EU accession only, or will it require specific policies in the new Member States?

Of course, EU entry and the certainty of the legal and contractual conditions for investors can be expected to be a magnet for foreign investors coming both from other EU countries and from outside. By investing in new Member States, foreign firms can exploit the local advantage of generally low labour costs and have free access to a market of nearly 450 million consumers. But actual inflows and their distribution among countries may strongly depend on policy environment. Under EU regulations, many specific FDI-supporting financial measures such as tax breaks and preferential treatment will no longer be available. However, state aid will remain available, provided it is in conformity with EU competition rules. What is crucial, however, is that public aid policy concentrates on establishing overall business-friendly administrative and legal environments, and on promoting investment in human capital.

Foreign direct investment of EU-origin may, in some cases, involve a direct relocation of production from current to new members and thus entail a relocation of jobs. To the extent that relocation indeed takes place, it enhances efficiency and in the longer term benefits the whole EU. Current EU members can be expected to re-deploy their free resources into higher value-added sectors, thus moving up the technology ladder and improving their competitiveness in longer term. They can also benefit from substantial spillover effects of FDI in the new Member States. However, these are only likely to occur over the medium term, with the—in several cases—non-negligible costs of restructuring occurring over the short term. Consequently, if social costs are involved in the process of restructuring, they can and should be alleviated through regional and structural aid. Generally, the efficiency-enhancing reallocation fostered by enlargement must not be hampered. In addition, it is difficult to demonstrate that the relocation of production activities away from a current EU Member State would not take place even without enlargement, since it is very likely that in many cases the shift would take place anyway, whether to future EU members or to other less prosperous countries. Under liberalised international trade rules, the true alternative faced by a corporation in deciding on the location of an industrial activity would usually not be between the territory of a current and a new EU member, but rather between the EU and regions outside with lower labour costs. For that reason, the FDI opportunities offered by the new Member States can paradoxically lead in some cases to retaining European production chains that might otherwise have relocated to other regions. Moreover, FDI is more often an additional investment induced by new opportunities, than the simple relocation of existing activities. The experience of earlier enlargements demonstrates that increased FDI inflows to new members (Spain, Portugal, Greece, Ireland) were not paralleled by any significant decline in investment ratios in other EU members (UNCTAD 2002).

Non EU-origin FDI in the new Member States is likely to increase as well, taking advantage of free access to the entire EU market and combining the benefits of harmonised legislation with low local costs. Again, this may further benefit the whole EU through spillovers, though the effects will likely be of a second order.

Human capital is essential for rapid and sustained growth. More educated people are generally more productive and more innovative than less educated people.[2] More educated people also tend to be healthier and more law-abiding, thus allowing for less provision of certain costly public goods (health

---

[2] On the role of innovation in the context of growth, see Chapter 4.

care, law, and justice). Thus, human capital contributes directly and indirectly to economic growth. How do the new members fare in this respect? Official statistics suggest that their human capital is relatively well developed—these countries register high levels of elementary and secondary education (much higher than Mediterranean countries in the 1980s). But these standard indicators conceal some structural deficiencies. The scope of tertiary education is generally narrower than in most of western Europe, while the university curricula still need updating and modernisation. Also, the lack of life-long learning and re-training systems makes the supply of labour less flexible, less mobile, and less productive.

Physical and human capital accumulation is the most direct and readily observable cause of economic growth. But behind it are other, more fundamental factors. As demonstrated by many studies (e.g. Easterly and Levine 2002; Rodrik et al. 2002), the most important among these 'non-standard' factors are institutions, including in particular the rule of law, property rights, and social capital. These studies have confirmed the earlier view by North (1990) that stable institutions, and in particular the rule of law and protection of property rights, are essential for establishing a favourable business climate and assuring investors that they can safely invest and retain the returns on their investment.

The establishment of stable, high-quality institutions can be achieved only through a long-term process of political interaction and sensible national policies, buttressed and supplemented by appropriate policies and incentives from the EU. The accession process has played an important disciplining role in shaping the institutional order in the new Member States over the past decade, but the current functioning of various institutions can still be substantially improved. Public administrations suffer from lengthy bureaucratic procedures, negative selection (civil servants are generally poorly paid compared to what the private sector can offer), bureaucratic bad habits inherited from the past, lack of established standards of an independent and professional civil service, and, in some cases, endemic corruption. This applies in particular to areas such as the working of the judiciary system, which is slow and overburdened, law enforcement authorities (police, prosecutor offices), protection of property rights, enforcement of competition rules, and the functioning of central and local government administration. In view of the positive contribution of a stable and business-friendly institutional environment to economic growth, support for strengthening and building institutions should become a key priority for EU cohesion policies.

One significant risk to be mentioned in this context is the enforcement of the *acquis communautaire* by the new members. The European Commission in its annual reports evaluates the progress of preparations for accession in individual countries. While most of the necessary formal legal and institutional changes have been implemented, or will be implemented by the time of accession, one area of concern is their actual enforcement. Clearly, it is typically much easier to promulgate a new law than to ensure its effective implementation in practice, given the current state of central and local administration in the new Member States.

8.1.2. *Convergence policies*

Income convergence between countries and regions has long been one of the priorities of EU policy. Traditionally, the EU has helped convergence in the low-income countries through policies that have concentrated on transfers to poorer regions in order to sustain their investment rates. To what extent these transfers added to key growth factors is a question that has been discussed at length in Chapter 4.

On the side of the newcomers, open access to EU convergence funds raises a number of immediate problems. It is uncertain to what extent their national administrations and economic agents are prepared to take full advantage of the opportunities offered. On the one hand, some experience has already been accumulated in the last decade in the process of participating in pre-accession financial support programmes such as PHARE. The relevant administrative authorities have become accustomed to the rules governing the use of EU funds and developed some expertise on how to apply for and use the pre-accession aid. On the other hand, the actual disbursement ratio (the ratio between the funds actually paid out and the funds allocated to a given country) is rather low (50–70 per cent of commitments) and substantial delays in using the funds are frequent—although part of the blame for this situation may lie with the EU side. The record with implementing projects financed from other pre-accession funds is even less encouraging. But the structural funds available after accession will be several times larger than pre-accession financing. This means a step change from the past and it means that the new Member States will need to make a great effort in order to benefit from the assigned EU funds—part of the efforts will also have to come from the EU side which needs to improve its mechanisms.

The limited administrative capacity of the new members manifests itself in two distinct areas. First, there is a chronic deficit of well-prepared projects that would be both part of a national development programme and meet the stringent substantive and procedural requirements imposed by EU rules on the use of its funds. The lack of good fundable projects has been the most frequent cause of low levels of disbursement of pre-accession funds. Second, the capacity of local administrations to evaluate projects and to interact between local agents and the EU authorities is limited. Some expertise on using EU funds has already been developed, but it is mostly concentrated in central government administrations; by contrast, local offices are largely understaffed, their personnel lack skills (language or knowledge of procedures) needed to process effectively and expeditiously all documentation pertaining to projects. The European Commission would also need to improve its expertise on the situation within the new Member States to ensure that their partnership is fully effective.

The obvious conclusion is that the institutional capacity of the newcomers has to be further developed—which suggests that EU assistance is urgently needed to enhance this capacity. Even then, however, it is likely that the Structural Funds will have to be phased in gradually to ensure efficient use of available resources. Lack of improvement in the institutional capacity may delay significantly the hoped-for benefits from these transfers as well as the overall positive impact on growth. Similarly the Commission should have its resources extended to provide high-quality and well-focused advice and processing of grants.

8.1.3. *Structural reforms*

For some time already the EU has been working on certain crucial structural reforms aimed at improving its ability to respond to the new challenges. Enlargement has further accentuated the pressing need for some of these reforms, including in particular the working of labour markets, and the structure and efficiency of the EU budget, especially the CAP.

Labour market reform is necessary to ensure a flexible reaction to opening borders across the enlarged Union and to extract maximum benefits from free movement of labour. Reforms should concentrate on increasing inter-sectoral and inter-regional labour mobility, through a combination of incentives for individuals to search actively for jobs, lower employment protection, temporary unemployment insurance, and more efficient systems of job-search assistance, training, and life-long learning. With labour mobility in the EU considerably lower than in the United States, the European Single Market continues to be less efficient and less competitive.

The cost of fully including new members in an unreformed CAP would probably boost EU budget spending well beyond the limit of 1.27 per cent of GDP. The EU therefore had two options: reform the CAP or pay farmers in the new members less than those in the current ones. It opted for the latter, offering direct payments of 25 per cent of those received by EU farmers. This result, together with the promise to increase gradually the direct payments to 100 per cent of EU level by 2013, makes all new members strong advocates of continuing with the unreformed CAP. Several new Member States could well team up with some of the current members in demanding that the high level of income transfers to farming continues.

8.1.4. *Migration*

The issue of migration has gained high visibility in the context of accession because of concerns related to the possible adverse impact of mass migration from the new members on labour markets and incomes in current EU countries.

The potential for migration from new members has been examined in a number of studies. A wide variety of approaches has been applied by various authors, including simple extrapolation exercises, historical analogies, static and dynamic models, and error-correction models (see Boeri et al. 2002, for a review). The results obtained differ widely, which should not be surprising given the number of necessary assumptions and the long-term nature of the exercise. Even if the obvious outlier studies are ignored, other studies still give a rather wide range of estimates. The findings suggest that the full liberal-isation of cross-border labour movement immediately after enlargement might have produced an annual flow of migrants from the eight new mem-bers in central and eastern Europe of somewhere between 250,000 and 450,000 during the first 1–2 years, falling to some 100,000–200,000 after-wards. Over the first decade, the cumulative number of migrants might have amounted to between 1.5 and 4 million, that is, 2–4.5 per cent of total population in the eight newcomers or 0.4–1.2 per cent of total population in the current Union.

Even if there is necessarily a considerable amount of uncertainty about these figures, they are rather small relative to the size of the EU workforce. More-over, there are arguments suggesting even lower levels of migration, especially in a context of ageing populations and low fertility rates in the new Member States. First, the experience of earlier enlargements shows that migration depends not only on income differentials but also on prospects of job and income opportunities and many other cultural and social factors. After all, the income differentials in the early 1990s were several times larger than now and still there was no mass migration. Second, most of those who wanted to migrate may well have done so already, as around 300,000 nationals from the new Member States, Bulgaria and Romania, combined already work in EU-15—in spite of strict restrictions imposed on labour mobility. Overall, rel-atively insignificant inflows of labour force are to be expected from the new member countries which are unlikely to entail significant perturbations on EU labour markets, both with respect to overall job opportunities and to wage levels. Moreover, there are distinct benefits to the new Member States from returning migrants with enhanced know-how and other valuable experience in western Europe. Maintaining EU-wide restrictions beyond 2004 would not therefore be required or justified.

If there is going to be no problem with the absolute number of would-be migrants—since mass migration is unlikely—the same cannot probably be said with respect to their geographic distribution. Migration is likely to be heavily concentrated in countries bordering on the new members, mostly in Germany and Austria. Already two thirds of migrants from new Member States reside in Germany and 14 per cent in Austria, representing respectively 0.5 per cent and 1.1 per cent of their workforce. If this distribution continues, the bulk of new migrants will settle in these two countries. The estimates of net migration to Germany in the initial post-enlargement years vary widely, ranging from

70,000 a year (Fertig 2001) up to 200,000–300,000 (Sinn et al. 2001), but declining in the following years. If the higher band prevails, the long-run migration stock in Germany would attain 2–3 per cent of the population after 15–20 years.

This raises the policy issue of how best to respond to the challenge posed by migration. The results of the accession negotiations grant the incumbent EU members the option of applying transition periods—initially for three years with a possible maximum of seven years. Several EU countries have stated that they would not resort to this option and that they are ready to remove all restrictions to free movement of labour immediately after enlargement in 2004 (Greece, Sweden, Spain, United Kingdom). Other countries, however, have made it clear they would opt for maintaining long transition periods (Germany, Austria).

8.2. Implications for macroeconomic stability

Enlargement will further increase the heterogeneity of the EU. The new Member States are not only poorer, they also have structural differences: some have large and inefficient farm sectors, others do relatively more trade with eastern neighbours in the Commonwealth of Independent States (CIS), most suffer from high structural unemployment, and their financial sectors remain insufficiently developed. Against this background, it can be assumed that their economic priorities may differ, not only from those in EU-15, but also among themselves. This poses a double challenge with respect to EU-wide macro-economic policy. The first is how to ensure a necessary degree of fiscal discipline and coordination in a grouping of twenty-five countries with diverse macroeconomic and structural characteristics. The other is how to conduct the single monetary policy in a euro area with increased economic heterogeneity (De Grauwe 2003*b*; Gros et al. 2002).

8.2.1. *Fiscal policies in the enlarged European Union*

At present, fiscal policy in individual EU member countries remains firmly in the hands of national governments. But, under the EMU fiscal policy rules, member countries have to respect the provisions of the Treaty and the Stability and Growth Pact (SGP).

The SGP is part of the *acquis communautaire* and its provisions are therefore mandatory for the new Member States. This means that both the deficit limit and the balanced budget requirement have to be observed. If a new member country fails to reduce its budget deficit below 3 per cent, the 'excessive deficit procedure' applies immediately upon entry into the EU. Sanctions would not apply as long as they remain outside the euro area, although, in the case of non-compliance with the targets set in their Convergence Programmes, they may lose access to the Cohesion Fund.

The application of the SGP to the newcomers raises a number of challenges (Buiter and Grafe 2003). The logic of the SGP is that countries bring their structural budget balances towards equilibrium so as to have a sufficient room for manoeuvre to let automatic stabilisers play in cyclical downturns without breaching the 3 per cent deficit ceiling. Such a framework is likely to lead to conflicting requirements. On the one hand, their larger exposure to country-specific shocks (due to the heterogeneity of their economic structure) would require that a large safety margin be created below the deficit ceiling. As shown in Table 8.3, while the fiscal stance varies from country to country, in some new members budget deficits in 2002 still exceeded the reference value by a wide margin. On the other hand, trying to reduce the deficits below the reference value immediately after accession and to continue the convergence towards close-to-balance structural positions may run counter to the goal of real convergence if it leads to a squeeze on public investment. Indeed, not-withstanding the undeniable need to reform their public finances, and especially the expenditure side of their budgets, most new Member States will need more rather than less public investment (also because of the co-financing needed for EU-supported projects). It may not be easy therefore to aim at fiscal consolidation while at the same time providing the necessary financing for new public investment, since this implies a reallocation within government spending which may be politically difficult in many cases.

Clearly, sound public finances are paramount if newcomers are to catch up, as they are essential to maintain stable macroeconomic conditions and to ensure high creditworthiness which, in turn, helps to attract FDI. Budget deficits will have to remain at manageable levels. However, in new member countries with low or very low levels of public debt (Table 8.3), temporary

Table 8.3. *Fiscal conditions in new Member States (% of GDP, 2002)*

	Budget balance	Public debt	Public investment
Cyprus	3.5	59.8	3.2
Czech Republic	− 7.1	27.1	4.6
Estonia	0.9	5.7	4.2
Hungary	− 9.2	56.3	6.1
Latvia	− 3.0	15.2	3.3
Lithuania	− 1.7	22.7	2.5
Malta	− 6.2	64.2	5.4
Poland	− 3.9	41.6	3.6
Slovakia	− 7.2	44.3	2.4
Slovenia	− 2.3	27.0	2.5
Total new Member States	− 5.2	39.8	4.0

Source: European Commission (2003*f*) and national data from pre-accession reports (DO ECFIN Enlargement Papers No.17, September 2003).

higher deficits used to finance public investment would not necessarily threaten the sustainability of their public finances.

How to square the circle of nominal and real convergence in an enlarged Union will be a major challenge for the EU's fiscal rules over the next several years.

8.2.2. *Monetary policy in the enlarged European Union*

The Maastricht Treaty makes it clear that all EU members—except Denmark and the United Kingdom—are expected to join EMU.

The EMU requirements as specified in the Maastricht Treaty were extended to new member countries at the European Council in Copenhagen in June 1993. The economic and political conditions for accession, as then formulated, included, among other things, the requirement for the candidate countries to be able to assume a wide range of obligations arising from full membership, including membership of the monetary union.

There are two issues here: the first concerns the optimal speed of transition by the new members towards full membership of the euro area; the second is how to run monetary policy in a (even more) diversified currency area.

As to the first issue (when should the new Member States join the euro area), the provisions of the Maastricht Treaty imply that a country can adopt the euro only after it has met the convergence criteria. Moreover, membership can be gained at the earliest two years after a new member has joined the EU. Prior to EU accession, candidate countries are free to adopt the exchange rate regime of their choice. However, sometime in the transition period between gaining EU membership and joining the euro area, new Member States are expected to enter ERM-2 (the present exchange rate mechanism), which is regarded by the EU as a useful framework to foster convergence. These requirements imply that the earliest possible date for euro area entry is 2007.

Should the new Member States accelerate their convergence process in order to enter the euro area as soon as possible? On the one hand, setting the objective of achieving early entry may have in many cases the advantage of providing strong incentives to pursue more vigorously domestic policies oriented towards fostering macroeconomic stability, while at the same time shortening the period over which their currency may be subject to speculative attacks. Newcomers also look forward to benefiting from lower risk premia on long-term interest rates. On the other hand, too short a transition to EMU may lead, in a number of cases, to foregoing prematurely the monetary and exchange rate flexibility which would otherwise be necessary to help foster real convergence by better accommodating the structural changes taking place in their economies. As pointed out above, fully respecting the SGP rules could also conflict with the high investment needs required to foster real convergence. All this would, in turn, make it more difficult for the newcomer to catch up under the single monetary policy.

In sum, given the significant differences in the economic situations of new members, the timing of entry into the euro area is likely to differ from country to country. It is nevertheless very important that the new Member States plan their transitional periods carefully, in a way which can both ensure a high degree of nominal convergence and guarantee a continuing process of real convergence once inside the euro area (see, for instance, Hochreiter 2000; Szapáry 2001; Eichengreen and Ghironi 2002).

The second issue concerns the implications of enlargement of the euro area for the conduct of the single monetary policy. With the entry of some accession countries into EMU, one can expect an increase in intercountry heterogeneity inside the enlarged euro area, which may pose a challenge to the conduct of monetary policy.

However several factors suggest that these concerns may be exaggerated. First of all, the relative weight of the new member states is small, with their GDP accounting for about only around 5 per cent of the GDP of the euro area. Second, they will join on a case-by-case basis and only after having achieved a high degree of sustainable nominal convergence. Third, although real convergence may lead to higher inflation rates in these countries through the well-known Balassa–Samuelson effects, this is an equilibrium phenomenon. Such higher inflation is confined to the non-tradable sectors and as such will not be 'exported' to other countries in the euro area. Finally, although intercountry differences will not disappear in the near future, the degree of heterogeneity is to some extent endogenous with respect to the single currency, and therefore the macroeconomic convergence of new Member States inside EMU can be expected to speed up as a result of EMU accession. See Table 8.4.

All in all, the challenges for monetary policy in a highly diversified euro area boil down to aiming at an appropriate inflation rate within the definition of price stability so as to allow a smooth intercountry adjustment within the currency area, and avoid that the large number of actors hamper the decision-taking process when setting interest rates. Beyond this, the potential problems raised by heterogeneity concern mainly the countries themselves and require that appropriate adjustment mechanisms be in place at the national level, particularly as concerns the flexibility of products and factor markets and the ability to carry out counter-cyclical fiscal policies with the SGP framework.

Table 8.4. *Inflation in the new Member States and the euro area*

	1997–2002	2002	Standard deviation 1997–2002
New Member States	7.7	2.7	2.5
Euro area	1.8	2.2	0.8

Source: European Commission AMECO database. The last column gives the average of national standard deviations.

Finally, in line with the enabling clause in the Treaty of Nice, the ECB Governing Council has proposed a reform to its own arrangements in order to accommodate enlargement, which has been endorsed by the European Council. In the new arrangement, the six members of the Executive Board will retain their full voting rights. On the other hand, a rotation system with three categories of members will be introduced, under which the national central bank governors from the larger Member States would sit on the Council more frequently and the number of governors with voting rights in any period would be limited to fifteen. A number of observers have raised concerns about the complexity of the system. Experience in an enlarged euro area will tell whether the system needs to be revised at some stage.

8.3. Implications for European Union governance

The analysis in Chapter 5 has identified a number of key weaknesses in the governance of the EU, which help to explain its disappointing economic performance. Our goal in this section is to revisit the governance issue with a forward-looking perspective.

8.3.1. *Adapting to number and diversity*

The model of governance of the EU was initially conceived for a Community that was (*a*) small and (*b*) homogeneous as regards levels of economic development. Enlargement is bound to represent a major shock in both respects.

First, it is very likely that the EU will be confronted with a tension between, on the one hand, the governance patterns based on intensive coordination which have developed in recent years, and, on the other hand, the logic of enlargement. The significant increase in the number of members will make methods of governance which rely on direct interaction and dialogue between Member States less efficient and calls for developing alternative methods which do not involve such high transaction costs. In terms of the categories of *delegation, commitment, coordination*, and *autonomy* presented in Chapter 6 (Table 6.1), this means either reducing the reliance on commitment or co-ordination which involve such transaction costs or making them deliver more than they have been able to deliver so far.

Second, enlargement is bound to lead to a very substantial increase in heterogeneity of preferences and needs. Heterogeneity may arise from different levels of development, different societal preferences, or be an inheritance of history, with the result that policy priorities differ, revealing troublesome differences in capacities to deliver shared rules. This is already apparent in areas such as environmental protection, product safety, or social protection, some elements of which are currently centralised in the name of the Single Market. Similarly, the difficulty of enforcing common disciplines for state aids is going to increase. Hence, the trade-off between efficiency and preference heterogeneity is bound to become more acute (Tabellini 2003).

The standard EU response to heterogeneity is to leave the *acquis communautaire* untouched while making room for long transition periods. The problem, however, is deeper. It is not necessarily the case that it makes sense for the transformation economies to replicate the policy trajectories of the economies of western Europe. Some argue in favour of a gradual institutional convergence and warn against the risks of adopting policies and institutions that are only appropriate at a later stage of development. Others advocate a kind of 'leapfrogging' and argue that new Member States would greatly benefit from adopting, say, the competition or monetary frameworks that have emerged from EU experience. This controversy is not likely to vanish and different pathways may deliver appropriate outcomes, taking account of a country's initial conditions and endowments, and mobilising a national consensus around shared policy goals (Ireland and Finland are instructive examples in this regard).

Those challenges are already apparent in a wide range of policy domains, ranging from regulatory policies to the macroeconomic field, where discussions on whether enlargement implies reforming the SGP have already started. They could trigger a hollowing out of the intermediate layer of *commitment* and *coordination* for the benefit of the two 'corner solutions' of *delegation* and *autonomy*, unless the EU is able to achieve significant efficiency gains in making coordination and cooperation work.

Responses are bound to involve trade-offs as the increase in the number of participants may call for stronger collective and uniform policies, while heterogeneity and idiosyncrasy naturally lead to preferences and pressures for decentralisation (Berglöf et al. 2003). Depending on the topic, they may imply:

(1) *transferring new policy responsibilities to the EU level* when heterogeneity of needs and preferences is limited and coordination methods are unable to deliver effective outcomes; or, alternatively, *strengthening the role of the Union as a coordinator or a facilitator* based on a transformation of governance methods;
(2) *moving policies back from the EU to the national level when heterogeneity in structures or preferences throws into question current arrangements*. A key, but politically sensitive, issue in this respect is the CAP, since the move to income support in lieu of price support combined with increased diversity as a consequence of enlargement weakens the rationale for retaining EU competence in agriculture;
(3) *developing a 'variable geometry' approach to integration*, whereby we would see in parallel some sets of basic common rules and policies, but also the emergence of arrangements among overlapping subsets of Member States. The EU has in fact already started to experiment with this kind of approach as monetary union can in some respects be regarded as a

case of de facto intensive cooperation among a subset of members (Coeuré and Pisani-Ferry 2003).

These challenges are especially substantial as regards the set of policies and procedures whose aim is to promote growth and social cohesion. From a substantive point of view, we have already pointed out that institutions and policies that are conducive to growth are not identical for economies in a catching-up phase and for economies that are closer to the innovation frontier. From a procedural point of view, the implementation of the objectives set out in the Lisbon Strategy relies heavily on techniques that involve high transaction costs. On both counts, the challenge of making Lisbon deliver is bound to become even greater.

8.3.2. *Coping with the deepening of integration*

Enlargement is a fact. Outlining other challenges of the future is by nature more speculative and open to debate. Nevertheless, current trends suggest that some of the foundations of today's patterns of governance may be weakened by the future dynamics of integration.

As integration develops within the EU, the current assignment of competences between the Union and the Member States is going to be increasingly challenged in a number of areas. It would make sense to allow patterns of governance to evolve as integration proceeds, that is, by moving competences from the national to the EU level, or indeed, where appropriate by the reverse process, or by adapting the functioning of regulatory networks and partnerships to the degree of effective market integration.

A key example here is market regulation. As explained in Chapter 6, new forms of network-based regulation have emerged in recent years, either of the more centralised 'steered network' type or of the more decentralised 'partnership' type. As market integration develops, models of regulation may further evolve. This could, for example, happen as regards securities markets, where the assignment of supervision to the national level is only defendable as long as cross-border holdings remain limited. For this evolutionary process to take place, however, the EU needs to retain a sufficient degree of flexibility in its decision-making procedures and its legal framework.

While such a development would remain consistent with the general thrust of market integration, other changes are likely to be more contentious. One of the key assumptions behind the division of labour, and hence of policy assignment, between the EU and the Member States is that citizens and especially workers remain essentially immobile. Although freedom of establishment and freedom of movement for individuals belong to the very basic principles of the EU, the mobility of persons has been so negligible that its impact on the Member States' ability to tax residents for financing public goods has remained of a second order. This allows Member States (*a*) to rely on general taxation to finance public goods, assuming that their benefits would essentially accrue to the taxpayers; (*b*) to provide free, or at a fraction of their cost, public services like education and healthcare, assuming that here again, externalities would remain minimal; (*c*) to maintain very different pension regimes which hardly communicate with each other and differ markedly in their rates of return; and (*d*) to implement redistribution through the domestic tax and benefits system, under the assumption that the relative generosity of the home system would have only a minor impact on migration. The no-mobility assumption thus justifies member countries retaining full autonomy in areas like personal income taxation, pensions and health insurance, education, unemployment insurance, welfare benefits, and so forth.

This assumption is less and less correct. While overall mobility remains low—even lower than in the 1950s and the 1960s—it is developing in some segments of the population: senior executives and high-level professionals; graduate students and young professionals; and migrants from non-EU countries. Anecdotal evidence shows that migration is already having an impact on the provision of certain categories of public services. Both 'health' and retirement migration are becoming familiar phenomena, the former backed by rulings from the European Court of Justice (Leibfried and Pierson 2000) and the latter based on the warmer sun in southern Europe. Tax policy discussions are also frequently affected by the spectre of tax-induced migration (Debonneuil and Fontagné 2003). Enlargement is generally expected to contribute to accelerating migration within the EU, albeit to a lesser extent than sometimes suggested.

Higher education is a key example of the likely implications of this changing pattern. The EU has begun intervening in this field to a limited extent, especially through its grants to encourage mobility, and through an insistence on recognising equivalence of qualifications. The basic assumption remains that education belongs to the core responsibilities of the Member States and should be preserved from external interference. However, this assumption is increasingly being challenged by current developments: professors and students have become increasingly mobile;[3] and the fragmentation of European higher education and research is proving detrimental to efficiency as it prevents the emergence of a few large-scale centres of excellence. Expectations have begun to change and it is increasingly envisaged that a kind of formal or informal European higher education area will emerge in the coming decade.

If these trends continue and accelerate, they could end up producing a sea change in the EU rules of the game, as an increasing number of public and

---

[3] A telling example is that French students outnumber Belgian students at the veterinary faculty of Liège. Another is the substantial presence in British universities of both undergraduate and postgraduate students from other EU countries, sometimes calculated as equivalent to the cost of providing four British universities.

social services would stop being of exclusive national concern. One outcome might thus be a kind of systems competition between Member States, especially in those public services where market-based factors operate. But a different outcome could be a growing call for significant changes in the allocation of competences, especially in areas like higher education and for redistribution. An even more significant pressure could be exerted on the assignment of responsibility for pensions as it also involves issues of fiscal sustainability (i.e. EMU-type externalities). Finally, these developments on the spending side could be accompanied by, or spill-over onto the revenue side, leading member countries to recognise that the case for preserving taxation from EU interference is severely weakened by the dynamics of integration.

In taking these changes into account, we should beware not to assume that integration would inevitably imply transferring additional competences to the EU level. This could be the case in certain areas, but there are strong reasons to believe that Member States will remain keen on preserving autonomy in areas that they perceive as essential for the domestic social contract. Rather, the aim should be for the EU to play the role of a facilitator in encouraging constructive reforms, while not interfering with national competences.

8.3.3. *Defining roles in a multi-level governance regime*

As integration has developed, transparency and clarity in the assignment of competences have increasingly been demanded by Member States and public opinion. Indeed, clearly assigned competences are conducive both to management efficiency and public accountability. In conformity with the mandate given by the European Councils of Nice and Laeken, the draft constitutional treaty transmitted to the European Council by the European Convention enumerates in its Articles I-11 to I-16 four categories of EU competences:

1. *Exclusive competences of the Union*, that is, areas where the Union is entrusted with legislative power. This category broadly corresponds to what we have called the delegation method. It covers a limited set of policy areas: the competition rules necessary for the functioning of the internal market, monetary policy for those members that have adopted the euro, the common commercial policy, customs union.

2. *Shared competences*. Here, both the Union and the Member States have the power to legislate, but the latter exercise their competence only to the extent that the Union has not exercised its. This category corresponds to areas in which the Union relies on commitment and coordination methods. Relevant policies include: internal market, agriculture and fisheries, transport, energy, specific aspects of social policy, cohesion, environment, consumer protection, common safety concerns in public health, plus research, technological development, and space policy (with specific provisions).

3. *The coordination of economic and employment policies* for which a special competence is assigned to the Union. The draft treaty explicitly refers to coordination through guidelines.

4. *Supporting competences* or, to be more precise, 'competence to carry out actions to support, coordinate, or supplement' the actions of the Member States. Here, competence belongs to the Member States and legally binding acts adopted by the Union may not entail harmonisation. This last category covers industry, health, education, vocational training, youth, and sport, culture, and civil protection.

It is apparent that this categorisation is essentially based on the relative legislative powers of the Union and its members. In some way, it resembles the distinction we have made in Chapter 6 between three governance methods (delegation, commitment, and coordination) and in our presentation of the roles of the EU in the same chapter. But, since effective policy competences do not exactly coincide with formal legislative powers, we should note that the draft treaty creates rather heterogeneous categories with respect to the methods used and the roles to be played by the EU. It is also open to question whether it makes sense to create a special category for economic and employment policy coordination, not least since the competences of the EU in this field are very uneven (e.g. compare, the excessive deficit procedure and employment policy coordination), a pattern not so different from what is the case in other policy fields. It is thus doubtful that a categorisation exclusively based on the legislative power criterion is sufficient to clarify in terms of effective and appropriate governance the respective roles of the EU and the Member States in the various policy areas.

From a procedural standpoint, decisions on an appropriate assignment of policy responsibilities involve a trade-off between, on the one hand, the intensity of externalities and economies of scale, and, on the other hand, the degree of heterogeneity of preferences and needs, which evolve over time and depend on the intensity of economic integration. The efficient assignment of competences is thus a function of market integration. Whether the EU will be able to decide flexibly on those matters without the decisions being hostage to institutional inertia is thus an important issue for the quality of its governance.

8.3.4. *Adapting institutions*

From an economic point of view, a striking characteristic of the EU institutional system is that institutions fulfil different roles in different fields, and sometimes even different roles in the same field. Thus, the Commission performs an executive function in the trade policy field, a quasi-judicial function in the competition field, and a supervisory function in the macroeconomic/budgetary field. The Council does not operate in a uniform way across domains either, and it is furthermore split into different council formations whose role and effectiveness vary a great deal. In some fields, the European Parliament has significant legislative or scrutiny powers, while in others very little. National institutions also vary a good deal among the current members in the ways that they are configured and in their organisational cultures. It is obvious that in the new Member States the core national institutions are themselves still settling down as frameworks for managing market economies.

At the same time, however, there is some redefinition under way across Europe of the role of public authorities as such, as a variety of experiments take place with new forms of agencies and new public–private partnerships. The tendency is increasingly to devolve regulatory powers to independent authorities that are able to act on the basis of a specific mandate in interaction with relevant professional and stakeholder communities and to entrust specific independent bodies with responsibilities for making decisions which directly affect specific private interests (e.g. as it is the case for competition policy). So far, the EU has—with the exception of the creation of the ECB—not followed this trend.

The combination of enlargement and additional responsibilities as a consequence of the endorsement of a growth programme for the EU risks creating a kind of institutional overstretch for the EU institutions. This, in turn, could weaken the ability of the institutions to perform in accordance with common goals and, for this very reason, weaken their legitimacy.

The proposals by the European Convention include significant reforms of the key institutions and how they interact with each other. However, they are mostly focused on the 'input' side of the political process, and have not been so attentive to the 'output' side and the issue of policy effectiveness. Nor should this constitutional reform distract attention from the need for 'non-treaty' reform of the various institutions or a continuous emphasis within each institution on improving performance and effectiveness. We think the challenge goes beyond simplifying the EU's legal order, clarifying the distinction between executive and legislative responsibilities, enhancing the role of the European Council, extending the scope for Parliament intervention or reducing the number of Commissioners.

Summing up, our assessment is that the EU is now confronting a fundamental choice: it must either abandon some of its present ambitions or seriously address governance weaknesses. One possible response would be to conclude that its ambitions should be scaled down to what it can credibly commit to deliver. Although this perspective is not the one we prefer, it should not be discarded on the ground that it would run against history. A streamlined, scaled-down Union that would concentrate on providing monetary stability, a pro-competitive environment, and development assistance to catching-up countries—but not endorse responsibility for growth, innovation, employment, or social cohesion—would certainly be preferable to an EU that claims to have higher ambitions but is not able to deliver. A Union that claims to live up to its commitment to growth, innovation, and cohesion needs to modify and modernise its governance methods.

9

Europe and the world

On May 2004, the European Union (EU) enters a new phase. An enlarged Union of twenty-five countries—with a population of 450 million and a quarter of world GDP—will have a huge impact on its neighbours in Europe and in the Mediterranean Basin. Beyond its immediate neighbourhood, enlargement will also change the EU's economic relations with the wider world. The EU already plays an important international role in the areas of trade and development assistance. With the successful start of the euro, it is also poised to play an increasing role in the area of international money and finance.

The EU must now be ready to take up the challenges of being the leading player in the Euro-Mediterranean region and an anchor for the global system.

9.1. Wider Europe—neighbourhood

The enlarged EU and its neighbours in Europe and in the Mediterranean Basin have approximately the same population. The two differ, however, in many important respects. First, per capita GDP measured at purchasing power parities (PPP) is about four times higher in the EU-25 than it is, on average, in the neighbouring region. This has obvious economic consequences for patterns of trade, investment and migration. Second, demographic perspectives differ: while those of European neighbours do not differ markedly from those of EU-25, the age structure of the Mediterranean countries is significantly different and population growth is much higher. This has implications for potential migration flows. Third, the land area in the neighbouring region is about five times larger than in the EU-25. Even allowing for non-arable land, it means that they are much more land-abundant than the EU-25, which has clear implication for agricultural production. Fourth, there are important differences between the enlarged EU and its neighbours in terms of energy consumption and production. The EU-25 consumes about twice as much energy per head as its neighbours, but produces four times less oil. Moreover, most of the world's oil production takes place in countries, which are directly contiguous with the EU's neighbours.

The main challenge for the EU vis-à-vis its neighbours is to foster their economic prosperity so as to ensure economic and political stability in the entire Euro-Mediterranean region. This raises the issue of the framework for

Table 9.1. *The EU and the world, 2000*

Region/country	Population (millions)	GDP (current) (€ billions)	GDP per capita (PPP) (€)	Old age dependency ratio (60 + /15 – 59)(%)
EU-25	452	8,935	17,694	34
European neighbours	339	1,064	4,994	26
Candidates and Western Balkans	124	289	6,185	20
European Free Trade Association	12	445	24,667	33
Belarus, Moldova, Russia, Ukraine	203	330	3,103	30
Mediterranean neighbours	154	388	3,852	11
Wider world	5,188	23,628	5,250	14
Africa, Sub-Sahara	671	345	1,377	9
China and India	2,310	1,686	2,683	15
Latin America	520	2,315	6,854	13
Japan	127	5,163	21,738	38
USA	286	10,806	30,371	26
Rest of the World	1,261	3,313	4,060	13
World total	6,133	34,015	6,118	17

Sources: European Commission and World Bank.

economic and political relations between the enlarged European Union and the rest of the region. At the moment, the EU divides the region into three groups of countries: candidate countries, that is, Bulgaria, Romania, and Turkey; potential candidate countries, namely the western Balkans (Albania and the former Yugoslav republics, other than Slovenia) and the members of the European Free Trade Association (EFTA) (Iceland, Norway, Switzerland, and Liechtenstein); eastern and southern neighbours, which at present have no prospects of EU accession, namely Belarus, Moldova, Russia, and Ukraine as well as Algeria, Egypt, Israel, Jordan, Lebanon, Libya, Morocco, the Palestinian Authority, Syria, and Tunisia.

Until recently, relations between the EU and the third group of neighbours lacked a comprehensive economic and political framework. In March 2003, the European Commission attempted to remedy this situation by issuing a communication on *Wider Europe—Neighbourhood: a new framework for relations with our eastern and southern neighbours*. In so doing, the Commission aims to create a zone of prosperity and good neighbourliness—a 'ring of friends' with whom the EU would enjoy close and peaceful relations based on cooperation. It suggests that in return for efforts and progress by those countries with political, economic, and institutional reform the EU should offer the prospect of a stake in the Single Market with free movement of goods, services, capital, and persons. The new framework will build on existing partnership and association agreements. In particular, the Commission proposes to extend the Single Market and its regulatory structures; to set up preferential trade relations and opening up markets; to offer prospects of lawful migration and movement of persons; to integrate its neighbours into transport, energy, and telecommunications networks and the European research area; to create new instruments for promoting and protecting investment; to support their integration into the global trading system; and to provide enhanced assistance (Emerson 2003).

The envisaged Euro-Mediterranean Single Market, which, in due time, might encompass the EU-25, the candidate countries, the western Balkans, the EFTA countries as well as the other eastern and southern neighbours, would constitute a gigantic entity, with a population of about one billion or roughly three times the size of the United States and even much larger than that of North American Free Trade Agreement (NAFTA). *Its total* GDP, however, would be about the same as that of the United States, which means that in per capita terms its GDP would be only about one-third the American level. This new entity and the United States would share the same demographic pattern, with an old age dependency ratio of about 26–28 per cent.

9.2. Wider world

The proposed relationship between the enlarged EU and its neighbourhood begs the question of the EU's relationship with the wider world.

The creation of a Euro-Mediterranean trading bloc would constitute a major development for the world trading system. It could well precipitate the reinforcement of two other equally formidable regional trading blocs: the Free Trade Area of the Americas (FTAA), for which a process has been under way since 1994; and an Asian trading bloc, which would include the current ten members of the ASEAN (Association of Southeast Asian Nations) Free Trade Area (AFTA), plus China and Japan, and perhaps India (Sapir 2000).

Nonetheless, as argued in Chapter 7, the trend towards more globalisation is likely to continue. Increased globalisation will create more economic opportunities, but also more economic frictions between countries. A crucial question, therefore, is whether the current wave of globalisation is sustainable, or whether it will end, like the first wave did in 1914, with severe international conflicts. In principle, the chances are considerably better this time because multilateral economic institutions—in particular, the Bretton Woods Institutions and the World Trade Organisation (WTO)—provide elements of global governance. In practice, however, the challenges are immense.

At a time when the global system is under stress from various quarters, the EU must serve as one of its anchors and help ensuring the success of the globalisation process. More effective action by the Union at the global level requires greater coherence on its part, including within and between the various multilateral economic institutions (Portes 2003). This is far from being the case at the moment. The EU speaks with one voice only at the WTO. In contrast, in the Bretton Woods Institutions, the twenty-five Member States of the enlarged EU are currently represented by no fewer then ten executive directors on the twenty-four member executive boards of the International Monetary Fund and the World Bank.

The Union also faces immediate challenges. One is to assume its responsibilities, along with other important players, to bring the ongoing Doha Development Round of trade liberalisation to a successful outcome. Another is to manage the euro as it develops the role and functions of a world currency.

PART III

RECOMMENDATIONS

10

Principles

10.1. Assessing past performance

Since the mid-1980s, the European Union (EU) has witnessed a 'big leap forward' in its integration process, with the establishment of the Single Market in 1993 and the introduction of the single currency in 1999. Judged by the progress made in the integration process, there is no doubt that this period has been a considerable institutional success.

Nevertheless, the verdict is more mixed from the economic viewpoint. While macroeconomic stability has significantly improved overall—as reflected, for example, in the marked reduction in inflation rates and budget deficits—and a high degree of cohesion has been preserved, the EU economic system has failed to deliver a satisfactory growth performance.

This underperformance is striking because it contrasts not only with expectations but also with past EU performance and recent US accomplishment. In the EU, there has been a steady decline of the average growth rate decade after decade and per capita GDP has stagnated at about 70 per cent of the US level since the early 1980s. The disparity between the EU and the United States has been particularly remarkable in recent years. For instance, over the period 1995–2001, the US economy accounted for over 60 per cent of the cumulative expansion in world GDP, while the EU, with only a slightly smaller economy, contributed less than 10 per cent.

The main reason for disappointing growth in the EU is quite clear. During the past decades, the economy has been confronted by a series of long-lasting shocks the information technology revolution, German re-unification, the opening up to the new market economies of central and eastern Europe, globalisation—which called for new organisational forms of production. The situation demanded less vertically integrated firms, greater mobility within and across firms, greater flexibility of labour markets, greater reliance on market finance, and higher investment in both R&D and higher education. In other words, this required massive change in economic institutions and organisations, which has not yet occurred on a large scale in Europe.

10.2. The challenges ahead

It is urgent, therefore, that the EU economic system is reconfigured so as deliver higher growth. Failure to do this would gravely endanger the sustainability of the European model, which puts a high premium on cohesion. This is especially the case in an environment with accelerating trends in population ageing, technological change, and globalisation, all of which greatly increase the demand for social protection. Fortunately, however, technological change and globalisation also hold the potential for higher growth.

The same applies to the forthcoming enlargement, which will make per capita income differentials between present and new EU members larger than ever before. Enlargement may add to the demand for social protection, but it is also a new source of growth for the EU as whole.

10.3. Rethink the European Union economic system

It is against this background that we, the authors of the present Report, make a series of recommendations. In our judgement, meeting these future challenges requires a major rethinking of the EU economic system. Three basic principles should guide the process:

Give priority to growth
There is a need to give higher priority to growth, because it is the means to achieve the economic, social, and environmental objectives of the enlarged Union. Growth is also crucial to help the Union fulfil its political objectives.

Reshape policy instruments and governance methods to fit the objectives
The EU economic system includes a wide variety of policy instruments and decision-making powers, ranging from microeconomic market regulation to macroeconomic policy and redistributive instruments, and applicable at local, national, and EU levels. Achieving the objective of higher growth requires a higher degree of coherence across the range of economic policies and across the different levels of decision-making powers. This implies improving the content of policies and the governance processes behind their implementation.

Adapt to a changing environment
The world is rapidly changing. In a dynamic environment, decision-making processes need to be characterised by commitment to stable objectives over an appropriately long time horizon. At the same time, economic policies and governance processes must feature commitment to change.

10.4. Redesign policies

We follow four principles in recommending new policy designs.

Set the right priorities
Expanding growth potential requires first and foremost reforms of microeconomic policies. However, there is also a need to revise some features of the

current macroeconomic policy setting and to redesign cohesion policies at both the EU and national levels. Growth and stability must go together. A well-designed macroeconomic framework helps to achieve sustainable growth. At the same time, significant growth is necessary to maintain stability. The same holds for growth and cohesion. Well-designed cohesion policies tend to foster growth and sustained growth is necessary to ensure cohesion.

Act at both the European Union and national levels
Well-functioning and competitive markets for labour, capital, goods, and services foster growth. Appropriate market regulation also plays a crucial role. This Report focuses on policies at the EU level and recommends redesigning EU policies that impinge directly on the functioning and regulation of product and factor markets. It makes no recommendation for reforming national policies in the area of social policy and taxation, even though we feel that appropriate national reforms in this area are absolutely crucial in order to ensure that the EU economic system delivers higher growth.

Avoid targeting several goals with one policy instrument
Quite often in the EU economic system, policy instruments are assigned two objectives at the same time: fostering growth and improving cohesion. Sometimes it may be possible for one instrument to help both objectives, but often it is not. It is better therefore to assign one objective to each policy instrument.

Focus on the enlarged European Union
The recommendations in this Report are meant to improve the functioning of the enlarged Union and geared towards increasing growth both in general and in the new Member States. The recommendations do not address a number of important transitional issues that will arise in the early years after the forthcoming enlargement. In particular, they do not cover transitional restrictions on labour movement nor transitional arrangements before membership of the euro area.

10.5. Revise modes of delivery: Governance methods and the budget

An underlying theme of this Report has been that the EU suffers from twin problems: some of its methods of governance are obsolete; and the system as a whole has become too complex and fragmented. Attempts to redress policy failures would make little sense, while leaving untouched the procedures and processes through which those policies are designed, decided, and implemented. Policy reforms can be expected to be successful only if implemented in conjunction with a restructuring of the methods of governance.

A clear definition of underlying principles of governance needs to be made in order to guide specific proposals for reform made by the Report's authors.

As authors, we outline four broad governance principles that should be used as an inspiration in the design of policy reforms.

Match methods to tasks

A continuing controversy and dichotomy between the so-called Community and intergovernmental approaches mar the EU debate on governance. Advocates of the former suggest that effective policies can be achieved only by reinforcing this. Supporters of the latter believe that soft forms of cooperation can both preserve Member States' autonomy and reap the benefits of coordinated action. This is a regrettable confusion.

We see merit in developing new methods of cooperation, provided that they are sufficiently structured, that the corresponding incentives can be specified, and that their scope is limited to those fields in which tighter forms of cooperation are not available.

Moreover, situations and policy contexts change, especially in conjunction with the progress of economic integration, and different methods may be needed to respond to new situations, since it would be foolish to freeze the processes of governance in a time warp. Some tasks need methods of delegation that are crystal clear, consistent and capable of well-specified implementation. Others depend on building up cooperation over time and on leaving space for decentralised experimentation and more local dynamics. Reflecting on which methods are appropriate to each policy task must be an integral part of policy-thinking for each of the tasks of European economic governance.

Develop incentives to conform to agreed strategy (more carrots, not only sticks)

Instead of a clear separation between the EU and the national remits, as was the case in the early days of the EC, there is an increasing overlap between the EU and the national or sub-national domains. EU priorities and policies are thus more and more often part of the varied policy environments in which decisions are taken at various government levels and in different countries, each with distinctive characteristics, as will be even more evident with further enlargement.

Effective implementation of EU policy thus frequently depends not only on the explicit cooperation of various national and sub-national government bodies in the implementation of common policies, but also on their willingness to set their own priorities and develop their own agenda in accordance with EU priorities, or to shape their local policies in the light of wider European reference points.

Furthermore, enforcement has frequently been neglected and many sensible and appropriate EU rules fail to bite because their implementation is sloppy.

In this evolving context, neither a pure command-and-control nor a monitor-and-punish approach is likely to be appropriate. What is required is a much more incentive-based approach that treats Member States as partners, which are willing to participate in forms of cooperation provided that they have a genuine interest in it. This is what we understand by the concept of *the EU as a facilitator*.

This leads us to emphasise the importance of developing a common agenda that commands support in the various Member States. Intellectual and policy legitimacy can be based only on first, high-quality policy analysis and evaluation and, second, on a process of continuous dialogue involving both Member States' governments and other players from civil society, including of course the economic stakeholders. The EU can—and should—certainly play an enhanced role in this policy-learning process, provided that the Commission is ready to allocate resources to policy analysis and to invest energy in policy dialogue.

Implementing this concept of the EU as a facilitator will, however, require more than knowledge and interchange. The design of the policy rules by which the Member States have to abide must take greater care of the incentive component.

This point also applies to the EU budget. As public spending by the Union represents barely 2.5 per cent of total EU public spending, its direct effect is bound to be dwarfed by those of national or sub-national programmes, unless (*a*) it is heavily concentrated on a narrow subset of policy domains, or (*b*) it serves as a catalyst for coordinating Member States' efforts. At present, EU spending is in effect concentrated on agriculture and regional development, and the incentive element is present through the supposed additionality of the Structural Funds. But there is considerable inertia in the allocation of EU spending and the choice of spending priorities does not square with the Union's present economic priorities. Hence, budget reform should be an integral part of a strategy of moving towards a more incentive-based approach. Above all, giving the utmost priority to growth implies that more expenditure needs to be channelled to growth-enhancing activities such as R&D and education. With a constant budget, this means reducing the share allocated to agriculture.

Increase Member States' ownership of European Union policies and systems

Whatever the incentives from the top, EU priorities can translate into policy actions by the Member States or by economic and social actors only if they develop a sense of shared ownership. As European integration affects a wide array of domains, national institutions need to consider EU priorities as their own. Politicians and policy-makers across the EU need to be engaged in the process. Economic and social actors need to have a sense that their own fortunes are tied up in the success of the European process.

This requires that national or sub-national institutions take a more proactive and more involved role than in the current system, in which they are either the implementing agents of policies in the definition of which they did not have much of a voice, or their activities are distinct from EU policies. Prospects for developing new patterns of EU policies are particularly promising in the various regulatory areas, where market opening and integration lend a European dimension to what hitherto have been national domains.

Adapt to numbers and to diversity

Enlargement is bound to challenge the governance of the EU in two major respects: it will very significantly increase the diversity of preferences and needs; and it will increase by two thirds the number of governments participating in the Council, thereby putting additional demands on already strained decision-making procedures. The traditional response to the first challenge—less delegation, more coordination, and commitment—is likely to conflict with the natural response to the second one—streamlined, simplified, decision-making procedures.

In an enlarged Union, variable geometry is likely to become a natural response to differences of situation or preference. In order to make it functional, clarity about a few organising principles will be of utmost importance. Hence we suggest spelling out more precisely the scope of policies and rules that must apply to all Member States and the procedures for making decisions in cases where not all are required to participate.

10.6. An agenda for a growing Europe

The EU has set two strategic economic goals for the decade to 2010. One is to become the most competitive and dynamic knowledge-based economy with sustainable economic growth, more and better jobs, and greater social cohesion. This was the objective set by EU heads of state and government when they met in Lisbon in March 2000. The second is to make a success of the pending enlargement by rapidly raising living standards in the ten new members, where the average income is less than half the EU-15 average.

Achieving these goals will not be easy. Above all, it will require a high degree of coherence, between EU policies and instruments on the one hand and between decision-makers at EU and national levels on the other. Our six-point agenda focuses on where EU policies and their economic management can make the greatest contribution. It is set out in more detail in Chapters 11 and 12.

10.6.1. *Policies for promoting growth*

Make the single market more dynamic

A dynamic Single Market is the keystone to Europe's economic growth. Much progress has been achieved in goods markets, but integration in services and in network industries remains very limited. A truly dynamic Single Market needs not only more integration, but also better regulation to facilitate entry by new players and the development of risk capital. Intra-EU and extra-EU labour mobility should be made much easier. (See Chapter 11, Section 11.1.)

Boost investment in knowledge
The integration of goods, services, and capital markets is only a first step. Innovation is a key driver of growth, calling not only for a dynamic market environment but also major investments in knowledge. EU funding for innovation and research can make a significant contribution here. (See Chapter 11, Section 11.2.)

Improve the macroeconomic policy framework
Now that Economic and Monetary Union (EMU) and the single currency have delivered price stability, it is time to consolidate this achievement. Some features of the way macroeconomic policy is set should be improved. The monetary and fiscal policy framework of EMU should be made more symmetric over the phases of the cycle. The implementation of the Stability and Growth Pact should focus more on long-term sustainability by taking into account both explicit and implicit public liabilities in the assessment of national budgetary positions. The policy framework for EMU should be upgraded to improve policy coordination among euro-area countries. (See Chapter 11, Section 11.3.)

Redesign policies for convergence and restructuring
The underdeveloped institutional capacity of the newcomers is a handicap to their ability to implement beneficial EU policies or even, in some cases, to draw on all the financial and technical assistance that is available. It risks delaying the catching-up process. This is why EU support should continue, as it did in the pre-entry period, to target the institution-building process. The EU should also promote restructuring. (See Chapter 11, Section 11.4.)

10.6.2. *Modes of delivery: Governance methods and the budget*

Achieve effectiveness
The EU should have more power to oversee the correct application of Single Market rules. Independent EU bodies should be created in certain specific areas, while more authority could be devolved to decentralised, but coordinated, systems of authorities which would operate within the same legal norms. Extending the scope for Qualified Majority Voting (QMV) in the economic field would also be vital for improving the overall performance of the EU system. (See Chapter 12, Section 12.1.)

Refocus the European Union budget
The economic component of the EU budget should better reflect the economic priorities the Union has set itself. Thus, budgets during the next financial

perspective period (starting in 2007) should redirect EU funding to the goals of creating a dynamic knowledge-based economy and of helping new Member States to catch up with the rest as rapidly as possible. But the EU budget is very small. It should act in unison with national budgets and act as a 'facilitator' to improve the composition of national public expenditure and revenue. (See Chapter 12, Section 12.2.)

11

Policies for promoting growth

Much has been accomplished during the past fifty years of European economic integration, culminating in the Single Market Programme and monetary union. The challenge today is for this unified economic area to function effectively to promote growth and employment and to integrate successfully the new Member States that are poised to enter the Union. As a result, our recommendations on growth address essentially two areas: measures to improve the functioning of policies adopted in the past and additional measures that go beyond and complement policies pursued up until now.

Although economic integration is an ongoing process, the context in which it takes place has been affected by the changing nature of markets. Tools of economic management that proved effective in the past no longer display the same efficiency with regard to the current situation. The nature of integration itself changes with an economy dominated by service industries and intangible investments compared with one dominated by manufactured products and tangible investments. Right of establishment and, therefore, foreign direct investment become more important relative to trade as does knowledge-creation through higher education. R&D gain in importance relative to gross fixed capital investment as motors of growth. Both European Union (EU) and national policies have to adjust to this more differentiated and more complex world.

Contrary to the post-war period where growth and catching-up with the United States could largely be achieved through factor accumulation and imitation, once European countries had moved closer to the technology frontier and also with the occurrence of new technological revolutions in communication and information, innovation at the frontier has become the main engine of growth. This in turn called for new organisational forms, less vertically-integrated firms, greater mobility both intra- and inter-firm, greater flexibility of labour markets, a greater reliance on market finance, and a higher demand for both R&D and higher education. However, these necessary changes in economic institutions and organisations have not yet occurred on a large scale in Europe and it is this delay in adjusting our institutions which accounts to a large extent for the EU's growth deficit.

11.1. A dynamic Single Market

In the new economic context, promoting the entry of new players requires particular attention. For product markets, this involves a substantial reduction of entry costs (administrative procedures, ...) and consistent anti-trust action against incumbents' attempts to prevent entry by others. For capital markets, it implies promoting those forms of equity-based capital which are particularly suitable for risky ventures with high growth potential for which traditional capital markets are ill-suited. For labour markets, promoting entry implies the ability to adjust rapidly and flexibly to changes in market conditions and to seize opportunities, even if subsequently some of these entries do not prove commercially successful. Finally, encouraging entry implies that both entrepreneurs and employees receive the high level of education required to exploit technological and market opportunities and receive appropriate rewards, too.

11.1.1. *Product markets*

The Single Market and active competition policy remain the cornerstone of efforts at EU level to improve European growth performance. They represent a foundation without which other efforts would be wasted. A general question with regard to these two policies relates to whether they adequately address the changing nature of markets as identified in this Report. There can be no simple reply to this question. Certainly, within the Single Market process there is a need for *innovation* and for *new entry* from start-ups and from firms not previously present in a sector to play a central role. Any product market regulation, including the Single Market legislation and regulation itself, should therefore be examined for its effects on innovation and new entry. At the present time, entry per se is not an objective of Single Market legislation, although sometimes it may be the result.

Whether or not a regulation encourages innovation and new entry can be tackled only on a case-by-case basis. Therefore, a general recommendation on regulation and entry must address the process by which regulations are formulated and applied so as to ensure that entry is adequately taken into consideration. To frame regulations appropriately with entry in mind requires an understanding of market structure and dynamics. Regulators therefore need to have access to the requisite expertise and can not rely on industry inputs alone since these by definition reflect the interests of incumbents.

Active competition policy plays an essential role in ensuring that market-opening does in practice lead to the achievement of potential gains. In the past, competition policy has been used effectively as a lever to open certain markets and to police anti-competitive behaviour. In the future, energetic efforts to ensure that markets become or remain competitive will be indispensable. When implementing competition policy, particular care should be taken to acknowledge the changing nature of markets in which innovation and new entry take place. Thus, when defining markets and assessing dominance, market dynamics, and potential competition—in particular the potential for competition from the newly-innovating-need to be taken into account. At the same time, the role of R&D in opening up competition—but also as including possible domains that restrain competition—needs to be considered.

A functioning Single Market requires more than the implementation of regulation. It also implies that the physical infrastructure for the exchange of people, goods, and ideas is put in place. Basic physical infrastructure is the responsibility of Member States. Nevertheless, there are substantial financial contributions for regional or national infrastructures from the EU Structural Funds and a much lower contribution from EU funds for 'missing links' between national systems. In order to connect up the broader European economy, regional and national infrastructure policies should be conceived appropriately. Enlargement makes this issue even more important since it adds an East–West dimension (including connections to the new neighbours of the enlarged Union) to the previous North–South one. What is essential, however, is that investments from a mix of EU and national funding should be based on careful assessments of need and close consultations between neighbouring countries.

11.1.2. *Financial services*

Given the crucial role of financial integration for growth, completing the Single Market for financial services is crucial. A number of specific proposals currently in the pipeline address issues identified in this Report. For example, credit markets and the financial system for innovation are the subject of the Risk Capital Action Plan and Financial Services Action Plans. We support the accelerated implementation of both these actions rather than bringing forward new recommendations in these areas. An effective regulatory system for financial services represents a requirement for the efficient functioning of the financial system. In general, the regulatory process needs to become much closer to, and more aware of, market developments in service sectors and utilities. Possibilities for self-regulation as a partial or complete substitute for statutory regulation need also to be explored.

11.1.3. *Improving labour mobility*

Lack of labour mobility, whether within countries, between EU countries, between the EU and third countries, or between firms, has been hindering the capacity of the European economy to adjust to the changed market conditions indicated in the introduction to this chapter. Very often, mobility is identified with increased insecurity and as a negative phenomenon instead of as a possibility to seek out better opportunities and to improve status and earnings.

In order for mobility to be viewed in a positive light, the correct combination of regulatory reform and supportive changes in welfare systems is required. Although the main responsibility in this area lies with, and will continue to lie with, Member States, the EU can act as a facilitator.

In order to make intra-EU mobility easier, the obstacles in terms of the non-transferability or non-compatibility of acquired rights in terms of basic provisions for health, pensions, and unemployment need to be removed. This aspect has received increasing attention and has been the subject of relevant proposals. It will be necessary for the European Parliament and the Council to adopt these proposals and to ensure that they are implemented fully in order to overcome the regulatory obstacles to mobility within the EU. In the context of enlargement, a general policy of liberalisation of cross-border labour flows between the current and new members will help to reap economic benefits from integration and strengthen political cohesion in the enlarged Union.

Because of both ageing and the important contribution of immigrants to entrepreneurship and innovation, Europe needs a positive attitude towards immigration from third countries. In a Single Market with free circulation of persons, it makes sense to set immigration policy, at least in its broad outlines, at EU level. This should address such issues as visas and border formalities. But it is also necessary to attract migrants and to ensure that they can be used most productively. An active policy to promote legal economic immigration has as a corollary that the necessary steps be taken to discourage illegal immigration in order not to undermine the process of greater openness.

11.1.4. *Our recommendations*

To make the Single Market more dynamic, the EU needs to update its approach by giving more consideration to the substantial changes that are taking place in markets and to the economic environment in which business operates. Promotion of innovation and entry should become a central aim of market opening. A financial system oriented towards risk will be required along with greatly enhanced labour mobility both within the EU and from third countries. Appropriate physical infrastructure underpins an integrated economic space. In parallel to the national authorities taking the appropriate measures to improve the functioning of product and factor markets, *we propose*:

1. Better coordination between regulatory and competition policies to encourage new entrants. Before a regulation is adopted, it is essential that a thorough and independent review of the effect on entry be carried out under an impact assessment procedure. The main challenge for the Single Market is to manage implementation more effectively. The recommendations on how to achieve this are to be found in the section on governance.

2. A more proactive role in facilitating intra-EU labour mobility. This addresses the non-regulatory aspects through a targeted programme of assistance. Such a programme should address barriers to labour mobility such as inadequate language skills, difficulties associated with job search in unfamiliar labour markets, problems with achieving acceptance of qualifications in the target country, and costs associated with relocation. Since this is a problem with a clear EU-wide dimension, it would be appropriate for such a programme to be partially financed out of the EU budget.

3. The issuing of work permits in the form of 'green cards' that allow free movement of third-country nationals throughout the EU once they have been legally admitted. Since current third-country nationals with legal residence in only one EU country do not benefit from the possibility of free movement of labour, this provision should be extended to cover them too.

4. Action to promote major infrastructure for connecting up the broader European economy and to expand EU budgetary financing to make this effective.

11.2. Boosting investment in knowledge

Europe underinvests in higher education and R&D compared to the United States. Both the relative importance attached to higher education and R&D in public policy and the absolute amounts of public investment are higher in the United States. At the moment, we invest 1.9 per cent of our GDP in R&D and 1.4 per cent in tertiary education. The EU would need to invest much more in both areas in order to obtain the level of knowledge required to reach a higher growth path. Targets of close to 3 per cent in each area seem appropriate in view of international comparisons. Member States and the EU as a whole need to invest *more* and also to invest *better* in higher education and research. Now, there are two main dangers that need to be kept in mind when contemplating an increase in public spending on higher education and research. First, neither Member State governments nor the EU should try to pick winners and adopt too much of a top-down approach. Second, public support for industrial R&D should be based on clearly-articulated public needs and avoid covert subsidisation of individual enterprises.

11.2.1. *Education*

The numbers of European school-leavers who go on to complete higher education are manifestly inadequate for the knowledge-intensive economy. Europe also suffers from a higher education system insufficiently open to international influence and insufficiently oriented towards the highest standard of excellence, particularly at the postgraduate level. This implies that incentives, performance evaluation, and benchmarking/competition should play a greater role in the organisation of universities and in the assignment of qualifications.

Encouraging larger numbers of school leavers to complete higher education remains essentially the preserve of Member States. Building on the successful Erasmus/Socrates programme, the EU can play a role in encouraging a more international outlook among institutions of higher education and greater mobility of both students and faculty across European universities. In particular, the effort towards establishing equivalence between undergraduate degrees and curricula across European countries should be pursued and intensified.

However, this is no longer sufficient, and special attention should now be given to promoting excellence at the postgraduate level as well as to favouring the emergence in Europe of top graduate schools or departments that would match the quality of the best US departments. Such centres of excellence would be in a position to attract the best faculty from anywhere in the world, including those who left European institutions for lack of a suitable environment. Young academic researchers should benefit from post-doctoral training grants or research grants, which would be allocated through a peer review process (e.g. following the example of the American National Science Foundation (NSF) or the more successful research councils in some European countries). At the same time, new centres of excellence or new clustering among researchers across several universities on topics of common interest should be encouraged through funding by both national agencies and European programmes. Such funding will be effective only if it is distributed purely on the basis of excellence irrespective of national origin. The budgetary implications of this recommendation are to be found in the section on the budget in Chapter 12.

11.2.2. *Research and development*

In terms of research and development, Europe suffers from a lack of private sector investment in R&D, substantial although diminishing levels of public investment in R&D and poor efficiency in the distribution of available public funds. These three deficiencies need to be addressed in different ways. First, with regard to the lack of *private* investment in R&D, the single most efficient instrument to stimulate investment has proved to be tax credits for R&D. Second, the growing inadequacy of public support for R&D needs to be addressed by a combination of increased national support in those Member States with below average expenditure and additional R&D investment at EU level provided that it follows the principles for effective expenditure set out below. Together, the national and EU public and private research efforts should combine to make an integrated European research community capable of performing to the highest standards. In essence, this is the objective of the proposed 'European Research Area'. However, this ambition is undermined by some of the structural characteristics of European research, in particular its fragmented character and the difficulty in getting the most out of Europe's undoubted scientific potential both in terms of the production of new knowledge and in terms of turning that knowledge into commercially-viable innovation. When the causes of this unsatisfactory situation are examined, it appears that the current dysfunctional models of research and higher education funding play a major role.

One such model is based on the allocation of funds on the principle of '*juste retour*' (getting out what one has paid in) rather than on the basis of scientific excellence. This leads to the dispersion of funds on a sprinkler principle (a little for everybody) without prioritisation and without proper evaluation. Here the distributional motive of ensuring that funding is evenly spread among institutions and countries is paramount. Another such model is that of centrally directed research programmes operated by public administrations. Here the funding system is subject to a lengthy bureaucratic process starting with programme priorities, followed by specific programmes to implement those priorities, and ending with projects that are considered eligible for financing. This generates detailed profiles of research to be financed and tends to give priority to big projects, which can quickly turn into white elephants. The worst situation arises when elements of both dysfunctional models are combined. Although the situation varies quite widely within Europe, some of these elements can be discerned at both national and EU levels. A more efficient organisation of research evaluation and funding at EU level could act as catalyst for spreading better practice across countries.

11.2.3. *Our recommendations*

European countries are investing too little and inefficiently in higher education and research. We propose that additional EU funding be allocated on the basis of excellence. Both by reorganising its own research policy and by contributing its additional funding, the EU can play an important role in fostering reform of postgraduate education and research systems in Member States. This implies competition for funding, peer review, and *ex post* evaluation by independent and internationally recognised researchers so as to avoid the refinancing of bad projects and the emergence of white elephants. These principles apply to publicly financed research in general, wherever it is undertaken. They also apply to specific programmes that aim to meet an identified public need and *bottom-up* research initiatives emanating from individual researchers or from groups of scholars who wish to create new centres and networks. In the latter case, the EU will both achieve a higher multiplier effect from its funding and help spread best practices. More specifically, *we recommend:*

1. A substantial increase in government and EU spending for research and postgraduate education, but at the same time putting the main emphasis on

excellence when allocating the new additional funds. Some funding should be allocated to attract the best faculty from anywhere in the world, including those who left European institutions for lack of suitable environment. To guarantee that the highest scientific standards are maintained, we recommend that the allocation of research grants be subject to open competition and a peer review process, and that the refinancing of existing projects or centres be decided through *ex post* evaluation by independent and scientifically-renowned researchers.

2. The creation of an independent European Agency for Science and Research (EASR), functioning on the model of the US NSF (but also the Nordic and British research councils), a model which we hope will be emulated by other Member States. The NSF has built up an enviable reputation both for independence and rigour in its appraisal processes based on peer review. The body should display the following features: (*a*) primarily a funding rather than an advisory body; (*b*) follow a bottom–up approach in stimulating proposals for funding; (*c*) cover all fields of science, including the natural sciences and engineering, the humanities and the social sciences, using a flexible approach; (*d*) base its decisions on scientific criteria and have a rigorous and transparent peer review process; (*e*) be accountable to its funders, but autonomous in its operations and run by highly respected scientists. Like the NSF, the EASR should focus on financing bottom-up academic research.

3. Tax credits to encourage private research investments, especially by small start-up firms.

11.3. Improving Economic and Monetary Union's macroeconomic policy framework

11.3.1. *A roadmap for reform*

The assessment of Europe's macroeconomic stability has identified a number of difficulties that need to be tackled to make Economic and Monetary Union (EMU) a lasting success. Three principles should be kept in mind when formulating policy recommendations:

1. *EMU's macroeconomic policy framework is and will have to remain rules-based.* Given the high negotiation costs, it is neither politically realistic nor economically desirable to shift to a system that would require a high degree of discretion. This especially applies to fiscal policies as coordination involves a large number of players. Hence, any new rule should as much as possible foster implicit coordination. The supranational character of EMU's policy rules should be taken into account when designing reform: rules which may be seen as first-best from a purely national standpoint, may be poor third-best in a supranational context where moral hazard problems are more important.

2. *Any new set of rules should not jeopardise the attained level of stability.*
Revisiting the current EU rules to improve upon their growth and cyclical
stabilisation properties should not risk throwing away the hard-earned
gains of monetary and budgetary convergence of the last decade. Both
monetary and fiscal rules—in their design and implementation—need to
ensure a symmetric behaviour over the different phases of the business cycle.
3. *Any reform should aim at making EMU's macroeconomic policy rules fit
for an enlarged Europe.* Reforms will have to make the EMU rules 'robust'
with respect to the Union and euro-area enlargement. Retaining a high level
of simplicity, which was key to the success of Maastricht, while limiting the
negative impact of one-size-fits-all rules, in a context of increasing heterogeneity, will be a challenge with enlargement. The right balance needs to
be found between discipline and flexibility.

These principles have implications for the way the single monetary policy,
national fiscal policies and macroeconomic policy coordination are run in
EMU. EMU's macroeconomic policy rules should enhance cyclical stabilisation while retaining a high degree of stability in an enlarged EU.

11.3.2. *Monetary policy: Ensure symmetry over the business cycle*

The monetary policy strategy adopted by the European Central Bank (ECB)
has succeeded in establishing its anti-inflationary credentials since the beginning of EMU. The definition of the price stability objective is a key element of
this strategy.

As stated in the EU Treaty, the primary objective of the single monetary
policy is to maintain price stability. The ECB has defined its price stability
objective as a year-on-year increase in the HICP for the euro area below 2 per
cent, to be maintained over the medium term.

The definition of price stability initially adopted by the ECB did not convey
enough guidance to markets and to the public, in general, for when the
inflation rate was judged by the ECB to be 'too low for comfort'. This also
probably led to the perception that while the ECB had clearly defined a rea-
sonable 'upper bound' (2 per cent) in its fight against inflation, the implicitly-
defined lower bound (0 per cent) was too low in the fight against deflation.
Consequently, there was a feeling among many observers that the ECB was
asymmetric in its aims in the sense of caring more about fighting inflation than
deflation. This feeling was probably exacerbated by the recent experience of
EMU, where growth has been very low in the euro area since 2001.

Indeed, given the definition of the price stability objective, there was the risk
that, unless the ECB were to aim continuously at being close to the upper end
(2 per cent) the resulting monetary policy stance could eventually become too
tight to accommodate the need for different countries to carry out the

necessary adjustments in relative national price differentials as well as to avoid the risk of any particular country entering into more or less prolonged deflationary periods. These potential problems would furthermore be heightened in light of the future enlargement of the euro area.

One thing which recent international experience makes clear is that central banks should be pre-emptive in fighting both inflation and deflation so that price stability is maintained over the medium run. In addition, it is very important that this symmetric attitude is clearly perceived by the public so that inflationary expectations are stabilised around appropriate levels and potentially economically destabilising situations are avoided.

Symmetry in the behaviour of monetary authorities vis-à-vis their price stability objective has the additional advantage of helping transform potential output gains from structural reforms into actual output growth. A policy that is perceived as being symmetric and forward-looking, and rightly so, can help stimulating structural reform by increasing the present value of corresponding welfare gains.

Conscious of these risks, the ECB carried out a thorough evaluation of its monetary policy strategy. In May 2003, it reached the conclusion that, while there are no solid grounds that could warrant changing the prevailing definition of price stability, there is nevertheless a need to clarify it by providing a clear indication of where, within the confines of the definition, is the single monetary policy aiming at. The message was that monetary policy will aim at an inflation rate close—but still below—2 per cent in the medium term, so as to dispel fears that the aimed rate of inflation could be 'too low for comfort' while also preserving the anti-inflationary reputation earned thus far.

While other formulations also aimed at conveying the idea of symmetry in monetary policy behaviour could have been envisaged, the announcement by the ECB is certainly an important and welcome step in the direction of making clear that symmetry governs the conduct of the single monetary policy, something which was not so clearly perceived so far. This should enhance public awareness that upward and downward risks to price stability are equally fought thus fostering macroeconomic stability in the euro area.

11.3.3. *Fiscal policy: Improve the stabilisation framework and combine short-term flexibility and long-term sustainability*

The basic reason for having fiscal rules in a monetary union concerns the potential spillovers of fiscal policy onto monetary policy. These spillovers have two dimensions. In the *short run*, inadequate fiscal policies would overburden monetary policy thereby leading to an unbalanced policy mix. This risk is particularly high in the event of a pro-cyclical budgetary behaviour in times of economic upturn. In the *long run*, an undisciplined fiscal policy, by leading to an unsustainable accumulation of public debt, would increase the risk of financial instability, create pressures for debt monetisation and threaten the independence of the central bank.

Both short-term and long-term spillovers are of direct concern also for the main goal of this Report, namely reviving economic growth in Europe: an unbalanced polity mix and rising public debt would result in high real interest rates which would stifle investment and growth.

EMU's fiscal rules need to respond to these concerns. Numerous authors have called for reforming the Stability and Growth Pact (SGP). Recent Commission communications and Council conclusions attempt, within the current rules, to rebalance the objectives of stability and growth, and the relative weight of public debt and deficits. Our policy recommendations build on such contributions.

Improve the stabilisation framework
The implementation of EMU's fiscal rules should foster a symmetric budgetary behaviour over the different phases of the business cycle. There are three complementary ways to address the problem of cyclical misbehaviour by fiscal authorities: (*a*) enhance budgetary surveillance to detect early slippage, especially in good times; (*b*) provide the right incentives for good fiscal behaviour; and (*c*) make sure that fiscal rules do not have an inherent pro-cyclical bias.

Early detection of budgetary slippage, especially in good times, is paramount to maintaining fiscal discipline. It requires tight budgetary surveillance. The European Commission should be the authority naturally in charge of fiscal surveillance. Its role should be reinforced and have more visibility. It should encompass the interpretation of the rules within specific guidelines set by the Council, the monitoring of the implementation of the rules, and the power to enforce the rules. In order to pursue these tasks effectively, the resources devoted to fiscal policy surveillance and analysis should be increased.[1] The visibility of the Commission's budgetary surveillance would be enhanced by regular high-level missions to countries, especially to those threatening to breach the agreed fiscal targets.

The effectiveness of a 'disciplinary' approach to restrain government's discretion would be enhanced by providing the right incentives to governments to correct their misbehaviour in good times.

Two options can be considered. An option to foster proper incentives would be to establish 'rainy-day funds' which are used in slowdowns and replenished in upturns. These funds would increase the incentive for governments not to waste budgetary surpluses in good times and increase the room for manoeuvre during slowdowns (see Box 11.1). Setting aside in a fund (part of) the surplus generated by the booming revenues and falling expenditure to be used in bad times would strengthen the hand of the finance minister in resisting pressures

---

[1] On recommendations to enhance rules' enforcement and strengthen national fiscal responsibility, see below.

Box 11.1. *Combining rigour with flexibility: Rainy-day funds*

The figure below sketches out how a system of rainy-day funds could work. Let us assume that the country has initially a balanced budget in structural terms. This implies that the actual deficit is zero when the output gap is closed. In a period of high economic juncture—which leads to a positive output gap—the country moves into surplus, part of which is set aside in a fund (the shaded area, implying that the budget balance develops along the dotted line, instead of the continuous line). These resources could then be used during recessions. In case a cyclical downturn—leading to a negative output gap larger than G′—would push the deficit against the 3 per cent ceiling, the country would withdraw resources from the fund (the shaded area) which would put a cap on the rise in the 'official' deficit so as not to exceed 3 per cent.

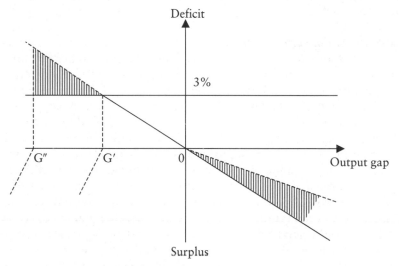

A simple example of how a system of rainy-day funds would work is provided in the following table. Here it is assumed that in year 0, the economy has a zero output gap, a balanced budget and a stock of debt of 60 per cent of GDP. As from year 1, it is assumed that growth accelerates from 2 per cent trend growth to 3.5 per cent, while inflation attains 2.5 per cent every year. If the sensitivity of the budget balance to the cycle is 0.5, under the current rules, the development of the budget balance and the debt is given in the left-hand side of the table. Under the assumption that, in the event of a positive output gap, half of the ensuing surplus is set aside in a fund, the budgetary developments behave as set out in the right-hand side of the table.

Time	Without rainy-day funds		With rainy-day funds		
	Govt budget balance	Debt	Govt budget balance	Debt	Fund
0	0.0	60.0	0.0	60.0	0.0
1	0.8	55.9	0.4	56.2	0.4
2	1.5	51.2	0.8	52.3	1.1
3	2.3	46.0	1.1	48.2	2.3

to give away the automatic fruit of growth. To avoid moral hazard, there should be some rule to ensure that resources are withdrawn from the fund only in the case of protracted slowdowns. A possibility is that the decision to set aside resources is made by the Member State, but that the decision to draw on the fund requires a 'double key', that is, approval of both the Member State and the Council (based on a Commission recommendation).

The creation of such funds is, however, not without cost as it would require a review of the current Common National accounting rules or their inter-pretation in the application of the Excessive Deficit Procedure. Hence, the pros and cons of such proposal need to be carefully considered. It would be clear that such move would be worthwhile only to the extent that a critical number of governments are ready to embrace it.

Another option, which would be conducive to the same end but would not require changing accounting rules, could be to introduce budgetary norms at the national level, which could apply in good years. Such norms would establish that all—or a pre-set percentage of—tax revenues in excess of what would be obtained in a 'normal' growth year should fully contribute towards a higher budget surplus. The drawback of such a norm is that it would rely on a disciplinary approach rather than positive incentives.

The Treaty prescribes that budget deficits should remain below 3 per cent of GDP unless exceptional circumstances arise. Provided that sound structural budgetary positions are maintained, such a ceiling need not be overly con-straining in normal cyclical slowdowns. However, in the event of severe recessions or protracted periods of economic stagnation, respecting such a constraint may imply damaging pro-cyclical policies. This could be avoided by re-defining the 'exceptional conditions' under which a temporary excess over the 3 per cent ceiling is allowed. The Council of the EU has established, as a rule, an excess over the reference value resulting from a severe economic downturn to be 'exceptional' only if there is an annual fall of real GDP of at least 2 per cent. This definition appears overly restrictive. A more sensible definition would characterise a severe economic downturn as simply an annual fall of real GDP.[2] This would imply a change in the text of the SGP legislation.

Combine short-term flexibility and long-term sustainability

It is commonly agreed that the SGP puts an undue weight on budget deficits, largely disregarding longer-term sustainability concerns. The stock of public debt and the implicit liabilities affect the long-run sustainability of public finances. While countries with high debt levels should make it a priority to reduce them fast by maintaining structural budgets close to balance or in

---

[2] There were forty-seven episodes of negative growth in EU countries over the period 1970–2002 (out of almost 500 observations), mainly concentrated around the first oil price shock (1974–1975), the second oil shock (1981–1982), and the recession of the early 1990s. Between 1993 and 2002, no country registered a negative annual growth rate. However in 2003 the Netherlands and Portugal had negative growth.

surplus, countries with low levels of debt could have more flexibility on their budget deficits.

A higher room for manoeuvre could be particularly suitable in the case of the new EU members, most of which have low debt levels. This implies that the structural position of these countries would not be jeopardised if deficits serve to finance their high investment needs. At the same time, it will be crucial for such countries to maintain sound public finances to enhance their credit-worthiness and attract foreign capital.

In line with the spirit of its recent proposals, the Commission in assessing compliance with the close-to-balance requirement of the SGP should take into account the overall debt sustainability of public finances. In particular, while countries should respect the close-to-balance or surplus objective, those with very low levels of public debt—say below 40 per cent of GDP—and contained implicit liabilities could be allowed to have a structural deficit of up to 1.5 per cent of GDP for the time span covered by their Stability or Convergence Programme (see Box 11.2). At the end of that period, the budgetary require-ments would be re-assessed. Implicit liabilities should be estimated on the basis of a commonly agreed method. Corresponding evaluations should be regularly published and become part of the fiscal sustainability assessment of each Member State.

Clearly, countries running a structural deficit of 1.5 per cent of GDP may see their budget deficits frequently exceed the 3 per cent of GDP threshold during periods of cyclical slowdowns. As the Excessive Deficit Procedure would continue to be applied, these countries would formally be in 'excessive deficit'. However, it might be accepted that the timing for the return of the deficit below the 3 per cent threshold might be longer than for the countries with a higher stock of debt. This approach would not require a change in the SGP that states that the excessive deficit must normally be corrected no later than a year following its identification. Indeed, there is the possibility of allowing a longer period for the correction as the Pact states that the above mentioned rule holds 'unless there are special circumstances'. This requires agreement that a very low level of debt qualifies as a 'special circumstance'.

11.3.4. *Make macroeconomic policy coordination more effective*

Macroeconomic policy coordination is envisaged in the Treaty as a key feature of Economic and Monetary Union, yet weaknesses in its current institutional set-up do not favour an effective process of coordination. Our assessment has identified three such weaknesses: (*a*) an inappropriate distribution of respons-ibilities between the Commission and the Council in the enforcement of the fiscal rules; (*b*) weak 'political ownership' of EU's coordination procedures; and (*c*) the coexistence within a single institutional setting of Member States who have adopted the euro and those who have not.

Box 11.2. *Economic and Monetary Union's fiscal rules and enlargement*

Two hierarchical requirements need to be met when designing fiscal rules for catching-up countries: (*a*) fiscal prudence needs to be ensured to enhance credit-worthiness and attract foreign direct investment (FDI); (*b*) the rules should be growth-friendly so as to foster the catching-up process. The first requirement is translated into attaining or maintaining a low level of public debt and relatively low budget deficits. The second condition implies that, provided that condition (*a*) is met, countries should be able to finance their high public investment needs, at least partly, by borrowing.

What follows illustrates quantitatively what these requirements could imply.

1. A low public-debt level could be defined as a stock of debt below 40 per cent of GDP. In 2002, five countries scheduled to join the EU in 2004 satisfied this condition (Czech Republic, Estonia, Latvia, Lithuania and Slovenia).
2. Countries with low public debt and high public investment needs could be allowed to have less strict medium-term budgetary targets. On the basis of the experience of EU countries in the 1960s and 1970s, a sustained net level of public investment of the order of 4 per cent of GDP appears to be required in a phase of catching up. However, EU transfers (cohesion and structural funds) will help finance such investment needs. On the basis of current experience, it is assumed that EU transfers will cover public investment to the order of 2.5 per cent of GDP. Allowing debt financing of the public investment net of EU transfers would imply structural deficits up to 1.5 per cent of GDP.
3. In order to compute the development of the budget deficit in bad times one needs to calculate the cyclical room for manoeuvre. Under the assumption of no discretionary policy, this depends on the sensitivity of the budget to the business cycle and on the volatility of output. Coricelli and Ercolani (2002) estimate an average budgetary sensitivity to the cycle for new EU members of 0.35, compared to 0.5, which is the average of current EU members. The output volatility of new members, however, is considerably higher: the average standard deviation in the 1990s was 4–4.5. In line with the calculations of the so-called 'minimal benchmarks' for the current EU members (Artis and Buti 2000), the cyclical room for manoeuvre can be computed by multiplying the budgetary sensitivity by twice the standard deviation. This gives a room for manoeuvre of about 3 per cent points of GDP. Hence, if the medium-term target were a structural deficit of 1.5 per cent of GDP, the deficit would soar to 4.5 per cent of GDP in bad times.

What do the above calculations imply? If, in an initial phase of catching up, the 'normal' annual nominal GDP growth is of the order of 8 per cent (say 5 per cent real growth and 3 per cent inflation), a structural deficit of 1.5 per cent of GDP implies that a country with a debt of 40 per cent of GDP will see its debt decreasing and converge to below 20 per cent of GDP.

Towards a more appropriate distribution of responsibilities

In the current setting, the Council is entrusted with both policy and surveillance functions, yet its inclination towards political compromise does not allow it to exercise the latter with the required degree of transparency and equity. The Commission has not been given the legal means to perform surveillance in an authoritative way, because its warnings and recommendations have to be endorsed by the Council. Hence, under the current EMU setting, enforcement of the rules risks being partisan: national authorities are supposed to apply the rules to themselves and hence have incentives for collusion and horse-trading.

In order to move to non-partisan enforcement, one has to distinguish between three types of decisions in the implementation of the SGP: (*a*) 'technical' assessments on the compliance with the rules; (*b*) 'political' decisions on how to prevent or correct an excessive deficit, and, in the latter case, at what speed; (*c*) application of sanctions. The Commission should be entrusted with the implementation of decisions, which mainly implies detection of compliance with the rules. It should be entitled not only to deliver Early Warnings, as proposed by the Convention, but also to determine whether an Excessive Deficit exists. The Council should take final responsibility on the other two types of decisions whose political nature is evident. This concerns what measures need to be implemented to prevent or correct a fiscal imbalance. It concerns also the application of sanctions in the event of a persistent excessive deficit. Such decisions clearly require that the Council take full ownership of them.

Enhancing the 'political ownership' of EU policy coordination

Lack of 'political ownership' of EU coordination processes undermines their effectiveness. This concerns even the SGP, in spite of its legally-binding character. In order to increase the Member States' ownership of budgetary policy coordination, two steps could be undertaken: (*a*) align the European coordination process and national budgetary processes, and (*b*) create or strengthen national institutions conducive to budgetary responsibility.

The current budgetary coordination cycle could be rendered more coherent. For the moment, establishing national Stability Programmes is to a large extent a purely national exercise. This does not mean that there is any guarantee that the programmes are based on consistent assumptions or that they take adequate account of the cross-country fiscal-monetary spillovers. In order to remedy this problem, and building on current practice, the Commission would set the external assumptions to be used when preparing national Stability Programmes and propose guidelines for the orientation of national fiscal policies taking into account both national and euro-area conditions. Once the national programmes of the euro-area Member States have been drawn up, they could be consolidated into an aggregate 'European Stability

Programme' which would serve to assess the overall fiscal policy stance within the area and help to determine whether adjustments to national programmes would be desirable.

Such a process would be facilitated by dividing the twelve-month calendar into a 'European semester', in which the priorities for the area as a whole are agreed, and a 'national semester', in which such orientations are factored into domestic policy-making. Furthermore, it would be an advantage in our view if national parliaments were asked to debate annually their countries' positions vis-à-vis the consolidated European Stability Programme before they decide on the national budget. Finally, Member States should commit to inform their partners and the Commission before announcing significant economic policy decisions with a potential impact on the euro area.

While the Commission is and would remain the main authority in charge of budgetary surveillance, strengthening national institutions is important to ensure greater transparency as regards the current and future budgetary situation and the consequences of taxation and spending decisions. Multi-lateral surveillance has a role in it, but transparency is essentially a domestic issue. We suggest establishing independent national Fiscal Auditing Boards (FABs). These boards would have no policy role, but they would be entrusted with the mission of auditing the quality of information on past and current budgetary situations and short-term forecasts and the accuracy of the governments' evaluations of the budgetary consequences of alternative policy options. Specifically, they should provide: (*a*) an independent auditing of budgetary forecasts for the current year; (*b*) an independent evaluation of the budgetary impact of policy decisions; and (*c*) an independent assessment of the implications of different economic assumptions. These assessments would be published. Countries might adopt a statute for the new body compatible with agreed norms that would indicate its goals and powers. In order to ensure effectiveness, FABs should rely on statistical institutes that are independent and have an established track record for the quality of budgetary statistics.

Different formulae are possible, not necessarily involving the creation of new institutions. Bodies that perform a similar role are in certain countries attached to Parliament, but a natural alternative would be to rely on the Court of Auditors. What is important is that those bodies should be independent and yet have access to relevant budgetary information.

Establishing appropriate differentiation among institutions
Currently, there coexist within a single institutional setting two categories of Member States (those which have adopted the euro and those which have not) with substantial differences in the rationale for and the requirements of coordination among them. Institutional differentiation has begun to emerge with the creation of the Eurogroup, but its systemic implications have not been clarified. The all-EU Ecofin Council is still responsible for all formal decisions,

but non-euro Member States do not participate in the vote on euro-only matters, such as exchange rate policy orientations, etc. This was a sensible arrangement as long as derogations were few and they were expected to be limited in time. It would be a source of inefficiency and confusion in a Union where roughly half the Member States will not for some time belong to the euro area.

A way forward would be to entrust a euro-area Council with decisions pertaining to the operation of the euro area. This Council should be made responsible for all policy decisions which are specific to the participants in the euro (e.g. the euro-area Broad Economic Policy Guidelines, macroeconomic policy recommendations to euro-area Member States, and exchange rate policy) and be given the right to amend and adapt rules that currently belong to the remit of the wider Ecofin, but are relevant only for euro-area members. It should obviously not extend beyond this specific domain to compete with the wider Ecofin and the rights of Member States not participating in the common currency should be preserved. In particular, amendments to rules should not lead to making entry more difficult for those currently outside the euro area. To that end, the Commission should, in accordance with its role as guardian of the treaties, be able to refer an issue back to the wider Ecofin if it feels that the euro-area decision might be contrary to the general interest of the EU. Similarly, countries currently outside the euro area should be regularly kept informed of discussion inside the euro-area Council and have the opportunity to ask for issues that may affect them to be discussed within the wider Ecofin.[3]

At the moment, there is no natural forum for exchanging views between the single monetary authority and the fiscal authorities of the countries sharing monetary sovereignty. In spite of its informal setting, the asymmetric composition of the Eurogroup (the ECB President facing currently twelve finance ministers and a Commissioner) does not favour dialogue. The reversed asymmetry is present when the Commissioner or the Council President attends the Governing or the General Council of the ECB. A solution would be that the president of the euro-area Council and the relevant Commissioner hold regular informal meetings with the President of the ECB. The objective of such a dialogue would not be to coordinate *ex ante* monetary and fiscal policies but to have an exchange of views on the assessment of the economic situation and policy challenges.

---

[3] A possible alternative would be that decisions could be adopted by the euro-area Council if they fail to win the necessary votes in the wider Ecofin (a system of this type was used with European Free Trade Association (EFTA) countries before they joined the EU). However, a significant difference here is that issues that would be brought to the euro-area Council would only interest non-euro-area members in their capacity as potential future members. Hence, it makes sense to leave the decision to euro-area members, unless this conflicts with the general interest of the EU.

11.3.5. *Our recommendations*

1. While the 3 per cent of GDP upper limit for deficits and the 'close to balance or in surplus' objective should be kept to steer fiscal discipline, the rules of the SGP should foster a symmetric behaviour of fiscal authorities over the phases of the cycle so as to prevent pro-cyclical policies. Consequently, the recommendations go in the direction of improving the incentives for countries to secure surpluses in good times while increasing the room for manoeuvre for fiscal policies in bad times within a framework of strengthened budgetary surveillance and more effective and flexible implementation of the SGP.

2. To detect slippage promptly, especially in good times, the Commission should reinforce budgetary surveillance, by devoting more resources to monitoring fiscal policies and carrying out regular high-level missions to Member States. Budgetary responsibility would be enhanced by establishing independent national Fiscal Auditing Boards entrusted with the mission of auditing the quality of information on past and current budgetary situations and short-term prospects, and the accuracy of the governments' evaluations of the budgetary consequences of policy measures. These boards should rely on independent statistical institutes to provide them with reliable budgetary statistics.

3. The role of the Commission should be strengthened to make more effective the implementation of the SGP. It should be entitled to deliver directly Early Warnings and determine whether an Excessive Deficit exists. Within specific guidelines set by the Council, it should have the responsibility of interpreting the rules. However, the Council would remain responsible for deciding sanctions.

4. A voluntary system of 'rainy-day' funds could improve the incentives to secure surpluses in good times while increasing the room for manoeuvre for fiscal policies in bad times. The advantages of setting up such funds should be assessed against the costs of revision of national accounting rules.

5. A higher degree of country differentiation should be introduced in the implementation of the SGP. Different levels of total public (explicit and implicit) indebtedness should be taken into account when evaluating national Stability and Convergence Programmes and in formulating recommendations in the case of an Excessive Deficit. Estimates of implicit liabilities should be computed on the basis of a commonly agreed method, regularly updated and published.

6. In order to attain more flexibility in the case of severe cyclical downturns, the 'exceptional conditions' under which an excess over the 3 per cent of GDP deficit threshold is allowed should be defined as simply a negative annual growth rate, rather than −2 per cent.

7. To increase the Member States' ownership of EU policy coordination, a closer alignment of the EU coordination process with national budgeting processes is needed. This would be facilitated by dividing the twelve-month calendar into a 'European semester', in which the common orientations are agreed, and a 'national semester', in which such orientations are factored into domestic policy-making. This would ensure that separate national fiscal policies add up to a consistent fiscal stance for the euro area as a whole.
8. A euro-area Council should be entrusted with all non-monetary policy decisions pertaining to the operation of the euro area and be given the right to adapt rules that are relevant only for euro-area members, while preserving the rights of Member States not participating in the single currency. The dialogue between the euro-area Council and the ECB needs to be upgraded via regular informal meetings between the president of the euro-area Council, the relevant Commissioner and the President of the ECB.

11.4. Convergence and restructuring in an enlarged European Union

Enlargement will mean an EU with much wider income disparities and, at least initially, it would leave practically unchanged the income disparities within EU countries. From an economic governance standpoint, policies for reducing the latter are traditionally in the remit of national authorities, while policies for reducing the former are traditionally in the remit of the EU. As a consequence, enlargement will pose a very great challenge to EU economic governance and it should force policy-makers to rethink their policies and instruments for achieving economic convergence.

Furthermore, deeper and wider economic integration together with innovation, technical change and globalisation will imply threats of job losses and an acceleration of economic restructuring. While it is clear that accelerating the pace of economic change in the EU is absolutely needed and that it will be welfare-enhancing, it is also clear that, at least in the short run, there will be losers in this process. Given that the causes for accelerating restructuring are more European (if not global) than national, and although the primary responsibility for alleviating the pain of job losses rests with the Member States themselves, there will be pressures at the EU level to smooth the consequences of restructuring.

The design and the implementation of the current EU cohesion policy are insufficiently focused. The largest part of the current EU cohesion policy focuses on regions (Structural Funds) and only a minor part focuses on countries (the Cohesion Fund). At present, all EU countries receive money under this policy and all countries, with the exception of Luxembourg and Denmark (the richest Member States) have at least one region labelled as 'low-income'. This is the result of the predominant regional focus of current EU cohesion policy and of the fact that its negotiations are driven by judgements about the net budgetary balances of Member States. Net-balance considerations find fertile ground in the current EU cohesion policy because the Council needs unanimity to agree on this policy, which gives to each and every government a significant bargaining power. National political constraints mean that each government worries more about being able to flag a negotiation success (i.e. obtaining a significant share of EU money to be spent in its own territory) than about being sure that money is spent on worthwhile projects, let alone those fostering convergence in the EU as a whole.

Indeed, not only does the current EU cohesion policy cover virtually all countries, but it can also finance a very wide and dispersed set of activities, without necessarily prioritising those investments with the greatest impact on growth. This unfocused policy design hampers the aim of fostering growth and economic development in the EU and it must be discontinued. Although some improvement has taken place in recent years, a quantum leap towards greater focusing of the use of money and the choice of beneficiaries is now certainly warranted.

The proposed new structure would represent a significant change from the current EU cohesion policy. Two new EU policies for achieving convergence and facilitating restructuring in the EU could be organised along the following lines.

11.4.1. *Convergence policy*

Reducing income disparities among Member States will be a matter of absolute urgency and priority in the enlarged EU. EU convergence policy cannot be a significant factor behind the needed economic convergence among members, if dispersed to small regions in different countries to care for different needs. Convergence policy can become an efficient tool of economic convergence only when accompanied by a set of financial and non-financial elements (labour market situation, investment opportunities, business climate, etc.), which are the result of national policies. Furthermore, several arguments, such as subsidiarity, coherence with national macroeconomic policy, equal treatment of equally prosperous countries, militate in favour of a country focus for the EU convergence policy. There is a solid argument for the new EU convergence policy to focus on countries, rather than on regions, using national GDP per capita (measured in Purchasing Power Parity) as an eligibility criterion. However, individual countries may decide to delegate implementation and monitoring of this policy to their regions.

It is obviously possible that, during the catching-up process, increasing regional disparities within the poorer countries may also emerge. However, this phenomenon may be mitigated by national growth and could be eased by national rather than EU policies (such as social transfer schemes, labour market and wage policy, etc). These national policies fall into the domain of the Member States but, to the extent that they concern the Common Market, they must be compatible with EU rules. In particular, regional policies involving subsidies to private or public companies that violate the rules against state aid would be inadmissible. Member State autonomy over regional policies should in no way provide a base for re-nationalising state aid policy. More generally, policies designed for mitigating regional disparities within Member States must not violate EU competition rules.

In addition to focusing EU convergence policy on countries, there is also a need for greater focus in the purposes of EU convergence policy. This policy should aim at reaching two purposes deeply related to the ultimate aim of fostering growth in a cohesive enlarged EU: one purpose should be institution-building, that is to help low-income countries to have a good and stable administrative capacity; and the other should be sustaining high investment rates in human and physical capital.

Priority to institution building

The experience of the new members during their period of economic transition from a command to a market economy and of the current EU countries during the last fifteen years shows that the quality of the institutions is a key pre-condition for growth in low-income countries. *A fortiori*, good and stable institutions are also a key precondition for a country to integrate into the EU economic system and to reap the benefits of the Single Market. Indeed, in order to be able to implement any policy, in order to attract investment, in order to build an environment conducive to business, a country needs a well-functioning legal and administrative system. Building legal and administrative capacity should therefore be considered as top priority in any convergence strategy across the EU.

These reasons provide grounds for earmarking part of the convergence money for institution-building. However, earmarking EU money, even for a top priority across a large group of countries, makes sense only if the EU level can effectively assess the needs and monitor progress in any country. Currently, as far as administrative capacity in the new Member States is concerned, the pre-accession negotiations have provided a useful toolbox to establish the legal and administrative needs and to monitor individual countries' progress and reforms. Financial resources have already been devoted to improving administrative capacity in the new Member States and several twinning programmes (between a current and a new member) have been launched to facilitate their taking 'ownership' progressively of these reforms.

It is appropriate to earmark part of the EU convergence fund to the purpose of improving administrative capacity, building on the expertise already acquired in assessing needs and monitoring progress. Receiving EU money for any other purpose could be made partly conditional on verified progress in improving administrative capacity.

Investment in human and physical capital

Growth enhancement is the main concern of this Report both in the enlarged EU and, *a fortiori*, in countries that lag behind. In particular, in these countries two types of capital expenditure are likely to have the greatest impact on growth: human capital investment (R&D, education, and training) and physical capital investment (infrastructure). The EU convergence fund should act as a catalyst for both types of capital expenditure so as to sustain high investment rates without crowding out domestic investment.

However, it is not imaginable that the EU level has the ability to decide which projects to support in the different EU countries. Therefore, the part of the convergence funds intended for investment in human and physical capital should be first pre-allocated to eligible countries, and then each country should be left free to decide how to allocate them across different projects of human and physical capital investment. In other words, no particular conditions (beyond the operational principles detailed below) should be attached to the use of EU money aimed at increasing growth in the low-income countries.

Operational principles

The main principles underlying the current EU cohesion policy (multi-annual programming of the expenditure; national co-financing of the EU money; and additionality of the EU money with respect to national money) were and still are sound. They have increased the political acceptability of the whole project by reassuring net contributors of the use of their money. They have avoided crowding out domestic investment by EU money. They have enabled the development of a set of coherent multi-annual programmes (the so-called Community Support Framework) which has proved useful in shielding investment expenditure from the economic cycle.

These elements—political acceptability, no crowding-out of domestic investment, and long-term investment plan—are likely to be even more important in the future enlarged-EU with a much greater number of low-income countries. It would be wise, therefore, to preserve their spirit and their logic.

However, the key principle of conditionality should be strengthened. Governments would be left free to choose the investment project to be financed by the EU convergence fund, but should declare *ex ante* the expected results of this investment project. The disbursement of a significant part of the money of the EU convergence fund could be made dependent upon reaching expected results. To evaluate results, one should follow an 'output' logic (e.g. having an additional Y per cent of schools linked to the internet, or having an additional Z per cent of public employees able to speak a foreign language) rather than an 'input' logic (having spent X million euros).

A country's eligibility for the EU convergence fund should be re-assessed at the end of each programming period. A country should be declared eligible for

the renewal of the EU convergence fund only if it meets the income requirement and has met the conditionality criterion on the use of previously allocated money.

11.4.2. *Restructuring policy*

Restructuring policy aimed at facilitating the process of resource reallocation
should cover, with no restrictions, all affected persons regardless of their
country of residence or their sector of activities. Indeed, resource reallocation
impacts on persons in different geographic locations and in different sectors of
activities. Eligibility for the restructuring fund should be limited in time with
the possibility for renewal.

This policy should cover the needs arising both in the industry and service
sectors and in agriculture.

Displaced workers in industry and services

Each year, several hundred thousand workers are laid off because of plant
closure or industrial restructuring. This happens as a consequence of technological change, intra-EU competition in the product markets, and—more
widely—globalisation. While they only represent a fraction of annual entries
into unemployment figures, those layoffs generally imply significant welfare
losses for those concerned. Research has shown that, although laid-off
workers generally do find a new job after several quarters, there is a cost in
terms of the present value of cumulated income losses. Furthermore, they
frequently need to go through a retraining process and/or to move to other
locations. In some instances, especially when large plant closures take place in
small cities or isolated regions, workers suffer additional costs arising from a
drop in the value of their real estate assets.

Our recommendations on the Single Market advocate more entry and
exit in the product market and more innovation and technical change and
acknowledge the impact of globalisation. This may imply further threats to job
security and an acceleration of restructuring. While we are adamant that
accelerating the pace of industrial change in the EU is absolutely needed and
that it will be welfare-enhancing, we fully recognise that there are losers in this
process and that they may have motives for opposing further integration and
competition, technical change, and globalisation.

The primary responsibility for alleviating the pain of job losses rests
with the Member States themselves. Adequate unemployment insurance,
effective retraining schemes, and active placement policies are among the key
ingredients that can help making restructuring less painful. More generally,
Member States should move from traditional employment protection to an
approach that puts emphasis on fostering transitions between jobs and on
supporting the individuals' employability and mobility. This requires resources
to increase the effectiveness of placement, on-the-job training, and retraining.

Comparison and benchmarking across Member States can be of significant help to assess what are the most effective ways of supporting unemployed persons. But there is a case for a more direct EU involvement in assisting displaced workers that would complement and not replace existing Member State schemes. To the extent that EU policies contribute to increasing job security, they could also contribute to alleviating the pain generated, inter alia, by wider and deeper EU integration. This could also help to gather support for the changes that the present Report is advocating. Thus, it is opportune to allocate part of the EU restructuring fund to a direct assistance scheme for displaced workers. This scheme could work as follows:

1. Workers in the EU losing their jobs as a consequence of a collective lay-off would receive through the local employment agency, a voucher worth six months of the minimum wage in their country of residence.
2. The voucher could be used for three purposes only: (*a*) retraining; (*b*) compensation for relocation costs; and (*c*) setting-up a new business.
3. Each Member State would designate an agency (presumably the employment agency) that would be made responsible for distributing the vouchers and assessing if workers are entitled to convert them into real support. The Commission would monitor those agencies.

Agricultural sector
The EU restructuring fund could also support a scheme destined for farmers and allowing beneficiaries to restructure both inside and outside the agricultural sector. Restructuring inside the sector would, namely, mean supporting investment in knowledge and equipment to increase agriculture sustainability, and favouring environmentally friendly and high-quality production methods rather than intensive farming with standard production methods.

Restructuring outside the agricultural sector would follow similar lines to the voucher scheme proposed for industry and services. This scheme should make it easier for farmers to move to other sectors, by helping them to meet the costs of: (*a*) retraining, (*b*) relocation, and/or (*c*) setting up a new business.

11.4.3. *Our recommendations*

1. The EU convergence policy should focus on low-income countries rather than low-income regions. The EU convergence fund should be allocated to a country on the basis of its GDP per capita level. The principles and the logic of multi-annual programming, additionality and co-financing should be retained. The principle of conditionality should be systematically strengthened.
2. A country's eligibility for the EU convergence fund should be re-assessed at the end of each programming period. A country should be declared eligible

for renewal only if it meets the income requirement and has met the conditionality criterion on the use of previously allocated money.

3. The EU convergence fund allocated to low-income countries should be used for two purposes:

    (i) Priority should be given to improving the administrative capacity of Member States. Part of the EU convergence fund should be earmarked for this use and cannot be used otherwise. Receiving EU money for any other purpose could be made partly conditional on verified progress in improving administrative capacity.

    (ii) Investment in human and physical capital. Each Member State should be left free to decide how to allocate across different national projects the part of the EU convergence fund aimed at sustaining high investment rates.

4. A restructuring policy for displaced workers in the industry and the service sector should be set up at the EU level to complement national policies. The EU policy should help displaced workers to re-enter the labour market via retraining, geographic relocation and/or assistance to set up a new firm.

5. Part of the restructuring policy should specifically cover the agricultural sector.

12

Modes of delivery: Governance methods and the budget

12.1. Achieving effectiveness in the governance of the European Union

Economic governance has developed incrementally in the European Union (EU) as new tasks have been built on the original foundations. The result is a mix of methods and approaches, combining some great strengths and some evident strains. The founders of the European Community put in place the initial institutional set-up that has demonstrated enough robustness to absorb a growing number of tasks. Nevertheless, our view is that the time has come to clarify and to reform economic governance. To this end, we address seven major issues and make proposals, designed to make economic governance more effective.

12.1.1. *Competence assignment*

A clear and appropriate assignment of responsibilities is crucial for the quality of EU governance. However, the current assignment of competences and the procedures for modifying it suffer from several shortcomings. First, there is a degree of confusion as to the responsibilities and roles of the EU vis-à-vis those of the Member States in the various fields in which it is active. Second, procedures for modifying the assignment of competences are not satisfactory for an EU of 25, since unanimity may become an excessively demanding rule for assigning new competences to the EU in domains in which the legitimacy of its involvement has already been recognised. Third, insistence on the inheritance of the *acquis communautaire*, introduced to protect integration from the consequences of enlargement, risks creating rigidities that impede devolution, and responsiveness to changing economic circumstances or differences of needs across the Member States.

The EU thus needs a more precise assignment of policy responsibilities and better procedures for deciding on how this should be done. The answer does not lie in cataloguing competences and enshrining them once and for all in a constitutional treaty. Decisions on the appropriate assignment depends on a trade-off between, on the one hand, the intensity of externalities and economies of scale, and, on the other hand, the degree of heterogeneity of preferences and needs; these evolve over time and depend on the intensity and impacts of economic integration. Rather, the aim should be to seek:

1. *A conceptually neater categorisation of the respective roles of the EU and the Member States.* Depending on the field, the EU acts as a rule-maker, a policy-maker, a regulator, a supervisor, or a facilitator. However, those roles are not precisely defined and this confusion is detrimental to accountability. We would prefer to define a limited number of homogeneous categories as regards the role played by the Union's institutions. The underlying concepts should be uniform, thus the same term (e.g. coordination) should have a similar meaning across sectors. A given policy domain should as far as possible be assigned to only one category.
2. *Precisely defined criteria and procedures for moving a competence up to the EU or down to the Member States.* Instead of the irreversibility created by the *acquis communautaire*, it should be possible for the EU to devolve a competence or task back to member governments or sub-national entities. The spirit of the *acquis* could be preserved by requiring a stronger supermajority for devolution than for centralisation. In both cases it is important to carry a persuasive consensus behind changes to the assignment of competence.
3. *A rearrangement of some existing competences.* The current messy allocation of responsibilities between the EU and the Member States contributes to complexity and may impede accountability. It would be desirable that the EU should not take on new responsibilities without being handed over corresponding policy instruments, either for carrying out policy or for effectively coordinating the policies of the Member States. This may call either for giving the EU the means to reach the goals assigned to it or for reducing the number of objectives it has been assigned.

12.1.2. *Devolution to autonomous bodies*

The Commission at present combines executive and quasi-judicial roles and has accumulated policy design, management, and enforcement functions. We advocate a clearer separation of roles through the creation of autonomous bodies for incentive-funding and for regulation. This would be consistent with developments that have taken place in many countries in Europe and elsewhere and would contribute to making governance more effective.

We see two main cases for delegating functions to autonomous bodies: first, the delivery of specific funding mechanisms could be delegated to separate organisations; and, second, regulatory functions could be delegated to independent authorities.

We have argued that the EU budget should be redirected towards growth-enhancing programmes and we have put particular emphasis on innovation. This requires that the corresponding programmes be managed in a highly professional way in interaction with the relevant communities. We have also called for ending the confusion between the allocative and distributive functions of the EU budget and argued that a significant part of that budget should be devoted to the financing of appropriate projects on the basis of quality criteria alone, that is, without deciding on an *ex ante* distribution of funds among Member States.

This has institutional consequences because the Commission is not well equipped to carry out such tasks. First, it would risk being overburdened by the micro-management of a series of specialised programmes. Second, the principle of separating allocative decisions from distributive ones is very difficult to implement for an institution that has to look in both directions.

We thus suggest hiving off the management of some specific funding mechanisms to independent European organisations. These would be given specific mandates and receive policy guidelines within that framework, but they would be fully independent and accountable as regards the implementation of their mandate. For example, the European Agency for Science and Research (EASR) would have in its mandate that funds must be allocated on the basis of quality criteria alone, on the basis of competitive processes and subject to peer review. It would still receive guidelines from the EU as regards sectoral or other priorities but would be responsible for implementation. It would be accountable to the Council and the Parliament on the execution of its mandate and the implementation of its guidelines.

As for implementing the regulation of the Single Market, we consider that the classical argument for independent authorities has full relevance at the EU level. The exact scope for independent regulatory authorities is a matter for discussion. Our view is that the EU can learn from successful experiences in the Member States and elsewhere, where independent regulatory authorities are increasingly seen as the best practice route to achieving rigorous and systematic results.

The enforcement of EU competition policy is the clearest example of a regulatory function that could be assigned to an independent European authority. We consider that responsibilities for traditional competition policy (prosecution of cartels and abuses of dominant positions as well as merger control)[1] could be allocated to an independent competition authority. Moreover, such an authority needs to be able to speak to, and operate in consistent fashion with, the counterpart authorities in the Member States. On the other

---

[1] The same logic might apply to anti-dumping.

hand, the Commission should retain responsibility for policy concerning state aids as well as the applicability of competition rules for enterprises providing services of general interest, because the application of EU rules in these matters requires assessments of political concerns of Member States that transcend the mere application of competition rules. To the extent that decisions concerning state aids or services of general interest rely on competition policy assessments, the competition authority should be involved in the deliberations.

More generally, we believe that there is a strong case for delegating regulatory powers to independent authorities when decisions:

(1) require specific technical expertise and frequent consultations with professional communities;
(2) must be made on the basis of a narrowly defined mandate without interference from other policy objectives (this especially applies to safety); or
(3) directly affect private interests (i.e. especially relevant when regulation involves attributing rights to private interests through auctions or other procedures—for example, frequency allocation in the telecoms business).[2]

Such independent regulatory authorities should have their mandates precisely defined and could receive non-binding guidelines. They should be fully accountable to Council and Parliament and be subject to periodic evaluation. In order to preserve continuity with the current regime, a fall-back provision could be introduced allowing the Commission, subject to careful specification, formally to override their decisions. Decisions on individual cases, in particular cases affecting private interests, should be subject to full court review, as in the current competition policy regime.

In making these two proposals we recognise that we are taking issue with some of the prevailing practices and doctrines within the EU as regards the scope for delegation and for the creation of 'agencies' with autonomous responsibilities. The discussions reflected in the Commission's White Paper on Governance of 2001 and in the jurisprudence of the European Court of Justice via the so-called Meroni doctrine have suggested that the scope for delegation is limited under the current treaty rules, which seem to rule out the granting of 'decision-making powers' to 'agencies'. Our reasoning, however, comes partly from valid precedents in individual countries and also from the successes of the European Investment Bank and the European Central Bank (ECB) as independent and function-specific bodies carrying out collective tasks on behalf of the Union as a whole. Hence, we would suggest that appropriate legal bases should be devised for the two kinds of independent bodies that we recommend above and that these should be put forward to the forthcoming Intergovernmental Conference on treaty reform.

---

[2] Another traditional motive is to protect the decision from political interference.

12.1.3. *Decentralised arrangements for market regulation*

In the preceding section, we have made the case for assigning certain tasks to autonomous bodies. This would not affect the degree of policy centralisation, only the division of tasks between the Commission and other bodies. A separate (but related) issue is that of an efficient approach to decentralised implementation of regulatory policies.

What the appropriate level is for market regulation in the EU depends on the degree of market integration, the size, and diversity of the Union, and the nature of the economic activity concerned. Increased market integration generally calls for centralisation while increased size and diversity call for decentralisation. In addition, some market regulation functions require not merely the consistent application of agreed rules but also a continuous adjudication and allocation, for example, in managing utilities and access to services, or a responsiveness to rapidly changing market processes, as in the case of financial services.

As developed in Chapter 6, the EU has not yet converged on a general model for adapting to these transformations, yet responses have emerged in various sectors such as central banking, competition, financial supervision, and the regulation of public utilities. We regard this approach as a positive development because we find significant benefit in involving national bodies in applying it and incorporating European reference points in their day-to-day contacts with, and surveillance of, economic agents. This should help to improve the quality of decisions, while at the same time increasing 'ownership' by national players and thereby the legitimacy of decisions. Furthermore, devolving tasks to specialised bodies and moving towards decentralisation can be regarded in many respects as complementary developments.

However, great care should be taken to preserve equality vis-à-vis the application of EU law and to avoid legal uncertainty. As explained in Chapter 6 in the context of competition policy, ensuring consistency of decisions across jurisdictions is especially important when cases involve cross-border externalities. Decentralisation could easily create legal uncertainty and give rise to confusing litigation.

A distinction should be made between:

1. *Steered networks* of national and EU bodies operating within the same legal framework to carry out a policy responsibility assigned to the EU. In this case, the ultimate responsibility rests with the EU institution to which national institutions are hierarchically related through codified procedures. Decentralisation is adopted because it is a more efficient way to implement a common policy. This may especially apply to the competition authorities.
2. *Partnerships* of national bodies that cooperate with each other and with EU bodies in a given policy domain but retain ultimate responsibility for policy implementation. This mode of decentralisation is preferred when the degree

of market integration is less intense, when there is a need to adapt to varying conditions and when the risks of conflicting decisions are limited. This may, for example, apply to the regulation of utility sectors and of financial services.

The network and partnership approaches should not be seen as mutually exclusive. One can think of hybrid arrangements where national bodies are independent and subject to obligations to the system as represented by the Commission and the other regulators, which ensure coherence of regulation across Member States of the European Union as well as adherence of each member to the principles of the Single Market. An example of such a hybrid arrangement is provided by the newly-introduced regulatory framework for telecommunications where all current cases are handled by national regulators acting under national laws, but certain decisions of principle have to be coordinated with the Commission and the other regulators. If such a hybrid form is used, it is important to have clear rules about the assignment of competences. Within a network or partnership, obligations of national regulators towards the system should be strict enough that any attempts to foreclose national markets can be easily prevented by the Commission and the other national regulators. At the same time, they should be loose enough to avoid giving the Commission and the other national regulators room for undermining autonomy in the day-to-day handling of individual cases. Clear rules will serve to reduce the detrimental effects of legal uncertainty as a barrier to competitive activity.

12.1.4. *Management of the Single Market*

Enlargement will make the Single Market programme much more complex to administer. First, the jump in numbers to twenty-five members brings with it an increasing administrative burden for the Commission in tracking transposition and potential infractions. Second, many of the new members have underdeveloped administrative and judicial resources to deal with implementation.[3] In addition, the nature of the Single Market evolves over time. Initially, the thrust was to interconnect previously separate national markets. However, firms operating on the Single Market create their own dynamic so that in certain sectors there are now a number of truly Trans-European firms operating. Furthermore, integration within the Single Market more and more concerns network industries and other sectors that are subject to specific regulation. Who should regulate these sectors and how, are questions that can no longer be avoided.

The European Commission's executive responsibilities cover policy development and verification of implementation, as well as other roles such as guardian of the treaties, but leave implementation itself largely up to the

---

[3] This aspect is developed in the recommendations on convergence and restructuring.

administrations of Member States. Now that the Single Market has been functioning for some time, a certain number of drawbacks to the present division of responsibilities are becoming clearer, which point to the need for a redefinition of responsibilities. In these cases, the governing principle would not so much be a centralisation of power in the Commission but delegation by both the Commission and Member States to specialised autonomous bodies operating with differing degrees of centralisation, as already argued.

Other areas of the Single Market require an undeniably high standard of safety in order for the good or service to be marketed at all. For instance, medicines and food, or transport safety fall into this category. Where safety standards cannot be guaranteed at the requisite level, the unity of the Single Market is inevitably undermined. In the past, problems related to food safety, inter alia with regard to BSE (mad cow disease), have indeed undermined the effective functioning of the Single Market. While it is always possible that, say because of taste differences, accepted safety standards in different countries diverge, an EU system, which opens markets for goods and services from all Member States without giving consumers a possibility to discriminate between states of origin, should also take regulatory action to achieve minimum standards of consumer protection across the EU.

At the present time, agencies to carry out risk *assessment* at EU level have been created in the areas of medicines and food. However, risk *management* remains in the hands of the Commission and Member States. As a result, there is a delay in taking decisions and greater probability of the process becoming embroiled in political considerations unrelated to safety. Regulation in these areas will have a chance of being more effective if risk management and risk assessment can be combined under the same authority. Medicines and food are the leading contenders for this type of approach, together with other areas such as the safety aspects of transport.

Effective operation of the Single Market implies that abuses and non-application are subject to the requisite sanctions. Faced with more Member States, the current infringement procedures are likely to prove less able to deal with problems of implementation. Possible solutions would be either to allow the Commission to decide itself on infringements,[4] subject to the requisite judicial review, or to involve more chambers of the European Court of Justice in handling infringement cases.

12.1.5. *Effective methods for achieving the Union's economic and social objectives*

As developed in previous chapters of this Report, 'Lisbon' has become a catchword for an objective, a strategy, and a method.

---

[4] Rather than requiring a case to go before the European Court of Justice.

We fully endorse the objectives set out at the Lisbon European Council in March 2000. Indeed, this Report has repeatedly stressed that priority should be given to growth, employment, and social cohesion.

We agree with the strategy, which emphasises the completion of the internal market, the promotion of innovation and knowledge, and the modernisation of the European social model. Our policy proposals essentially aim at detailing some of its components or at complementing them as regards the role of macroeconomic stabilisation and the implications of enlargement. We also see merit in coordinating the corresponding reform efforts, because their short-term impact is stronger in an environment where monetary policy is able to reap the benefits of better functioning markets. The immediate benefit from reforms is larger when they are undertaken simultaneously in individual EU countries and for that reason, we support coordinating their timing in the different Member States.

However, we doubt that relying on the 'Open Method of Coordination (OMC)' alone, that is, by issuing guidelines, agreeing benchmarks, and comparing performance, would be sufficient to implement the strategy and reach the objectives. It is clear from experience so far that the outcome will continue to depend on what can be achieved within individual countries and for that reason, implementation of the Lisbon Strategy must rely on the joint efforts of the Union and the Member States. To claim that soft coordination will suffice to reach the objectives partly implies that obstacles on the way are minor ones, when the reality is that a very great deal needs to be done in the Member States and by all concerned. We stress that the gap between objectives and means must be bridged for the EU to fulfil its commitments and for the real returns to be achieved for the European economy.

Time is short because the commitment to growth and full employment has already lost credibility since the 2000 European Council, as neither the performance nor the efforts have matched what should have taken place. We therefore propose:

1. *To focus the scope of the OMC and to strengthen its implementation.* We consider that there are potential benefits to be drawn from this method provided it is not considered a convenient substitute for traditional Community methods but rather a technique specifically designed for areas in which the EU plays only a supporting role, such as labour markets, taxation and welfare, education, innovation and R&D. Furthermore, forms of coordination should be developed only where they can bring clearly identified benefits.[5] In these areas, we support the goals recently set out by the

---

[5] Alongside this we endorse the value of promoting in parallel cross-country comparisons and benchmarking as a form of recurrent dialogue over time in order to stimulate new thinking, exchanges of experience, and the promotion of best practices—but here dialogue should be the objective rather than coordination.

Union: focus on a limited set of objectives; adopt streamlined, more stable, and outcome-oriented guidelines; improve monitoring and Commission assessment; publish 'league tables' and rankings to put pressure on worst-performing Member States. Among all these goals, we especially emphasise the quality of assessment, because the very value of cross-country comparison hinges on the ability to identify best-performing and worst-performing institutions and policies.

2. *To rely more on incentive-based methods and on delegation.* While the OMC is a natural approach when policy responsibility rests with Member States and spillovers are limited, more effective methods can be used in fields where there is a rationale for stronger EU involvement. For research and higher education, we have suggested complementing the Member States' efforts with incentive EU financing, targeted at the promotion of world-class research and graduate education. We also see a case for direct EU responsibility in creating conditions for effective labour mobility across the EU, through the traditional instruments of the Community method.

3. *To develop incentives for Member States to direct budgetary priorities towards growth-enhancing spending categories.* Meeting the Lisbon objectives requires Member States to spend more on (higher) education, research, and innovation. In the medium run, this additional spending should mainly be financed through spending redeployment (and possibly additional taxes). But redeployment takes time, while this investment should be as much as possible front-loaded for the EU to see results before 2010. At the same time, the coming years are bound to be dominated by budgetary adjustment in a number of countries in order to meet the 'close to balance' target by 2006. This could have the unfortunate consequence of delaying investment in knowledge and productivity. The EU thus faces a conflict of objectives.

We do not support the proposals that have been made to introduce some form of golden rule into the Stability and Growth Pact (SGP) and to make the judgement on excessive deficits dependent on the nature of public expenditures. The purpose of the Pact is to ensure the sustainability of public finance and this objective should not be mixed up with others. However, we recognise that there is a conflict of objectives for the coming years. We would thus find merit in offering member countries incentives to give priority to growth-enhancing spending items and in taking into account *additional* public spending on education, research, and innovation in the evaluation of efforts made towards reaching a 'close to balance' position. This is particularly important for countries which do not yet satisfy the 'close to balance' requirement of the SGP and must therefore reduce their structural budget deficit in the coming years. For these countries, we thus suggest that *during the next five years*, supplementary spending on growth-enhancing categories be taken into account in the planned reduction of the structural budget deficit.

12.1.6. *Institutions*

There is a tension in the economic governance of the EU between, on the one hand, the need to set and to review strategic policy goals and priorities, and, on the other hand, the need to deliver agreed policies, their rules and mechanisms, as effectively as possible. As we have argued above, many of the latter tasks can be better delivered by well-adapted and function-specific bodies, sometimes by a Trans-European body dealing with relevant tasks across the whole of the Union, and sometimes by networks (or partnerships) and coordination among relevant national bodies.

A crucial reason for our recommendations for decentralisation and devolution is that we firmly believe that energies need to be released so that the strategic policy capabilities of the Union can be enhanced. There is an over-arching importance for moving forward the agenda for growth in the European economy and for harnessing the best endeavours of policy-makers from across the Union in this direction. To achieve a more effective grasp of strategic policy requires action on three fronts: in the Commission, in the Council, and in the Member States. Our particular concerns are with those areas of macroeconomic and microeconomic policies, and the socio-economic policies, which are so important for achieving sustained structural reforms, and for promoting innovation.

As regards *the Commission*, we have three main proposals:

1. The Commission should pull together its strategic resources for addressing the growth issues. The Lisbon Strategy has a much greater chance of succeeding if there is a leading Commissioner with a clear mandate for taking forward the agenda of the Competitiveness Council and the spring meetings of the European Council, and for anchoring processes of benchmarking, targeting, and coordination with partners from the member countries.
2. The implication of our recommendations on decentralisation and devolution is that a leaner Commission would be better adapted to the strategic tasks, which we see as its primary purposes. The logic would be a Commission of, say, fifteen members, with well-focused portfolios, able to provide both a steering capacity for the independent bodies we have in mind, and a effective stimulus to the Member States.
3. The staffing of the Commission services needs to be reinforced to provide absolutely first class expertise in all core policy areas that we have discussed in this Report, as well as a deep understanding of the situations in each of the Member States, especially in the light of enlargement. This implies enabling the Commission to hire experienced professionals instead of assessing abilities and skills on the basis of a uniform recruitment procedure. We also suggest creating a small Council of Economic Advisers to the President of the Commission, which would participate in policy planning and evaluation inside the Commission.

As regards the *Council and the European Council*, it is vital that these two organs drive forward the growth agenda. Together, they provide the interface between the Union's policies and national policies, and have to deliver the impulses both to underpin Union-wide rules and policies, and to keep up the pressures for domestic reforms in the Member States. Already the Council, through Ecofin, has made a good deal of progress in providing direction to the macroeconomic stabilisation agenda.[6] But the Council and European Council have so far been less successful and less consistent in pulling together the microeconomic and socio-economic reform agenda. Thus,

1. The spring European Council must hold to its task of strategic overview and not degenerate into a limp ritual.
2. The newly formed Competitiveness Council [unfortunately overlooked by the Convention on the future of Europe] must be given a chance to develop a sense of momentum, both to develop corollary Union measures where these are appropriate and to act as a bridge to more effective governance in the Member States.
3. Beneath the level of ministers, the relevant high-level groupings of officials from the Member States and the Commission need to develop cohesion and momentum in the evaluation of policy options and the preparation of decisions comparable to what has been achieved for macroeconomic policy.[7] We see a role here for a strengthened Economic Policy Committee.

As regards the *Member States*, it is vital that in each of these the focus on growth be made much sharper. This is a tricky subject since governmental organisation varies a good deal among EU countries and there is no single template that is likely to work in each of them. Nonetheless progress with the reform agenda is likely to be sticky unless and until domestic energies can be better harnessed to support both domestic reform and the Union's core economic goals. The logic of our argument in favour of a sharper focus on the growth agenda in the Commission and the Council, and an enhanced role for the Competitiveness Council implies that this focus should also be developed in the Member States so that governments take ownership of what they have to deliver in order to enhance their own economic prospects. This requires that each government assigns clearer responsibilities to, and coordinates among, its own ministers for playing their parts in the Competitiveness Council and delivering the growth agenda.

Our discussion here addresses in particular the need for more effective governance as regards strategic policy choices and hence stresses the roles of the Commission, the Council and the European Council. In addition and very

---

[6] We have made further comments on how this direction might be made more effective in Section 11.3.

[7] A relevant example is the Economic and Financial Committee, which prepares all Ecofin decisions.

importantly, our emphasis on budgetary restructuring and more effective policy delivery has considerable implications for the European Parliament and the European Courts.

It is vital that the new autonomous bodies that we propose both for operating funding for growth and for implementing regulation should be systematically and rigorously held accountable for carrying out their mandates effectively, appropriately, and with clear value added for European citizens. Hence, the European Parliament would need to rise to the challenge of supervising these new bodies and ensuring that they perform to the highest possible standards.

It is equally vital that the legal system of the Union should be able to deliver effective judicial enforcement of all relevant legislation and policy operating systems. The European Courts, with their counterparts in the Member States, already perform a hugely important role in doing this, but often much too slowly because of the volume of cases before them. Delays in delivering judicial decisions carry clear economic costs and create uncertainties for market operators. Hence, the capacity of the judicial system needs to be increased in order to deal with a workload that can only increase with more members, as well as with the likelihood of needing to take account of some differentiation among them, as we have argued throughout this Report.

Finally, we consider that extending the scope for voting by qualified majority (QMV) on EU economic decisions is vital for the effectiveness of governance. Experience has shown that unanimity generally implies considerable delays before a compromise can be reached. It is therefore an important cause of institutional inertia, which results in the persistence of legislation, structures, and policies long after they have lost justification. Furthermore, unanimity frequently results in decisions that are in the interest of all members being hijacked by countries seeking to gain concessions in other, sometimes wholly unrelated, fields. Both factors are detrimental to the quality and effectiveness of EU governance and therefore to its overall performance. This report is not the place to discuss in detail where the EU should move to on QMV. However, we are adamant that progress on this front is an integral part of an effective governance reform agenda.

12.1.7. *More intensive cooperation*

There is a broader issue which is relevant to how the economic governance of the Union develops as a whole, namely the question of which policy regimes require the participation of all members and which can appropriately be developed by fewer than the full membership. This issue takes on greater importance in the context of the current enlargement.

For those policy areas which involve setting rules for the Union as a whole and for the Single Market, for which Member States do not exhibit major differences in preferences or capabilities, and where there are clear spillovers across all countries, all should continue to be fully involved in setting the rules and enforcing them. Similarly, as regards funding measures designed to stimulate innovation and to provide incentives for growth, all Member States would be included in the process, although as we have argued earlier, we recommend that the allocations to be made on the basis of clear economic criteria, and not on the basis of a distributional formula. As for coordination and dialogue in the context of the Lisbon strategy it also makes sense to involve all members, since the aim of the strategy is to stimulate dynamic reforms across the whole of the Union.

However, there are circumstances in which it makes sense for only some members to take forward a particular policy regime. Economic and Monetary Union (EMU) already shows a working example whereby not all EU countries participate in the single currency, and where there is already therefore more intense involvement in policy-making for Eurogroup members. We expect that Member States participating in the euro will extend and intensify their sphere of cooperation as corollaries to the single currency are set in place. We also recognise that care needs to be taken to ensure that the legitimate concerns of those outside any such arrangement for intensified cooperation are taken into account.

We thus suggest adopting a flexible attitude towards the formation of groupings for intensified cooperation of any possible size (we do not see a rationale for the current threshold of eight participants) provided they obey a set of general principles: consistency with the Union's aims and principles; authorisation by a vote in the Council acting on the basis of a Commission recommendation; full transparency vis-à-vis the Union's institutions; openness to all Union members, possibly subject to qualification criteria; and the possibility for the Council to reject amendments to the rules of the intensified cooperation arrangement if they risk jeopardising the interests of non-participant members.

12.1.8. *Our recommendations*

1. The assignment of competences between the EU and national levels of governance should be more flexibly and coherently defined. To this end, the various roles of the EU institutions—those of rule-maker, policy-maker, regulator, supervisor, or facilitator—should be clarified; procedures for assigning a competence to the EU or devolving it back to the national level should be made more flexible; and within any given policy area, consideration should be given to limiting the overlapping of competence between the EU and the Member States.

2. There is a case for devolving funding, economic law enforcement, and regulatory functions to independent European bodies instead of concentrating on policy and management responsibilities within the Commission. Management of specific funding mechanisms should be assigned to bodies operating within EU guidelines, subject to Commission oversight,

and accountable to Council and Parliament, but independent in the implementation of their mandate. Responsibility for enforcing EU competition policy (except state aids) should be assigned to a European competition authority accountable to Council and Parliament, whose decisions could be subject to formal override by the Commission. Sectoral regulation should also be assigned to independent authorities.

3. The enlarged EU should move further towards decentralised implementation of market regulation by developing both steered networks of national and EU bodies operating within the same legal framework and partnerships of autonomous national bodies cooperating with each other and with EU bodies. In steered networks, ultimate responsibility remains with the relevant EU institution, hierarchically related to relevant national bodies, whereas in the partnerships, ultimate responsibility remains with each national institution. Choices between these models—or any hybrid thereof—should depend on the degree of market integration, the kind of regulatory coordination that is needed (e.g. harmonisation versus information exchange) as well as the need to be close to the markets.

4. The obligations of EU and national regulators should be strictly defined in such a way that any attempts to foreclose national markets or to depart from commonly agreed principles can be effectively prevented by the Commission and national regulators. The Commission and national regulators should have no room for undermining independent day-to-day handling of individual cases.

5. The management of the Single Market needs to be improved. Product and service safety should become an integral part of EU competence, and responsibility for both risk assessment and risk management should be delegated to the same agency. More effective methods for sanctioning non-application of Single Market directives should be adopted.

6. EU methods for implementing the common growth and social cohesion agenda must be strengthened. The scope of the OMC should be limited to the areas where there are no alternatives and its implementation should be streamlined. In areas in which there is a case for stronger EU involvement, more effective methods such as incentive-financing and Community method should be relied on. Incentives should be given to Member States to direct budgetary priorities towards growth-enhancing spending categories, especially in the next few years as there is a need for catching-up on the objectives set out in 2000 by the Lisbon European Council.

7. Institutional reform should be directed to strengthening strategic capabilities. A leaner Commission of fifteen with focused portfolios should pull its resources together for addressing the growth issue, giving a leading Commissioner a mandate for taking forward the corresponding agenda. Its staffing should be improved by giving it the possibility of hiring relevant professionals. The Council should devote to the growth agenda the same

resolve it has shown in the macroeconomic field. We see a role here for the Economic Policy Committee. Focus on the growth agenda should also be developed in the Member States. This requires assigning corresponding responsibilities to minister(s) taking part in the Competitiveness Council. Finally, we emphasise that extending the scope for QMV in the economic field is vital for improving overall performance.

8. Possibilities for developing more intensive cooperation among subsets of Member States should be extended, without defining an a priori threshold. Procedures for setting up such arrangements should ensure transparency and guarantee that the rights of all EU Member States are preserved.

12.2. Mobilising the European Union budget

As it stands today, the EU budget is a historical relic. Expenditures, revenues, and procedures are all inconsistent with the present and future state of EU integration.

Half its spending goes on supporting a sector whose economic significance is declining and little is used to provide economic or non-economic public goods typically featuring large economies of scale, while convergence policy is very dispersed across EU countries and is not focused regarding the activities it should support.

More than 90 per cent of the EU budget is financed through national contributions linked to national treasuries, rather than from taxes levied on EU-wide fiscal bases.

Finally, the procedure for adopting the EU Financial Perspectives (the multi-annual frameworks, which determine the maximum amount for every item of expenditure in the EU annual budget) is driven by narrow national calculations of self-interest, bolstered by unanimity voting.

For these reasons, the successive negotiations to renew the Financial Perspectives for a five- or seven-year period have always followed the line of least resistance, which consists of modifying, at the margin only, the financial allocations of the previous period. As a result, the current budget is more the expression of different deals and attempts by governments to claw back in receipts as much of their contribution as possible (*juste retour* again!) than a coherent set of measures aimed at pursuing EU objectives.

Instead of being tied to the past, the EU budget should be a crucial tool to help achieve the current economic objectives of the Union. It must, therefore, be sufficiently flexible to permit redeployment according to new priorities.

If the Union is serious and determined to achieve growth and solidarity in an enlarged Europe, the EU budgetary envelope should move away from the present inertia, which allows for only minor tinkering, and be radically restructured.

Provided this restructuring takes place, the purely economic and social objectives, that are the focus of this Report, can be funded by an amount similar to that allocated to economic and social objectives in today's budget (about 1 per cent of the EU GDP), which, therefore, can be easily accommodated under the current budget ceiling for EU revenues (1.27 per cent of GNP). It is outside the scope of this Report to examine whether this ceiling would also be sufficient for financing policies beyond narrow economic and social issues, such as policy towards neighbours, foreign and defence policy, development aid, justice, and home affairs, or those economic policies with a dominant external dimension, such as trade policy.

The present analysis covers the three areas of expenditure, revenues, and procedures. The resulting recommendations are the budgetary translation of the recommendations endorsed by this Report with respect to growth, convergence, and restructuring.

12.2.1. *Expenditure*

A major overhaul of the expenditure financed by the EU budget is needed. In particular, the EU budget should focus spending on those economic and social areas where it is best able to make a contribution to growth and solidarity in Europe. This implies a shift away from traditional expenditure (such as the Common Agricultural Policy (CAP)) and could be achieved by regrouping EU budget spending into three new instruments (or funds), organised as follows:

1. A fund for economic growth within the EU area. This would then be subdivided further into R&D and innovation, education and training, and infrastructure.
2. A convergence fund aimed at helping low-income countries catch up with the rest. This fund would divide into two main items: institution-building and human and physical capital.
3. A restructuring fund aimed at facilitating the process of resource reallocation that would be required as a result of deeper and wider economic integration. This would also be in two parts: aid to the agricultural sector and aid to displaced workers in general.

The allocation of money should respect the principle of 'one fund for one goal'. Growth and solidarity goals should be clearly divided across the different funds. The growth fund should be allocated in a 'competitive way' with no particular implicit or explicit a priori allocation of money across countries, and with no constraints other than maximising added value of the investment. Conversely, the convergence fund would be allocated to a subset of countries determined on the basis of their relative income. This is not always the case at present, since the allocation of money, for example, for R&D purposes, often tries simultaneously to serve both growth and solidarity.

Growth fund
The growth fund should be destined for those projects that would make the greatest contribution to the EU growth objective. It should cover, in particular,

three areas of spending which have been identified as the most efficient and relevant growth engines at the EU level: R&D and innovation, education and training, and infrastructures connecting national markets.

Research and development and cross-border infrastructures are two clear cases where the size of the EU budget is so small compared to the declared objectives that its intervention becomes economically significant only if accompanied by national (private and public) expenditure. EU Member States have agreed on numerical targets of expenditure, both for R&D and for infrastructure projects, to be reached by a joint action involving EU, national, and private financing. In the future, the EU budget should play a role greater than today in helping the EU system meet those targets. By acting as a catalyst for national expenditure, the EU budget can also provide an incentive to governments to improve the quality of national public finances.

International comparisons of spending on education suggest that spending per student is higher in the United States than in the EU, where (at the tertiary level) it reaches only about 60 per cent of the American level. Tertiary education is a very valuable input for EU growth, especially if its European dimension could be reinforced. There is therefore a ground for EU budget intervention in this domain to foster excellence and stimulate the development of high-quality doctoral and postdoctoral studies. This would help close the gap with the United States. Money from the EU budget could facilitate exchanges of students and professors across the EU, provide international training opportunities for both students and workers, and support the development of a dozen world-class universities within the EU.

Convergence fund

It will be a matter of urgency to reduce the range of income disparities across EU countries brought about by enlargement. The convergence fund should be allocated to low-income countries in need of above-average growth in order to converge towards the rest of the EU. It could be used for two purposes: institution-building and investment in physical and human capital.

The experience of the new Member States during the period of economic transition from a command to a market economy and that of the current EU countries during the last fifteen years shows that that the quality of institutions is a key precondition for growth and convergence. *A fortiori*, good and stable institutions are also a key precondition for a country to integrate into the EU economic system and to reap the benefits of the Single Market. This alone justifies the need to earmark part of the convergence fund to improve converging countries' administrative capacity.

High investment rates, both for human and for physical capital, have been identified as the most direct source of economic growth. The EU convergence fund should help a country to sustain these high rates of investment. To avoid crowding out of domestic investment by EU money, the 'additionality' principle should be strictly respected. National authorities should be left free to decide how to allocate the EU money across different investment projects.

Restructuring fund
The restructuring fund, aimed at facilitating the process of resource reallocation due to deeper and wider economic integration of the EU area, should be available, with no restrictions, to all workers adversely affected by change, irrespective of their country of residence or their sector of activity. Affected workers could use the restructuring fund to cover three main needs: (a) retraining; (b) compensation for relocation costs; and (c) setting up a new business. Eligibility for the restructuring fund should be limited in time with the possibility for renewal. This fund would cover persons occupied either in manufacturing and services or in the agricultural sector. Farmers could also obtain aid to restructure their business.

A shift away from agricultural expenditure
The structure of the budget sketched above implies a very sizeable reduction in the amount devoted to agriculture. This is a radical step away from the present situation. Four reasons justify this reduction. First, the present share of the CAP is so large that unless it is brought under tighter control, no significant reallocation of resources within a EU budget of the current size is possible. Second, the CAP moved away from being an allocative policy, promoting efficiency and production, towards being a distributive policy for a particular group of citizens. Already in 1987, the Padoa-Schioppa Report had noted that:

This represents a systemic anomaly, since the Community [...] is not well suited to executing distributive policies at the level of individual persons or small enterprises. Efficient income distribution requires detailed administration at the level of the individual, and coherence with features of income tax and social security systems, and the Community cannot assure this. The Community has thus switched role with the Member States, counter to the basic principles of subsidiarity and comparative advantage. (Padoa-Schioppa et al. 1987)

Third, the large spread of income, population density, and climate across the enlarged Union implies a large heterogeneity of preferences that makes it very difficult to conduct a single rural policy from Brussels. The same holds for interpersonal redistribution. A fortiori, interpersonal redistribution for a sector of activity is a very daunting task at the EU level. Fourth, the CAP does not seem consistent with the Lisbon goals, in the sense that its value-for-money contribution to EU growth and convergence is lower than what is targeted for most other policies. Continuing to fund the CAP at present levels would amount to discounting its reduced contribution to the Lisbon goals compared with potentially much greater contributions from the other growth-enhancing policies of the type described above.

There is therefore a solid argument for decentralising to Member States the distributive function of the CAP, as is already the case for all other individual distributive policies. At the same time, decentralised national aid to farmers should abide by Community state aid rules and not distort competition or be incompatible with the common market.

12.2.2. *Revenues*

The changes advocated on the expenditure side of the EU budget require a parallel and consistent change on the revenue side. By 2006, 90 per cent of EU budget revenue will be financed by national contributions. The overt character of national contributions, which have a very clear link to the national treasuries and no link to EU-wide tax bases, feeds the tendency of national governments to focus the debate on the net balance or *juste retour* issue, thus preventing an economically rational allocation of the EU budget.

To redress this situation, the EU should target those sources of revenue that have a clear EU dimension rather than those with an obvious national label. Revenues directly accruing (partially or totally) to the EU budget might be either related to an EU policy so that they cannot meaningfully be reapportioned nationally or might have a very mobile tax base within the EU.[8] Further economic integration is likely only to increase the number of sources of revenues that have a clear EU dimension and that could therefore directly accrue to the EU budget.

12.2.3. *Procedures*

Procedures are certainly a key tool to facilitate the transition of the EU budget towards an instrument of EU economic governance, which should, inter alia, also provide incentives to improve the quality of national public finances. In particular there are three areas where procedures should be improved.

Transparency, efficiency, and flexibility
Resources allocated in the budget for a given policy should also cover the 'delivery' costs of that policy, that is, the administrative costs of designing, implementing, monitoring, and *ex post* evaluating any given policy. This should demonstrate which are cost-efficient policies and the good management practices. Monitoring and evaluation should follow an 'output' logic (e.g. having an additional X per cent of schools linked to the internet) rather than an 'input' logic (spending X million euros). The programme evaluation, the methodology, and the data requirements should be made explicit. Evaluation should be both at the micro level of the project and at the macro level of the policy design. Evaluation should also be applied to the financial and

---

[8] An example of the former would be the seignorage earned from issuing euro banknotes. An example of the latter would be capital income taxes or stock exchanges taxes. The size of the EU budget is so small that even a partial allocation to the EU budget of any of these possible taxes would suffice to cover the financing needs.

management practices according to criteria specified *ex ante*. Monitoring and evaluation should allow the disbursement of EU money to be made conditional on its past efficient use. Monitoring and evaluation should also allow for the reallocation of unused resources within the budget. For such unused funds, the flexibility of the EU budget across budgetary headings and across financial years should also be enhanced. This could be done through a swift budgetary procedure that would reallocate unused funds from one to the other budget item.

Responsibility for implementation

At present, Article 274 of the Treaty lays down that 'The Commission executes the Budget under its own responsibility'. This has been criticised because, in economic terms, responsibility should be at the level of the action concerned, while in political terms it seems at odds with subsidiarity. This Report has argued for more decentralisation of the expenditure: both by operating more effectively through national authorities and by creating some new EU purpose-specific agencies. It is only consistent that the different bodies, agencies, or institutions operating the different funds of the budget should carry their own share of responsibility. This means that the legal provision of Article 274 should be changed accordingly.

Getting rid of unanimity

No matter how radical the changes to the expenditure side of the EU budget, there is little hope of a genuine debate on the value added of the EU budget unless the voting procedures for adopting the medium-term Financial Perspectives is changed. At present, the Council adopts these budgetary guidelines by unanimity. The rigidity of the system gives little opportunity to take the advice of the Parliament and it can sideline the Commission. Setting the Financial Perspectives is precisely one area where compatibility and consistency should be sought between national and EU budgetary planning.

12.2.4. *Our recommendations*

1. A radical restructuring of the EU budget to support the growth agenda proposed by this Report in line with the Lisbon objectives. The budget should be organised into three funds:

(a) a fund to promote growth through expenditure for R&D, education and training, and infrastructure;
(b) a convergence fund to help low-income countries catch up; and
(c) a fund to support economic restructuring.

2. Meeting the growth agenda implies, if the overall size of the budget remains the same, a sharp reduction in EU agricultural expenditure.

3. Within each fund resources should be allocated in a way which best meets its objective. Resources for growth should be allocated on a competitive basis. Resources for convergence should be allocated to countries on the basis of their income level. Resources for restructuring should be allocated to individuals anywhere in the EU based on their economic circumstances.
4. The relative weight of national contributions to the EU budget should be reduced in favour of revenue sources with a clear EU dimension.
5. A radical change in budgetary procedure towards: more *ex post* evaluation of expenditures based on meeting criteria specified *ex ante*; devolution of responsibility for budget execution to relevant local, national, or EU actors; qualified majority voting for the adoption of the multi-annual budgetary guidelines.

Box 12.1. *The economic and social part of the EU budget for the next financing period: an illustration*

This box aims at illustrating a possible numerical structure of the EU budget for the next financing period (from 2007 to 2011, or possibly 2013). In line with the conclusions of the Copenhagen European Council (December 2002), it is assumed that the EU will by then have twenty-seven members. Possible synergies between the EU budget and national budgets are taken into account to determine the quantitative role of each. Two transitional measures for phasing out EU involvement in two areas are foreseen for the next financing period: one for aid to low-income macro-regions in countries with a GDP per capita above the eligibility threshold for the EU convergence fund; the other for aid to the agricultural sector. These should be one-off measures expiring at the end of the next financing period (i.e. 2011 or 2013).

Growth

1. EU heads of state and government endorsed, in March 2002, the objective of spending 3 per cent of GDP on R&D to be roughly divided into 2 per cent for the private sector and 1 per cent for the public sector. The EU could contribute 25 per cent of the public sector expenditure in R&D. This would translate into 0.25 per cent of EU GDP being devoted to research.
2. EU contributions to expenditure for physical infrastructure with an EU dimension must also be assessed against the overall declared needs. These are estimated at about €500 billion over ten years, or about €50 billion per year. The EU could cover 25 per cent of this expenditure, which amounts to 0.125 per cent of the EU GDP per year.
3. The EU budget could also cover part of the gap between the EU and the US public investment in tertiary education. In percentages of GDP, EU public expenditure, for tertiary education, is 1.1 per cent, while the US public expenditure is 1.4 per cent. The EU budget could devote some 0.075 per cent of the EU GDP to cover 25 per cent of the public investment gap, including training.

Continued

Box 12.1. *Continued*

The whole growth part of the EU financial package would thus be worth 0.45 per cent of the EU GDP. This translates into a very significant increase in the EU financial involvement in R&D, education, and infrastructures connecting national markets.

Convergence

1. The European Council of Berlin, in March 1999, indicated that the constraint posed by administrative capacity made it difficult for any country to be able to absorb more than 4 per cent of its GDP in terms of convergence funds. Given that the new Member States represent about 5 per cent of the EU GDP, the total expenditure in convergence funds for them under this formula would amount to 0.20 per cent of EU GDP.
2. Fixing the eligibility threshold for the EU convergence fund at the level of 100 of the EU-27 per capita GDP, Greece, Portugal, and Spain would also be eligible (based on 2001, the latest available figures). Since their population is slightly more than half that of the twelve new members, they might receive the equivalent of about 0.10 per cent of EU GDP. Obviously, in purchasing power terms, this would mean a lower funding for them than for the new Member States.
3. Finally, a transitional period to phase out the EU budget assistance to the two large macro-regions of southern Italy (Mezzogiorno) and the eastern *Länder* of Germany should also be foreseen in the 2007–2011 financial period. This is justified by the fact that these macro-regions are too large compared to the size of their respective country to impose a sudden end to EU funding. Considering that the population of these two macro-regions is somewhat more than half the population of Greece, Spain, and Portugal, their share could be of the order of 0.05 per cent of EU GDP.

Hence, in total, about 0.35 per cent of the EU GDP could be devoted to convergence expenditure.

Restructuring

1. Assistance to displaced workers. This assistance is meant to complement national policies to support them. Assuming a grant of, on average, €5,000 per worker affected (equivalent to about six months of the average minimum wage) and assuming that about 1 million EU workers qualified for it, the total expenditure would be €5 billion or some 0.05 per cent of the EU GDP.
2. Assistance to the agricultural sector. In 2002, farming employed around 14 million persons. Assuming that between 5 and 10 per cent of them would be entitled to EU restructuring aid, of the order again of €5,000, this would amount to about 0.05 per cent of EU GDP.
3. Finally, the heavy legacy of the past is such that EU involvement in agriculture cannot be ended abruptly and a phasing-out period should be foreseen. To meet this need, about 0.10 per cent of EU GDP could be allocated, on a transitional basis, as EU support to agriculture.

Hence, restructuring expenditure would be a total amount of 0.2 per cent of the EU GDP.

Expenditure	Financial period 2007–2011 % of EU GDP
Growth	*0.45*
(R&D)	(0.25)
(Education & Training)	(0.075)
(Infrastructure)	(0.125)
Convergence	*0.35*
(For new Member States)	(0.20)
(For old Member States)	(0.10)
(Phasing out for macro-regions)	(0.05)
Restructuring	*0.20*
(For displaced workers)	(0.05)
(For agriculture)	(0.05)
(Phasing out of agricultural expenditure)	(0.10)
Total economic and social activities	*1.00*

This structure estimates the budget cost of the EU economic and social activities at about 1 per cent of the EU GDP, which is equivalent to what is foreseen in the current financial plan for the period 2000–2006. At the same time, this structure would increase the involvement of the EU budget in growth-enhancing and in solidarity expenditure and reduce drastically its involvement in agricultural expenditure.

References

Acemoglu, D., Aghion, P., and Zilibotti, F. (2002). 'Distance to Frontier, Selection and Economic Growth', NBER Working Paper No. 9066.

Akerlof, G., Dickens, W. T., and Perry, G. L. (2000). 'Near-Rational Wage and Price Setting and the Optimal Rates of Inflation and Unemployment', *Brookings Papers on Economic Activity*, 1: 1–45.

Aghion, P. and Howitt, P. (1998). *Endogenous Growth Theory* (Cambridge, MA: MIT Press).

——Meghir, C., and Vandenbussche, J. (2003). 'Growth, Education and Distance to the Technological Frontier', mimeo.

Alesina, A., Angeloni, I., and Schuknecht, L. (2001). 'What Does the European Union Do?', NBER Working Paper No. 8647.

Allsopp, C. (2002). 'Macroeconomic Policy Rules in Theory and in Practice', Bank of England Monetary Policy Committee, External MPC Unit Discussion Paper No. 10.

Andrés, J., Hernando, I., and López-Salido, D. (2000). 'Assessing the Benefits of Price Stability', Banco de España, Estudios Económicos No. 69.

Artis, M. J. and Buti, M. (2000). 'Close to Balance or in Surplus'—A Policy Maker's Guide to the Implementation of the Stability and Growth Pact', *Journal of Common Market Studies*, 38: 563–92.

Auerbach, A. (2002). 'Is There a Role for Discretionary Fiscal Policy?', in The Federal Reserve Bank of Kansas City (ed.), *Rethinking Stabilization Policy (Symposium at Jackson Hole)*, FRB of Kansas City.

Baldwin, R. E., Francois, J. F., and Portes, R. (1997). 'The Costs and Benefits of Eastern Enlargement: The Impact on the EU and Central Europe', *Economic Policy*, 12: 127–70.

Barro, R. (1996). 'Inflation and Growth', *Federal Reserve Bank of St. Louis Review*, 78: 153–69.

——and Lee, J.-W. (2000). 'International Data on Educational Attainment: Updates and Implications', CID, Harvard University, Working Paper No. 42.

——and Sala-i-Martin, X. (1991). 'Convergence Across States and Regions', *Brookings Papers of Economic Activity*, 1: 107–82.

Bean, C. R., Bentolila, S., Bertola, G., and Dolado, J. J. (1998). *Social Europe: One for All?*, Monitoring European Integration No. 8 (London: CEPR).

Beetsma, R. and Uhlig, H. (1999). 'An Analysis of the Stability and Growth Pact', *Economic Journal*, 109: 546–71.

Begg, D., Canova, F., De Grauwe, P., Fatás, A., and Lane, P. (2002). *Surviving the Slowdown*, Monitoring the ECB No. 4 (London: CEPR).

Berglöf, E., Eichengreen, B., Roland, G., Tabellini, G., and Wyplosz, C. (2003). *Built To Last: A Political Architecture For Europe*, Monitoring European Integration No. 12 (London: CEPR).

Bertola, G., Jimeno, J. F., Marimon, R., and Pissarides, C. (2001). 'Welfare Systems and Labour Markets in Europe: What Convergence Before and After EMU?', in

G. Bertola, T. Boeri, and G. Nicoletti (eds.), *Welfare and Employment in a United Europe* (Cambridge, MA: MIT Press).

Blanchard, O. and Wolfers, J. (2000). 'The Role of Shocks and Institutions in the Rise of European Unemployment: The Aggregate Evidence', *Economic Journal*, 110: C1-33.

Bloom, N., Griffith, R., and van Reenen, J. (2002). 'Do R&D Tax Credits Work? Evidence from an International Panel of Countries 1979–1997', *Journal of Public Economics*, 85: 1–31.

Blundell, R. and Preston, I. (1998). 'Consumption Inequality and Income Uncertainty', *Quarterly Journal of Economics*, 113: 603–40.

Boeri, T., Bertola, G., Brücker, H., Coricelli, F., de la Fuente, A., Dolado, J., Fitzgerald, J., Garibaldi, P., Hanson, G., Jimeno, J., Portes, R., Saint-Paul, G., and Spilimbergo, A. (2002). *Who's Afraid of the Big Enlargement?*, CEPR Policy Paper No. 7, (London: CEPR).

Boldrin, M. and Canova, F. (2001). 'Inequality and Convergence: Reconsidering European Regional Policies', *Economic Policy*, 16: 207–53.

Bourguignon, F. and Morrisson, C. (2002). 'Inequality among World Citizens: 1820–1992', *American Economic Review*, 92: 727–44.

Breuss, F. (2001). 'Macroeconomic Effects of EU Enlargement for the Old and the New Members', WIFO Working Paper No. 143/2001.

Brunila, A., Buti, M., and in't Veld, J. (2003). 'Fiscal Policy in Europe: How Effective are Automatic Stabilisers?', *Empirica*, 30: 1–24.

Buiter, W. and Grafe, C. (2003). 'Reforming EMU's Fiscal Policy Rules: Some Suggestions for Enhancing Fiscal Sustainability and Macroeconomic Stability in an Enlarged European Union', in M. Buti (ed.), *The Interactions between Monetary and Fiscal Policies in EMU* (Cambridge: Cambridge University Press).

Buti, M. and Giudice, G. (2002). 'Maastricht's Fiscal Rules at Ten: An Assessment', *Journal of Common Market Studies*, 40: 823–48.

——— and Nava, M. (2003). 'Towards a European Budgetary System', Paper prepared for the 2003 International Institute of Public Finance Conference, EUI Working Papers RSC 2003/8.

——— and van den Noord, P. (2003). 'Discretionary Fiscal Policy and Elections: The Experience of the Early Years of EMU', OECD Economics Department Working Paper No. 351.

Calmfors, L., Corsetti, G., Flemming, J., Honkapohja, S., Kay, J., Leibfritz, W., Saint-Paul, G., Sinn, H.-W., and Vives, X. (2003). *Report on the European Economy 2003 of the European Economic Advisory Group (EEAG)* (Munich: CESifo).

Coeuré, B. and Pisani-Ferry, J. (2003). 'A Sustainability Pact for the Eurozone', mimeo.

Coricelli, F. and Ercolani, V. (2002). 'Cyclical and Structural Deficits on the Road to Accession: Fiscal Rules for an Enlarged European Union', CEPR Discussion Paper No. 3672.

Corsetti, G. and Pesenti, P. (1999). 'Stability, Asymmetry, and Discontinuity: The Launch of European Monetary Union', *Brookings Papers on Economic Activity*, 2: 295–358.

Davies, S. and Hallet, M. (2002). 'Interactions between National and Regional Development', HWWA Discussion Paper No. 207.

Debonneuil, M. and Fontagné, L. (2003). *Compétitivité*, Conseil d'Analyse Economique, Report No. 40 (Paris: La Documentation Française).

De Grauwe, P. (2003*a*). *The Economics of Monetary Union*, 5th ed. (Oxford: Oxford University Press).

De Grauwe, P. (2003*b*). 'The Euro at Stake? The Monetary Union in an Enlarged Europe'. *CESifo Economic Studies*, 49: 103–21.

Drèze, J., Wyplosz, C., Bean, C., Giavazzi, F., and Giersch, H. (1987). 'The Two-handed Growth Strategy for Europe: Autonomy through Flexible Cooperation', European Commission Directorate-General for Economic and Financial Affairs, Economic Papers No. 60.

Easterly, W. and Levine, R. (2002). 'Tropics, Germs, and Crops: How Endowments Influence Economic Development', NBER Working Paper No. 9106.

Eichengreen, B. and Ghironi, F. (2002). 'EMU and Enlargement', in M. Buti and A. Sapir (eds.), *EMU and Economic Policy in Europe. The Challenge of the Early Years* (European Commission and Cheltenham: Edward Elgar).

Eijffinger, S. C. W. and de Haan, J. (2000). *European Monetary and Fiscal Policy* (Oxford: Oxford University Press).

Emerson, M. (2003). 'The Shaping of a Policy Framework for the Wider Europe', Centre for European Policy Studies Brussels, CEPS Policy Brief No. 39.

European Central Bank (2002). 'Recent Findings of Monetary Policy Transmission in the Euro Area', *Monthly Bulletin*, October.

European Commission (1985). 'Completing the Single Market: White Paper', COM(85) 310.

—— (1988). *The Economics of 1992*, European Economy No. 35 (Luxembourg: Office for Official Publications of the European Communities).

—— (1998). 'Risk Capital: A Key to Job Creation in the European Union', SEC(1998) 552.

—— (1999). *Italy's Slow Growth in the 1990s: Facts, Explanations and Prospects*, European Economy–Reports and Studies No. 5 (Luxembourg: Office for Official Publications of the European Communities).

—— (2000). *Public Finances in EMU—2000*, European Economy—Reports and Studies No. 3 (Luxembourg: Office for Official Publications of the European Communities).

European Commission (2001*a*). *Unity, Solidarity, Diversity for Europe, its People and its Territory: Second Report on Economic and Social Cohesion* (Luxembourg: Office for Official Publications of the European Communities).

—— (2001*b*). *Financial Report 2000* (Luxembourg: Office for Official Publications of the European Communities).

—— (2001*c*). 'The Economic Impact of Enlargement', Enlargement Papers No. 4, June.

—— (2001*d*). 'Compte de gestion et bilan financier afférents aux opérations du budget de l'exercice 2000', SEC(2001) 528.

—— (2001*e*). 'Company Taxation in the Internal Market', Commission Staff Working Paper, SEC(2001) 1681.

—— (2002*a*). 'Nineteenth Annual Report on Monitoring the Application of Community Law (2001)', COM(2002) 324 final, June.

—— (2002*b*). *The EU Economy 2002 Review*, European Economy No. 6 (Luxembourg: Office for Official Publications of the European Communities).

—— (2002c). 'Strengthening the Coordination of Budgetary Policies', COM (2002) 668, November.

—— (2002d). *European Union Public Finance* (Luxembourg: Office for Official Publications of the European Communities).

—— (2003a). 'Choosing to Grow: Knowledge, Innovation and Jobs in a Cohesive Society. Report to the Spring European Council, 21 March 2003 on the Lisbon Strategy of Economic, Social and Environmental Renewal', COM(2003) 5 final, January.

—— (2003b). 'Commission Staff Working Paper in Support to the Report from the Commission to the Spring European Council in Brussels (COM(2002) 5 final) ("The Spring Report"): Progress on the Lisbon Strategy', SEC(2003) 25, January.

—— (2003c). 'Second Progress Report on Economic and Social Cohesion', COM(2003) 34 final.

—— (2003d). *Public Finances in EMU—2003*, European Economy-Reports and Studies No. 3 (Luxembourg: Office for Official Publications of the European Communities).

—— (2003e). 'Single Market News: 10th Anniversary Special', Directorate-General Internal Market.

European Convention (2003). 'Draft Treaty Establishing a Constitution for Europe', CONV 820/03, submitted by the President of the Convention to the European Council meeting in Thessaloniki on 20 June.

Fatás, A. and Mihov, I. (2003). 'Fiscal Policy and EMU: Challenges of the Early Years', in M. Buti and A. Sapir (eds.), *EMU and Economic Policy in Europe: The Challenge of the Early Years* (European Commission and Cheltenham: Edward Elgar).

Feldstein, M. (ed.) (1999). *The Costs and Benefits of Price Stability* (Chicago: University of Chicago Press and NBER).

Fertig, M. (2001). 'The Economic Impact of EU-enlargement: Assessing the Migration Potential', *Empirical Economics*, 26: 707–20.

Fondazione BNC and Censis (2003). 'Impresa e criminalitá nel Mezzogiorno', Censis Ricerche, February.

Furman, J., Porter, M. E., and Stern, S. (2002). 'The Determinants of National Innovative Capacity', *Research Policy*, 31: 899–933.

Gali, J., López-Salido, D., and Vallés, J. (2000). 'Technology Shocks and Monetary Policy: Assessing the Fed's Performance', Banco de España, Working Paper No. 0013.

Geroski, P. A. (2000). 'What Do We Know about Entry?', in D. B. Audretsch and S. Klepper (eds.), *Innovation, Evolution of Industry and Economic Growth* (Cheltenham: Edward Elgar).

—— and Jacquemin, A. (1985). 'Industrial Change, Barriers to Mobility, and European Industrial Policy', *Economic Policy*, 1: 169–218.

Giavazzi, F. and Pagano, M. (1990). 'Can Severe Fiscal Contractions Be Expansionary?', in O. Blanchard and S. Fischer (eds.), *NBER Macroeconomics Annual* (Cambridge, MA: MIT Press).

Giersch, H. (1985). 'Eurosclerosis', Institut für Weltwirtschaft Kiel, Discussion Paper No. 112.

Gosling, A., Machin, S., and Meghir, C. (2000). 'The Changing Distribution of Male Wages in the UK', *Review of Economic Studies*, 67: 635–66.

Gros, D., Castelli, M., Jimeno, J., Mayer, T., Thygesen, N., and Hobza, A. (2002). *The Euro at 25*, Special Report on Enlargement by the CEPS Macroeconomic Policy Group (Brussels: CEPS).

——, Jimeno, J., Monticelli, C., Tabellini, G., and Thygesen, N. (2001). *Testing the Speed Limit for Europe*, Third Annual Report by the CEPS Macroeconomic Policy Group (Brussels: CEPS).

Hallet, M. (2002). 'Income Convergence and Regional Policies in Europe: Results and Future Challenges', Paper presented at the Congress of the European Regional Science Association (ERSA) in Dortmund/Germany, 28 and 29 August, available at www.ersa2002.org.

Herce, J. A., Sosvilla-Rivero, S., and de Lucio, J. J. (2001). 'Growth and the Welfare State in the EU: A Causality Analysis', *Public Choice*, 109: 55–68.

Heston, A., Summers, R. and Aten, B. (2002). 'Penn World Table Version 6.1', Center for International Comparisons at the University of Pennsylvania (CICUP).

Hochreiter, E. (2000). 'Exchange Rate Regimes and Capital Mobility: Issues and some Lessons from Central and Eastern European Applicant Countries', *North American Journal of Economics and Finance*, 11: 155–71.

Hodson, D. and Maher, I. (2001). 'The Open Method as a New Mode of Governance: The Case of Soft Economic Policy Co-ordination', *Journal of Common Market Studies*, 39: 719–45.

Honohan, P. and Lane, P. (2003). 'Divergent Inflation Rates in EMU', *Economic Policy*, 18: 357–394.

Hurst, C., Thisse, J. F., and Vanhoudt, P. (2000). 'What Diagnosis for Europe's Ailing Regions?', *EIB Papers*, 5: 9–30.

IMF (2003). 'Deflation: Determinants, Risks, and Policy Options—Findings of an International Task Force', Study, available at: www.imf.org/external/pubs/ft/def/2003/eng/043003.htm.

Issing, O., Gaspar, V., Angeloni, I., and Tristani, O. (2001). *Monetary Policy in the Euro Area: Strategy and Decision Making at the European Central Bank* (Cambridge: Cambridge University Press).

Keuschnigg, C. and Kohler, W. (1999). 'Enlargement of the European Union: Costs and Benefits for Present Member States', Study for the European Commission, available at: http://europa.eu.int/comm/budget/financing/enlargement_en.htm.

Krugman, P. (1991). *Geography and Trade* (Cambridge, MA: MIT Press).

Lamfalussy, A., Herkströter, C., Rojo, L. A., Ryden, B., Spaventa, L., Walter, N., and Wicks, N. (2001). 'Final Report of the Committee of Wise Men on the Regulation of European Securities Markets', Report to the European Commission, available at: http://europa.eu.int/comm/internal_market/en/finances/general/lamfalussyen.pdf.

Landesmann, M. (ed.) (2003). *Shaping the New Europe — The Challenge of EU Eastern Enlargement* (Basingstoke: Macmillan).

Lawrence, R. and Schultze, C. (eds.) (1987). *Barriers to European Growth: A Transatlantic View* (Washington D.C.: The Brookings Institution Press).

Leibfried, S. and Pierson, P. (2000). 'Social Policy: Left to Courts and Markets?', in H. Wallace and W. Wallace (eds.), *Policy-Making in the European Union*, 4th edn., (Oxford: Oxford University Press).

Leonardi, R. (2003). *Regional Policy in the European Union: The Role of Cohesion in the Building of a United Europe* (Basingstoke: Palgrave).

Maddison, A. (1995). *Monitoring the World Economy 1820–1992* (Paris: Development Centre Studies, OECD).

Mairate, A. and Hall, R. (2000). 'Structural Policies', in L. Tsoukalis, *Competitiveness and Cohesion* (Oxford: Oxford University Press).

Martín, C., Velázquez, F. J., and Funck, B. (2001). 'European Integration and Income Convergence: Lessons for Central and Eastern European Countries', World Bank Technical Paper No. 514.

Martin, P. and Ottaviano, G. (2001). 'Growth and Agglomeration', *International Economic Review*, 42: 947–68.

Mélitz, J. (2000). 'Some Cross-country Evidence about Fiscal Policy Behaviour and Consequences for EMU', in European Commission (ed.), *Public Debt and Fiscal Policy in EMU*, European Economy-Reports and Studies No. 2 (Luxembourg: Office for Official Publications of the EC).

Midelfart-Knarvik, K. H. and Overman, H. G. (2002). 'Delocation and European Integration: Is Structural Spending Justified?', *Economic Policy*, 17: 321–60.

Ministero dell'Economia e delle Finanze (2003). *Quinto rapporto del Dipartimento per le Politiche di Sviluppo 2001–2002*, Rome.

Molle, W. (2001). *The Economics of European Integration: Theory, Practice and Policy*, 4th ed. (Aldershot: Ashgate).

Morrisson, C. and Murtin, F. (2003). 'Inequality among Europeans (1970–2000)', Report for the European Commission, mimeo.

Murphy, K. M., Riddell, W. C., and Romer, P. M. (1998). 'Wages, Skills and Technology in the United States and Canada', NBER Working Paper No. 6638.

Neven, D. and Gouyette, C. (1995). 'Regional Convergence in the European Community', *Journal of Common Market Studies*, 33: 47–65.

Nicoletti, G. and Scarpetta, S. (2003). 'Regulation, Productivity and Growth: OECD Evidence', *Economic Policy*, 18: 9–72.

North, D. C. (1990). *Institutions, Institutional Change and Economic Performance* (Cambridge: Cambridge University Press).

Padoa-Schioppa, T., Emerson, M., King, M., Milleron, J. C., Paelinck, J. H. P., Papademos, L. D., Pastor, A., and Scharpf, F. W. (1987). *Efficiency, Stability and Equity: A Strategy for the Evolution of the Economic System of the European Community* (Oxford: Oxford University Press).

Pelkmans, J. (2001). *European Integration*, 2nd ed. (Harlow: Financial Times Prentice Hall).

Perotti, R. (2002). 'Estimating the Effects of Fiscal Policy in OECD Countries', European University Institute, mimeo.

Portes, R. (2003). 'The Euro and the International Financial System', in M. Buti and A. Sapir (eds.), *EMU and Economic Policy in Europe: The Challenge of the Early Years* (European Commission and Cheltenham: Edward Elgar).

Puga, D. (2002). 'European Regional Policies in Light of Recent Location Theories', *Journal of Economic Geography*, 2: 373–406.

Rodrigues, M. J. (ed.) (2002). *The New Knowledge Economy in Europe: A Strategy for International Competitiveness and Social Cohesion* (Cheltenham: Edward Elgar).

Rodrik, D., Subramanian, A., and Trebbi, F. (2002). 'Institutions Rule: The Primacy of Institutions over Geography and Integration in Economic Development', NBER Working Paper No. 9305.

Sala-i-Martin, X. (2002). 'The Disturbing "Rise" of Global Income Inequality', NBER Working Paper No. 8904.

Sapir, A. (2000). 'EC Regionalism at the Turn of the Millenium: Toward a New Paradigm?', *World Economy*, 23: 1135–48.

——(2001). 'Who's Afraid of Globalization? Domestic Adjustment in Europe and America', in R. B. Porter, P. Sauvé, A. Subramanian, and A. B. Zampetti (eds.), *Efficiency, Equity, and Legitimacy: The Multilateral Trading System at the Millenium* (Washington: Brookings Institution Press).

Saxenian, A. (1999). 'Silicon Valley's New Immigrant Entrepreneurs: Skills, Networks, and Careers', MIT Sloan School of Management, Task Force on Reconstructing America's Labour Market Institutions, Working Paper No. 5.

Scarpetta, S., Hemmings, P., Tressel, T., and Woo, J. (2002). 'The Role of Policy and Institutions for Productivity and Firm Dynamics: Evidence from Micro and Industry Data', OECD Working Paper No. 329.

Scharpf, F. W. and Schmidt, V. A. (eds.) (2000). *Welfare and Work in the Open Economy, Volume II: Diverse Responses to Common Challenges* (Oxford: Oxford University Press).

Seabright, P. (2001). 'Ten Years of Merger Control', Beesley Lecture, Institute of Economic Affairs and London Business School, available at: http://www.idei.asso.fr/English/ECv/CvChercheurs/PageEcvSeabright.html.

Siebert, H. (ed.) (2002). *Economic Policy for Aging Societies* (Heidelberg: Springer).

Sinn, H.-W. (2003). *The New Systems Competition* (Oxford: Blackwell).

——, Flaig, G., Werding, M., and Hänlein, A. (2001). *EU-Erweiterung und Arbeitskräftemigration: Wege einer schrittweisen Annäherung der Arbeitsmärkte*, ifo Beiträge zur Wirtschaftsforschung No. 2 (Munich: ifo Institut für Wirtschaftsforschung).

Steinherr, A. (2000). 'Europe's Unemployment: No Policy Issue? A Policy Issue for Europe, or for Member States, or for Both?', *Ifo Studien*, 46: 123–37.

Svensson, L. O. (2002). 'Inflation Targeting: Should It Be Modeled as an Instrument Rule or a Targeting Rule?', *European Economic Review*, 46: 771–80.

Szapáry, G. (2001). 'Maastricht and the Choice of Exchange Rate Regime in Transition Countries during the Run-Up to EMU', Centre for European Policy Studies Brussels, ENEPRI Working Paper No. 6.

Tabellini, G. (2003). 'Principles of Policymaking in the European Union: An Economic Perspective', *CESifo Economic Studies*, 49: 75–102.

Tsoukalis, L. (1997). *The New European Economy Revisited* (Oxford: Oxford University Press).

UNCTAD (2002): 'Outward FDI from Central and Eastern European countries', Study, available at: http://r0.unctad.org/en/subsites/dite/pdfs/CEE_outward_en.pdf.

United Nations Population Division (2002). *World Population Prospects: The 2002 Revision*, www.un.org/esa/population/unpop.htm.

van Ark, B., Inklaar, R., and McGuckin, R. (2002). 'Changing Gear: Productivity, ICT and Services: Europe and the United States', Research Memorandum GD-60, Groningen Growth and Development Centre, University of Groningen.

Viñals, J. (1998). 'Monetary Policy and Inflation: from Theory to Practice', in J. L. Malo de Molina, J. Viñals, and F. Gutierrez (eds.), *Monetary Policy and Inflation in Spain* (London: Macmillan).

—— (2001). 'Monetary Policy Issues in a Low Inflation Environment', in A. García Herrero, V. Gaspar, L. Hoogduin, J. Morgan and B. Winkler (eds.), *Why Price Stability?* (Frankfurt: European Central Bank).

von Hagen, J., Hughes-Hallett, A., and Strauch, R. (2002). 'Quality and Success of Budgetary Consolidations' in M. Buti, J. von Hagen and C. Martinez-Mongay (eds.), *The Behaviour of Fiscal Authorities* (Basingstoke: Palgrave).

Wallace, H. and Wallace, W. (eds.) (2000). *Policy-Making in the European Union*, 4th ed., (Oxford: Oxford University Press).

Wyplosz, C. (2003). 'Fiscal Discipline in EMU: Rules or Institutions?', in European Commission Group of Policy Advisers (ed.), *Economic Policy-making in the European Union*, Proceedings of the First Four Meetings of the Group of Economic Analysis (Luxembourg: Office for Official Publications of the European Communities).

Young, A. R. and Wallace, H. (2000). *Regulatory Politics in the Enlarging European Union* (Manchester: Manchester University Press).

Index